AF522335

Future Library Technology

Future Library Technology

Anurag Ghosh

Future Library Technology

ISBN 978-93-5111-556-4

Published in 2015 in India by

RANDOM PUBLICATIONS

4376-A/4B, Gali Murari Lal, Ansari Road
New Delhi-110 002
Phone : +9111-43580356, 011-23289044, 011-43142548
e-mail: sales@randompublications.com,
info@randompublications.com, randomexports@gmail.com
Reprinted 2019

Type Setting by : Friends Media, Delhi-110089
Digitally Printed at : Replika Press Pvt. Ltd.

Preface

Today's digital library systems cooperate in manifold ways. They exhibit a varying internal organisational structure, e.g. given by the introduction of specialised sub-collections or by extraction of project-specific reference libraries. Furthermore, different business models also including the ability to count the cost of library access have to be taken into account. Against this background, the ability to map intra- and inter-institutional requirements to the underlying digital library system as presented is of paramount importance. Libraries including resources other than traditional library documents like e.g. resource collections in e-science or health information systems emerge. This calls for the determination of detailed strategies not only for searching these collections but also for replication of both resources and services.

In library information system, information technology has had a clear and persuasive impact in almost every area of the library. The most significant development in information technology over the last few years or so is digital technology.

Digital technology is revolutionizing the traditional concepts of preservation and access in library and archive communities. The applications of digital system and computing system in the libraries have been a subject of interest to present day professional librarians.

The digital revolution driven by ICT innovation has transformed academic libraries fundamentally. It has impacted on every sphere of academic library activity, e.g., the form of the library, collection development strategies, library buildings and consortia. Information and communications technology have changed the academic library in a profound way. Computers and networked electronic resources had become an integral part of the academic library the past decade.

This has been underscored by the phenomenon of knowledge or information commons in academic libraries, which refer to a specific environment in the library where a designated number of PC workstations, networked to databases and other e-resources, are made available to students. Every sphere of the academic library is being affected by ICT quite radically.

The book will be highly useful for students, teachers and all those concerned.

I would like to thank my team for standing beside me throughout my career and writing this book. My special thanks go to "Random Publications" who have published the book.

–Anurag Ghosh

Contents

Preface .... *v-vi*

1. Digital Libraries of the Future **1**

Introduction 1
Diligent 2
The Future of Public Libraries in an Internet Age 7
Technology and Telecommunications 13
From Consumption to Creation 14
Open Data, Internet Resources Web sites and Literacy 15
Four Priorities for the 21st Century 16
Public Library Service 16

2. Libraries - An Investment in Our Future **34**

Universal Recommendations -For All Libraries 35
Training and Support to users 37
Use of Public Library Services 42
Integrating Predications: Biomedical Knowledge Repository 49
Technology and the Information 56
Market Place 56

3. Library Information Technology on Information Professionals **63**

Introduction 63
Information Technology in Libraries 76
Developments in Computer and 77
Microprocessor Technology 77
Developments in Communication and Network Technology 79
A conceptual Schema of Information Access 81
Distributed Search across in Digital Libraries 84

4. Library Information and Communications Technology **106**

Introduction 106
Internet-based Communication Services 115
The Communication Process 119
Non-verbal Communication in Organizations 119

Organizational Channels and Directions of Communication ... 120
Barriers to Communication ... 122
Overcoming Barriers to Communication ... 123

5. Library Information Science and Technology ... 127

Information Science ... 127
Information Retrieval ... 133
Different Types of Information Service ... 143

6. Information Technology-based Library Services ... 155

OPAC and WebPAC ... 155
Library Services ... 159
IT's Role in Managing Organisational Change ... 166
Role of Information in Contemporary Economy ... 170

7. Library Information System and Information Technology ... 193

Introduction ... 193
Information Explosion and the Direct Relation of Information To Developments . 195
Information Storage, Organisation, and Retrieval ... 205
Systems Based on Sets and Subsets ... 206
Space Analogues ... 209

8. Use of Computer-based System in the Libraries and Information Units ... 220

Digital Initiatives at J.N.N. College of Engineering Library ... 220
Role of Open Source in Higher Education ... 223
Role of Open Source in Higher Education ... 226
Man-Computer Interaction in Pro-Cognitive Systems ... 228
The Physical 'Intermedium' ... 229
Man-Computer Interaction Languages ... 233
Computer Techniques and Procedures in Library ... 246
Web Based Library Service ... 253

9. ICT Advancements and the Future of Libraries ... 262

Educational Digital Libraries ... 263
Facilitating Institutional Visibility ... 266
Facilitating Scholarly Communications ... 268
Development of IT Skills for Information Professionals ... 271

***Bibliography* ... 276**

***Index* ... 278**

1

Digital Libraries of the Future

INTRODUCTION

According to the most recent understanding, the DLs of the future will be able to operate over a large variety of information object types - far wider than those maintained today in physical libraries and archives. These information objects will be composed of several multi-type and multimedia components aggregated in an unlimited number of formats. These, for example, can mix text, tables of scientific data and images obtained by processing earth observation data, or they can integrate 3D images, annotations and videos. These new information objects will offer innovative and more powerful means to researchers for sharing and discussing the results of their work. In order to be able to support these objects, the DL functionality has to be appropriately extended far beyond that required to manipulate the simple digital surrogates of the physical objects. In order to support these objects the DL may need considerable resources.

For example, the creation and handling of the new documents may require access to many different, large, heterogeneous information sources, the use of specialised services that process the objects stored in these sources for producing new information, and the exploitation of large processing capabilities for performing this tasks. New DLs are also required to offer a much richer set of services to their users than in the past. In particular, they must support the activities of their users by providing functionalities that may range from general utilities, like annotation, summarisation or co-operative work support, to very audience-specific functions, like map processing, semantic analysis of images, or simulation. The availability of this new DL functionality can, in principle, change the way in which research is conducted.

By exploiting such types of DL, for example, a scientist can annotate the article of a colleague with a programme that extracts useful information from a large amount of data collected by a specific scientific observatory. This programme, executed on demand when the annotation is accessed, can complement the content of the paper with continuously refreshed information.

In the new DLs users are not only consumers but also producers of information. By elaborating information gathered through the DL they can create new information objects that are published in the DL, thus enriching its content. The new DLs are thus required to offer services that support the authoring of these new objects and the workflows that lead to their publication. In parallel with the evolution of the role of DL systems, we are now observing a large expansion in the demand for DLs.

Research today is often a collaborative effort carried out by groups belonging to different organisations spread worldwide. Motivated by a common goal and funding opportunities, these groups dynamically aggregate into virtual research organisations that share their resources, *e.g.* knowledge, experimentation results, or instruments, for the duration of their collaboration, creating new and more powerful virtual research environments. These virtual research organisations, set up by individuals that do not necessarily have great economic power or technical expertise, more and more frequently require DLs as tools for accelerating the achievement of their research results. This new potential audience demands less expensive and more dynamic DL development models.

They want to be able to set up new DLs that serve their needs for the duration of their collaborations in an acceptable timeframe and with an acceptable cost. The current DL development model cannot satisfy this large demand; a radical change is needed if we want to be able to address these new emerging requirements. A great contribution towards the satisfaction of all the requirements can certainly come from the introduction of mechanisms that support a controlled sharing of resources among different organisations. Sharing in this context is not only applied to repositories of content, as is usually meant today, but can be extended to any type of resource needed to build a DL, *i.e.* language and ontology resources, applications, computers and even staff with the necessary skills for supporting the DL development, deployment and maintenance.

Supporting this type of sharing requires the introduction of appropriate solutions at both the technological and organisational levels. These two levels are not independent; instead they strongly influence each other. In fact, the availability of a good technological solution favours the creation of an appropriate organisation, and vice-versa, a successful organisation stimulates the development of new supporting technologies. We present the DILIGENT infrastructure as an example of a technological solution for these new DLs. The organisational aspects stimulated by the introduction of this technology are briefly discussed afterwards.

DILIGENT

DILIGENT (DIgital Library Infrastructure on Grid ENabled Technology) is a three-year Integrated Project funded by the European Commission under the 6th Framework Programme for Research and Technological a Digital Library Infrastructure that will enable members of dynamic virtual research organisations to create on-demand transient digital libraries that exploit shared resources. Resources in this context are multimedia and multi-type content repositories, applications, and computing and storage elements. Following the understanding of DLs expressed in Borgman *et al.*, this project focuses on the development of DLs that "are not ends in themselves; rather they are enabling technologies for digital asset management, electronic commerce, electronic publishing, teaching and learning, and other activities".

From an abstract point of view, the DILIGENT infrastructure can be understood as a broker serving DL resource providers and consumers. The providers are the individuals and the organisations that decide to publish their resources under the supervision of the broker, according to certain access and use policies. The consumers are the user communities that want to build their own DLs. The resources managed by this broker are content sources (*i.e.* repositories of information searchable and accessible through a single "entrance"), services (*i.e.* software tools that implement a specific functionality and whose descriptions, interfaces and bindings are defined and publicly available) and hosting nodes (*i.e.* networked entities that offer computing and storage capabilities and supply an environment for hosting content sources and services).

Providers register their resources and give a description of them by exploiting appropriate mechanisms provided by the infrastructure. The infrastructure also automatically derives other properties of the resources that are used to enrich the explicit description. The infrastructure manages the registered resources by supporting their discovery, monitoring and usage, and by implementing a number of other functionalities that aim at realising the required controlled sharing and quality of service. A user community can create one or more DLs by specifying a set of requirements. These requirements specify conditions for the information space (*e.g.* publishing institutions, subject of the content, document types), for the operations that manipulate the information space (*e.g.* type of search, tool for data analysis), for the services for supporting the work of the users (*e.g.* type of personalised dissemination, type of collaboration), for the quality of service (*e.g.* configuration, availability, response time) and for many other aspects, like the maximum cost, or lifetime.

The broker satisfies the community's requirements by selecting, and in many cases also deploying, a number of resources among those accessible to the community, gluing them appropriately and, finally, making the new DL application accessible through a portal. The composition of a DL is dynamic since the DL broker continuously monitors the status of the DL resources and, if necessary, changes them in order to offer the best quality of service. By relying on the shared resources many DLs, serving different communities, can be created and modified on-the-fly, without big investments and changes in the organisations that set them up. In order to support the transactions between the providers and the consumers, the DILIGENT infrastructure exploits the virtual organisations (VOs) mechanism that has been introduced in the Grid research area. This mechanism models sets of users and resources aggregated together by highly controlled sharing rules, usually based on an authentication framework. VOs have a limited lifetime, are dynamically created and satisfy specific needs by allocating and providing resources on demand. Through the VOs mechanism the DILIGENT infrastructure glues together the users and the resources of a DL.

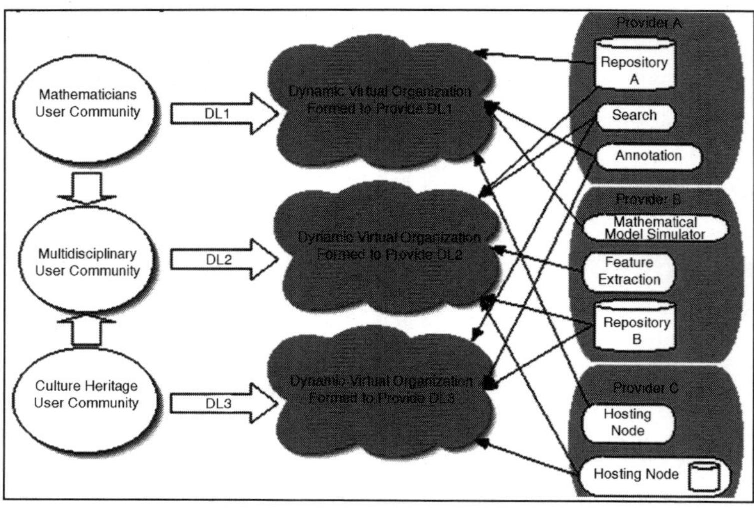

Fig. The Role of Virtual Organisations in DILIGENT

Figure graphically illustrates the role of VOs in supporting the brokerage model. The consumers, *i.e.* the user communities that require DLs to support their needs. The providers, each of which makes a number of resources available, are on the right. The infrastructure acts as a mediator by maintaining a framework where multiple virtual organisations, active on the same shared resources, can co-exist. The DL development model proposed by DILIGENT is radically new. Within the described framework each DL consumes the required resources only for the time it needs them.

This opens a lot of new opportunities for the creation of the functionalities required by the new "knowledge commons" environments. In particular, the exploitation of more effective, but also very computationally expensive algorithms becomes viable at an acceptable cost for many communities. For example, thanks to sharing, the use of the high processconsuming algorithms that automatically extract features from multimedia objects can be exploited in a large number of DLs. Moreover, in the framework established by the new development model, the user communities can easily, and in a timely manner, create and maintain their own DLs with limited resources since the management of the DL is automatically and transparently carried out by the infrastructure. The system that implements the functionality of the DILIGENT infrastructure is being built by integrating DL and Grid technologies. The motivation for this design choice relies on the similarity between many of the problems encountered through our new notion of DLs and the issues addressed by the most recent research in the Grid domain.

From the functional point of view, the DILIGENT system is divided into five functionality clusters:

- *DL Creation and Management:* is responsible for the dynamic construction and maintenance of the transient DLs and for the controlled sharing and management of the resources that are used to implement them. The functionalities offered by this cluster allow users to express the requirements that the DL must fulfil. Moreover, they automatically identify and arrange the pool of resources needed to satisfy these needs.
- *Content and Metadata Management:* implements the handling of DL content and related metadata, the consistent and distributed management of annotations, and the integration of external content and metadata sources.
- *Process Management:* manages the creation of user processes composed of existing services, the validation of their correctness, the automatic optimisation of their definition according to the resources available and the service characteristics, and their reliable execution. Thanks to this feature, the DILIGENT system can easily be enriched with additional operational workflows to meet new user requirements.
- *Index and Search Management:* is responsible for enabling cost-efficient search and retrieval of information in DLs, while satisfying the level of quality required for the overall data retrieval and delivery operations.
- *Application Specific Functionality:* provides the functionality needed to support user-specific scenarios, like portals, document visualisation, or features extraction.

From the architectural point of view, the DILIGENT system is designed as a Web Services Resource Framework (WSRF) application built on top of the gLite Grid middleware released by the Enabling Grids for Escience in Europe (EGEE) project. gLite hides the heterogeneous nature of the computing elements (*i.e.* services representing a computing resource) on the one hand and storage elements (*i.e.* services representing a storage resource) on the other hand by providing an environment that facilitates and controls their sharing. The DILIGENT services are being initially deployed on a project-proprietary gLite infrastructure. Architecturally, this infrastructure is completely interoperable with the EGEE infrastructure. EGEE is currently the largest European Grid infrastructure ever built.

A number of other recently funded projects will extend this infrastructure to other geographic regions, like Mediterranean countries, Latin America, or China. The interoperability with the EGEE infrastructure will allow any authorised virtual community that wishes to create DLs to also exploit the resources made available by this vast Grid infrastructure. During the project timeframe, the DILIGENT infrastructure will be populated with a number of important archives and software applications provided by the two communities that are participating in the experimentation with the results of the project, one from the environmental e-science domain and one from the cultural heritage domain.

The first community is Impact (Implementation of Environmental Conventions) and includes leading players in the environmental sector. This community will use DILIGENT to support the organisation of conferences and the preparation of projects and periodical reports. Through DILIGENT this community expects to improve accessibility, interoperability and usability of environmental data, models, tools, algorithms and instruments, integrating the distributed data sources with specialised data handling services. The second community, ARTE, is a community of scholars located in different parts of the world, working together to establish a new discipline that merges experiences from research in medicine, humanities, social sciences and communication.

In order to achieve their objectives, these researchers require instruments to ease the construction of multimedia artefacts and to improve support for education. At the time of the writing of this paper initial experimentation with the features of a DILIGENT DL has already been conducted by implementing simplified services for preparing environmental reports, as required by the ImpECt environmental agencies. Through the exploiting of rich information sources, ranging from raw data sets to maps and graphs archives, these agencies periodically prepare reports on the status of the environment. Currently, this task is performed by first selecting the relevant information from each of the multiple and heterogeneous sources available, then launching complex processing on large amounts of data to obtain "products", like graphs, tables and other summarised information and, finally, producing the required report by assembling all the different parts together.

This process, which is repeated periodically, requires a lot of work due to the complexity of interfacing the different sources and tools. Despite the effort expended, the resulting reports do not completely fulfil the requirements of their readers, who would like to have a picture of the environmental status which is updated at the time the report is accessed. A DILIGENT DL offers a more effective framework for the creation and maintenance of these reports. In our experimentation, for example, we have built a DL which exploits content maintained in both repositories including textual documents and archives of Earth observation raw data provided by the European Space Agency. In this DL, which is accessible through a single user interface, all the different kinds of information necessary for creating the reports can be found.

By combining this information and by defining how to derive the associated "products" (images, tables, or graphs) from raw data, the users can create their reports much more easily. Moreover, a specialised user interface allows authorised users to access these composite reports by choosing static or dynamic generation. The selection of dynamic generation triggers associated process workflows which, by combining appropriate applications, generate the required products on demand by processing both the raw data and other intermediate products stored in the DL repositories. The dynamically generated products are obtained by running those applications that are computationally intensive on the Grid.

In this way the complex processes required to generate the products are executed in few minutes at a limited cost to the community that is exploiting them. In order to obtain the same performance without the Grid, an institution would have to equip its digital library with a great number of computers, while in the case of DILIGENT the institution can also exploit computer capabilities made available by third party organisations. The same is true for storage capacity. Maintaining raw data, intermediate products and high resolution images requires a large amount of storage capacity. By exploiting the Grid technology, part of this information, especially the temporary part, can be maintained in third-party storage systems.

THE FUTURE OF PUBLIC LIBRARIES IN AN INTERNET AGE

With the Internet reshaping so many aspects of our lives, it has become common for prognosticators to speculate about the ultimate demise of all sorts of institutions that many of us have come to take for granted. So when Public Agenda set out to investigate public and civic leaders' thinking about public libraries today, we were not at all certain what we would hear. The first message that came was loud and clear: there is a future for public libraries in the Internet age. Even with the vast and growing amount of information available on the Internet and more competition for public funding, Americans say that public libraries will continue to play a vital role in communities.

A strong majority say that if their public library were to shut down, they would feel "that something essential and important has been lost, affecting the whole community" (78 per cent). The feeling that libraries are central to healthy communities is even more common among those who are most actively engaged in communities: the voters, volunteers, and contributors who make communities strong and can usually be counted on to raise a ruckus when things go wrong. In our recent report on the research, "Long Overdue: A Fresh Look at Public and Leadership Attitudes About Libraries in the 21st Century", Public Agenda documents the strong beliefs people have that their communities must have wellfunctioning public libraries in order to be healthy and strong. Large majorities said that all children should have a good, safe, appealing library in their neighbourhood; that libraries play a crucial role in preserving permanent and unalterable records; and that government should support the wiring of libraries so that low-income people can have access to the Internet.

AMERICANS SAY LIBRARIES ARE A GOOD PUBLIC INVESTMENT

At a time of broad concern about wasteful public spending, and as we hear of communities refusing to pay more taxes for public education or "essential services", 71 per cent say that libraries spend public money well. Fifty-two per cent say that if their local library needed additional funding, they would favour a tax increase to generate the necessary resources— significantly more than the number who favour charging users (32 per cent) or reducing services (16 per cent) as options for solving a financial shortfall. In many ways, people believe that libraries are more essential now than ever before. Americans say that since so many businesses are selling information, we absolutely need public libraries to provide vital information free of charge to anyone who needs it.

They also strongly agree that libraries are an important, quiet oasis from fast-paced, stressful lives. In an age when people are often deeply cynical about the performance of all sorts of public services, from public education to the police to cultural institutions, public libraries are rated A more often than any other public service we asked about. Indeed, public libraries seem almost immune to the distrust that is associated with so many other institutions. More than one hundred years ago, the philanthropist Andrew Carnegie saw the potential of the public library to be the center of enlightened learning in every community. He offered to build libraries if communities would contribute land, furnish money for annual maintenance, and exercise governance and oversight.

He gave communities the incentive to participate in a national movement and between 1881 and 1917 invested the equivalent of $3 billion to build 1,689 libraries across the nation. The result of Carnegie's investment and the involvement of communities helped educate generations of Americans. His commitment helped fix the library in the American consciousness as a significant public institution that needed and deserved broad public support. A century after this compact with American communities, nearly 90 per cent of library funding derives from local public dollars—which can be seen as either a curse or a blessing.

LIBRARIES FOR TODAY, LIBRARIES FOR TOMORROW

When people think about their expectations of libraries today, they generally think about the traditional services that most libraries carry out so well. Topping the public's list of priorities is that the basic services they have come to expect from libraries remain free of charge to the public. They also expect libraries to have enough current books for children; numerous reference materials; and friendly, knowledgeable librarians available. Libraries should offer convenient reading hours and special programmes for children, and they should have well-maintained buildings along with books and information that are organised for easy self-service. The top-ten list of public priorities for libraries also includes making available safe and productive gathering places for teenagers, being open on evenings and weekends, and having plenty of current books for adults.

For the most part, these public expectations are matched by libraries' performance, the public told us. People give especially high grades to their public libraries for having buildings that are well maintained; comfortable places to read; and enough friendly, knowledgeable librarians to supply help when needed. Although people clearly want libraries to ace the basics—materials, hours, and service—they also expect more and more from libraries in this age of the Internet. "Long Overdue" reveals a great deal about libraries and technology. Libraries are anything but relics of the past. They are viewed as key players in our digitised future.

Two-thirds of survey respondents say that having enough computers and online services for people should be a high priority for their local library. Seven in ten favour wiring libraries so that those who might not be able to afford a computer in their home can learn computer skills and get online. Those who think that libraries are merely becoming "information resources of last resort" for those who can't afford a home computer seem to be mistaken. Advanced computer users and families with higher income are even more likely to use public libraries and the technology services they offer. But, not surprisingly, people with few computer skills are the most likely to say wiring libraries to provide for "have-nots" should be a high priority.

WHERE IS THE LOVE

Public libraries are beloved institutions, but they can't survive on accolades alone. With the advent of computers and search engines, digital libraries, and the Internet, some question if libraries are essential and whether they should command priority in the competition for public dollars. Public Agenda's research shows public libraries are not seen as objects of nostalgia, but rather as essential community players in the effort to increase equity, opportunity, and community development in the information age. A growing number of communities are determined to keep their libraries at the leading edge of technology: affording small businesses the resources to compete globally; giving residents access to credible, current health information; and making libraries vital information access points for everyone.

These communities reveal the vast potential of libraries for the future. But only a small percentage of communities invest in public libraries to the extent necessary to produce maximum dividends. In those communities where the case for libraries is less clear and competition for public funds is high, there are disturbing indicators that support for libraries is slipping. The precarious financial condition of the nationwide public library system (to the extent that there is a cohesive system at all) that we heard about from library advocates was reinforced in our interviews with civic leaders across the nation.

Civic leaders do see the great strengths of the public library as being an information center in the digital age, an important resource for those who have the fewest resources available to them, and the "go to" place for all manner of public functions (including health information, job services, immigrant acculturation, and adult literacy training). But they also see challenges for libraries that need to be addressed by library supporters. Many civic leaders pointed to public libraries' seemingly infinite variety in governance structure as a major stumbling block. Public libraries' lack of marketing, impassive advocacy, and isolation from the community were also cited as shortcomings in library performance. Our research identified four specific areas where civic leadership, public citizens, and library leaders all seem to agree that there is a major opportunity for public libraries to step in and address community needs:

- Developing better programming and services for teens,
- Addressing illiteracy and poor reading skills among adults,
- Offering ready access to information about government services (including making public documents and forms quickly and easily available), and
- Permitting much greater access to computers for all.

Yet venturing into these areas would likely require financial resources that many libraries do not currently have. The civic leaders we spoke to questioned whether a groundswell of citizen support for public libraries would emerge in their communities. "Long Overdue" suggests that there is, in fact, strong potential for vocal support from activist citizens who could argue effectively for consistent and reliable financial support for public libraries. But library supporters, especially leaders with governance responsibility, must take the steps necessary to harness this potential and make it a reality.

LEVERAGING PUBLIC GOODWILL FOR FINANCIAL SUPPORT

There are people in every community who make things happen but don't necessarily hold any official post. These are the folks we refer to in our research report as "community soldiers", because no battle can be won without them. The good news for libraries is that these citizens—who nearly always vote in local elections and involve themselves in community organisations and activities—are heavy users and big fans of libraries. But even though they may be considered champions of libraries, currently they are not very aware of the potential financial vulnerability of their local libraries. Although 45 per cent of the civically engaged think their local government has not furnished enough money and assistance to the public libraries in their communities, 42 per cent think they have, and 13 per cent say they simply do not know. It appears that those citizens who can be counted on to rally to the cause if libraries are in financial peril are no more likely than the general population to be aware of the challenges facing libraries today.

Public lack of awareness of the financial challenges libraries face aside, there are other reasons everything is not milk and honey in the land of libraries. Libraries face real challenges today. Only 35 per cent of survey respondents say their local library gets an A when it comes to having convenient hours so people can use the services; only 28 per cent give libraries an A for offering access to catalogues and databases through the Internet; 26 per cent give an A for having enough computers and online services in the library for the people who want to use them; and just 24 per cent give an A for making available reading hours, homework help, and study space for children and teenagers. These are services that the public rate among the highest priorities for libraries. Clearly there are opportunities to improve service delivery on the part of local libraries.

Library leaders would like to do much more in the way of customer service and innovative programming. But as our interviews with public leaders attest, finances are always a challenge. The civic leaders we interviewed generally share the public's high regard for libraries but are more conscious of the tenuous financial condition of many public libraries. Some public libraries are comfortable with the funding they receive, but the vast majority are not so well supported. Though the public remains largely unaware of the fiscal pressures on libraries today, civic and business leaders believe that public libraries are often first on the chopping block when state and local budgets are cut.

Recent history in Salinas, Calif., a community that closed almost all of its libraries (and is profiled in our study), points to the passion for libraries that can emerge when a funding crisis imperils a treasured institution. But since the vast majority of the public do not sense that their own libraries may be at risk, most people do not see a reason to raise their voice in concern. It is simply not something on their radar screen today. The "canary in the coal mine" metaphor has a place here. Leaders have pricked up their ears to the distressed calls of the canary, but the public seems to hear only a sweet song and no hint of impending trouble.

LIBRARIES: ESSENTIAL COMMUNITY PROBLEM SOLVERS

To identify the most favourable potential opportunities for libraries to strengthen public support, Public Agenda asked the public about their priorities for urgent action in their communities and in which areas they think government should be more effective because current performance is relatively poor. Researchers explored the same terrain in the interviews with national and local leadership.

Four areas of opportunity resonated most with the public and leaders alike:

- *Providing stronger services for teens*: The public is greatly concerned about teenagers and feels (72 per cent) that offering safe and productive activities for teens should be a high priority for their communities. This is also an area where the public potentially holds local government accountable, believing local government both can and should do more for teens. In the public's reckoning, libraries can potentially fill the gap: three out of four Americans (74 per cent) believe providing services for teens should be a high priority for libraries.
- *Helping address illiteracy and poor reading skills among adults*: Another major opportunity for libraries to fill community needs is with supplying literacy and reading programmes for adults, which many civic leaders tied to strengthening workforce skills and economic development. Sixty-eight per cent of the public said adult literacy programmes should be a high priority for the community, very few said it was something their community was doing a very good job of providing, and a large majority (68 per cent) said it should be a high priority for their local library.
- Affording ready access to information about government services, such as making available government forms or information on literacy programmes.
- Ensuring even greater access to computers for all. Almost two-thirds of Americans say having enough computers and online services for the people who want to use them should be a high priority for libraries.

For public libraries today, the greatest challenge is not in convincing the public of their worth—in the present or for the future. People clearly see many valuable roles for libraries to play. Our research yields ample evidence that libraries are highly valued public institutions serving multiple needs that, the public notes, will certainly continue to be needed with changing times.

A TIME OF RECKONING

America's public libraries are facing a pivotal time in their history. There is a rich tradition of public service that infuses citizens with great respect for the mission of libraries. Libraries have received significant public and private financial support over the years, ranging from local property tax support to state budget funding and a high level of private philanthropic funding. But funding level and mechanisms vary tremendously from one community to the next—and that's part of the problem. During the past several decades, there has been a major effort to upgrade technology and Internet access to bring the benefits of these new technologies to all citizens, regardless of economic circumstances. This has added further to public approval of the allimportant contributions of libraries.

Of course, libraries have also long held a position of special importance in educating schoolchildren and older students. The kind of action required for libraries to position themselves securely in the future will demand active and engaged governance. When change happens in communities, it is often a product of the passion of engaged citizen leaders who demand change from elected officials. But our research into a variety of library environments would suggest that libraries may suffer in some cases from a kind of "benign neglect" on the part of those who are most civically engaged. The reasoning here may be a variation on the theme that if it ain't broke, don't fix it. Although the public's strong feelings about how well libraries are doing their job make clear that libraries aren't broken, this doesn't mean there aren't cracks in the foundation.

Those who are most passionate about the importance of libraries in communities, if they are to secure their future, must make certain that the local and state governance structures that determine funding understand all that libraries are able to do for citizens and just how successful their constituents perceive them to be.

TECHNOLOGY AND TELECOMMUNICATIONS

Less than two years ago industry projections suggested that there would be 150,000,000 tablets, smart phones and e-reader devices sold in North America by the year 2015. The North American market passed the 150,000,000 milestone last fall. It took less than half the time that industry experts had predicted. Estimates suggest that there are now more than 200,000,000 devices in the hands of North American consumers and that by the end of 2016, there may be 8 billion cellphones worldwide. This trend will affect public libraries. Data plans for these smartphones and other devices are more frequently bought by wealthier Canadians. There are also more free wi-fi zones in wealthier neighbourhoods. There is an implication for libraries. It is possible that libraries might provide more users with information access by supplying wifi outside their walls than by offering some current services inside their walls. Public libraries have a unique opportunity. Canarie (the Canadian Advanced Research and Innovation Network) has partners in every province.

The British Columbia partner is BCNet. Canarie recently changed its definition of research organisations (those allowed to use their service) to include both public libraries and school boards. In some provinces, Canarie, along with a provincial partner, now helps to provide inexpensive, high-speed

Internet access to K-12 school boards and to public library systems, provided they can reach a Canarie hub. A Canarie programme called the Infrastructure Extension Programme has a statement of purpose which says they are to... enable national and international collaboration, improve access to knowledge, and contribute to the development of cyberinfrastructure and e-research in Canada. Specifically, connections to government laboratories, educational institutions and other facilities are to be supported.

Very few K-12 school boards or public libraries currently take advantage of this amazing opportunity. Canarie/BCNet may be able to provide British Columbia K-12 school boards and public library systems with improved bandwidth at a reduced cost. In Ontario, one public library system is planning to use Canarie access (through the Ontario partner, Orion) to provide recreation centers with free wifi zones. Recreation centers are open more hours than public libraries. Technology and technologically-based solutions to problems will be peppered throughout this report. The most important message is that school boards and public library boards need more knowledge about how people use technology when they seek information, and libraries need to ensure that their mandate fits that world. As an example, the Cleveland Public Library has just started to offer library card holders free cloud storage space that is protected from commercial invasion and that ensures privacy is preserved. Wow.

FROM CONSUMPTION TO CREATION

An emerging trend, with a youth focus, is shifting the role of public libraries from a place focused only on information that is consumed (usually by taking it home to read or view) towards places where people gather, learn from each other and then use new skills. This trend is reflected in the American Library Association report mentioned in the Introduction. The shift towards library as community creativity hub is more developed in northern Europe but some initiatives are taking place in North American.

The Fayetteville Free Library in New York is receiving deserved attention for its Fab Lab, featuring a 3D printer that people can use to *print* plastic objects. The 3D printer is not expensive (less than $2,000) but is having a huge affect on how youth and older customers view their library system. The District of Columbia Public Library has a recording studio in its Central Library teen area. The Chicago Public Library has a YouMedia Center where young adults can:

- *Hang out* (talk to each other in informal sessions with no adults telling them to be quiet or to take their feet off the tables),
- *Mess around* (Experiment with new technologies),
- *Geek Out* (Teach each other about ways they have learned to use music and video editing equipment, etc.)

These three "goals" come from research conducted by the MacArthur Foundation. The research identifies ways that teens and youth can learn from each other. YouMedia labs are now being established in other U.S., cities. The provision of creation spaces in public libraries is pervasive in northern Europe. Researcher visited a Swedish library where people bring projects to the library, learn how to use relevant software tools and then reserve large blocks of computer time for weeks into the future. In contrast, the North American model for public computer use is based on shorter blocks of daily time and an assumption that people are using the computers to search for information. The Helsinki Library system and other Scandinavian libraries provide video and music editing rooms as well as staff expertise. The Finnish creation movement started with a national initiative to reconnect alienated youth. The public library portion of this initiative has proven remarkably successful.

COMPUTERS AND INDIVIDUALISATION

Library computer areas are often designed to resemble quiet reading rooms, but:

- School boards and teachers stress group projects and collaborative work. To complete their work, young people want to cluster and want to talk as they work.
- Some computer applications have noisy, interactive elements.
- People do not always want to use computers while sitting in chairs and at the same kind of desks as the people next to them. They want options.
- The presence of wifi in libraries means that one area cannot be set aside for computer use. Instead, all areas of the library now house technology and all staff need to provide assistance.

The photos to the below tell the story. The first photo is from the Amsterdam Central Library and shows one of their many seating options available to people using library computers. The Amsterdam photo shows an option designed for teens and the way they sit. The second photo is from Mohawk College in Ontario and it shows one of many types of collaboration spaces where teams can work together on projects.

Today, the computer is a phone, a gaming device, a movie screen, a radio and a videoconferencing tool. These are not quiet uses.

OPEN DATA, INTERNET RESOURCES WEB SITES AND LITERACY

The public, graphic Internet is a young technology. It is so young that it has only endured one significant change. It has morphed from being a passive information tool where large companies and organisations posted documents and has become, as well, a place where anyone can and does contribute opinions about events and thoughts or their personal lives. We are beginning to see a third major change in the web. This change is characterised by people being sent information that their profile suggests they might like to receive. Singles Around Me (SAM) is a dating app for smartphones. It links to social media profiles and lets users know when single people who match their interests are physically close, in any city. This is a huge shift from a web that provided passive web pages waiting to be viewed.

FOUR PRIORITIES FOR THE 21ST CENTURY PUBLIC LIBRARY SERVICE

- Place the library as the hub of a community.
- Make the most of digital technology and creative media.
- Ensure that libraries are resilient and sustainable.
- Deliver the right skills for those who work for libraries.

The key issues emerging in this research are similar to those we handle with the wider arts and cultural sector. It is because there is such a close fit with the Arts Council's five long term goals that we will be able to develop solutions to these challenges from which both libraries and arts organisations can benefit.

Place the Library as the Hub of a Community

We know that, in future, many people are likely to lead more isolated lives. More will work from home and more will live alone. Opportunities to meet in free public spaces for a wide variety of purposes will be increasingly important. Our findings show that libraries will continue to be valued as trusted, safe, democratic places that offer valuable resources and expertise to support the activities of the people who use them.

Libraries' physical space will be more flexible and integrated with a virtual presence that includes web-based reading groups, social networking and links to other online resources. People will engage in creative and cultural activities as well as reading and learning, exchanging ideas, conversation and knowledge.

Space shared with community based services (such as council, health, business support, and learning organisations) will be better for local people, and will bring benefits such as skills exchanges, reaching more people and cutting costs.

The challenge: the use of a library's space:

- Re-think the way library spaces are used to encourage shared and creative activity while continuing to welcome those who want to explore on their own
- Integrate the library's physical and virtual spaces
- Sustain enough spaces offered by libraries to meet the needs of their communities

Make the most of Digital Technology and Creative Media

Digital technology is developing rapidly and will continue to have a major impact on the way we obtain and consume information, culture and the written word. Beyond the library building, people will expect a more interactive experience and to be able to gain access to library services all day, every day, particularly while on the move.

Libraries should be at the heart of digital innovation. They should develop their role in actively connecting communities and helping people to experience, experiment with and master new technologies. Digital technology will be the key to future library service delivery but our research points out that its true potential will not be achieved unless the principle of an open, enabling ICT infrastructure is agreed by local authorities and library services.

This would allow libraries to innovate, and to share or jointly adopt services more efficiently. By making it easier to develop national services and enable local innovation, people will get access to more resources, information and support. Many assume that digital information sources and online services are accessible to everyone. But a digital divide still exists because a significant number of people lack the confidence, the necessary skills or the desire to make effective use of technology. Some who do, are held back by poor digital connections or can't afford them. Public libraries will ensure that no-one needs to be left behind or excluded.

The challenge: using technology:

- Improve the quality and consistency of the virtual library experience
- Develop an open ICT infrastructure that encourages innovation and better service
- Enable libraries to lend the full range of e-books, including remotely

Ensure that Libraries are Resilient and Sustainable

Our research, along with reductions in public expenditure, makes clear that libraries will need to reduce costs and find other sources of funding to supplement local authority support. Alongside this, communities are becoming more involved in the design and delivery of library services. To find the right solution, councillors in local authorities are considering whether they should change the way their library service is governed, or whether they can share aspects of their service with others.

Our research indicates that, as with many other public services, this trend will continue and grow, and the debate about community involvement in public libraries needs to be seen in this wider context. We do not suggest that any one approach is the right one in all circumstances but we have published guidance, based on experience to date, that we suggest should be taken into account.

Some library services are already doing this and we believe that they could be role models, not just among libraries, but for all public services. This kind of community involvement will become seen not as a cost-cutting tool but as a normal way of working, with staff and users developing ideas and creating services together.

The challenge: cutting costs, finding new sources of funds and new ways of working:

- Create a positive environment for communities and individuals to become actively involved in the design and delivery of their library services
- Encourage the development of new approaches to governing and managing libraries that make it more likely that they will survive and succeed
- Equip libraries to be commissioned to deliver other public services, and to commission other organisations to deliver library services

Deliver the Right Skills for those Who Work for Libraries

Our research indicates that one of the major challenges facing public libraries in the future is ensuring that library staff have effective leadership and delivery skills for a rapidly evolving service. Librarians will need to be active in their communities, encouraging people to get involved with their library. That involvement will include local people identifying what their priorities are as well as volunteering and community managed services.

Supporting people in using digital resources competently and confidently will become increasingly important. Those who work in libraries will need to improve their skills in organising and helping users to find their way through complicated information sources. They will become more pro-active in inspiring new services in partnership with others, and their leaders will need to be more entrepreneurial and adept in communicating and marketing their services.

Our research indicates that not enough people working in libraries are equipped to tackle these changes and take on these roles, and that current training is not always relevant for the current and future needs of those working in public libraries.

The challenge: developing the skills of those who work in libraries:

- Ensure those responsible for libraries have the right range of skills and experience to lead their services successfully
- Encourage those working in libraries to offer creative and innovative ways to use library spaces, books and other resources
- Ensure that library staff have the skills to develop and respond to digital developments and to support digital users

THE ROLE OF THE ARTS COUNCIL IN DEVELOPING THE LIBRARY OF THE FUTURE

We also recognise that to build an effective 21st century library service, we will need to work in partnership with a range of agencies, who have their own distinctive responsibilities:

- Department of Culture, Media and Sport where the statutory oversight of public libraries in England sits.
- Local Government Association who represent the local authorities with the statutory responsibility and democratic mandate to ensure public library services are provided.
- Society of Chief Librarians who are the leaders of public library services.
- Chartered Institute of Library and Information Professionals who are the professional organisation for librarians.
- British Library the national hub of knowledge, information and expertise.

This is only the start and we will be inviting other partners from across the library, cultural, commercial, voluntary and academic sectors to work with us to make real this ambition for public libraries in England. We are confident that we now have a robust set of evidence to provide a framework for what happens next. We want this evidence to inspire a collaboration that will make it possible for the public library service to change and develop with confidence.

By combining our resources we expect to be making progress on a shared programme of activity by the end of the year. So we invite all those involved in libraries and those who care about their future to embrace the findings and to work with us on the next stage of their development.

THE ROLE OF LIBRARIES IN FUTURE DLs

In the framework envisaged by DILIGENT, libraries play an important role at the organisational level. In particular:

- As providers of resources, they can help to enhance the amount of available resources by making stakeholders aware of the importance of sharing. In particular, as far as the sharing of content is concerned, they can operate by promoting digitisation campaigns and the Open Access approach. These actions may result in a vast amount of new digital information accessible online which can be exploited by advanced services.
- Also within a digital framework, libraries are certainly the best candidates for carrying out content description, maintenance and preservation of resources. By exploiting their large experience acquired in the past, they can contribute to the long-term availability and to the quality of the resources disseminated by the DLs.
- Long-term availability also requires the implementation of models able to support the sustainability of the resources provided. Libraries, either alone or as members of library consortia, can also act as the organisations deputed to define and put in place these models.
- As main resource providers, libraries can work jointly on the definition

of common policies and standards. An agreement on these aspects would strongly contribute towards facilitating the design and development of the new complex services required to fulfil the emerging user needs.

- In the future envisaged by DILIGENT, libraries can also play an important role as mediators between the infrastructure and the user communities. In particular, they can proactively promote and facilitate the creation of DLs that respond to the needs of the user communities. They can also assist users by providing, if necessary, the skills required to select, update and exploit the DL content and services.

FUTURE DIGITAL LIBRARY MANAGEMENT SYSTEMS

One major goal of grid computing is to establish highly flexible and robust environments to utilise distributed resources in an efficient and transparent way. Due to the highly dynamic nature of such environments where computational nodes may leave or join in, it is essential to bind service invocations to concrete service instances at run-time. This allows to flexibly reacting to changes in the environment. In a service-oriented world, application logic is encapsulated by means of services.

Standards like SOAP over HTTP can be used for the invocation of services, and WSDL for accessing information on the capabilities of services. When several instances of the same service exist in a grid environment, then it should be possible to dynamically make use of as many service instances as possible by parallelising a service call and by submitting requests in parallel to them. The goal of this parallelisation is twofold and depends on the characteristics of the services which are subject to parallelisation.

First, we aim to make use of as many services as possible to increase the quality of the result. This is particularly true for the access to data sources, encapsulated by dedicated services. Second, having multiple service instances accessible opens the possibility to speed up the processing of computationally intensive tasks. Whereas examples for the latter have been presented in detail in and large scale experiments with more than 2500 worker nodes have been demonstrated in using MW class library, this work focuses on the goal of enhancing the quality of the request when accessing data sources by means of services.

The contribution of this work is to introduce architecture of a service seeming to be an ordinary, callable service to the outside world, which is able to adopt its behaviour controllable by optional quality of service criteria, and the resources available on a grid. In short, such dynamic services use Meta information on the currently available service providers and their capabilities and partition the original request into a set of simpler requests of the same service types.

These requests are then submitted in parallel to as many service providers as reasonable, and their responses are finally integrated and returned as the result of the original request. In particular, this parallelisation shall be carried out without the need to modify existing functionality or interfaces, and transparently to the user and developer. Due to its master/slave nature, it is especially suitable for grid environments. To better illustrate the benefits of such an approach, the following scenario describes how these dynamic services can be used in health care applications.

A SAMPLE SCENARIO

GENOTYPE/PHENOTYPE CORRELATION

Donald, a patient, consults his family doctor telling him about pain in his chest, shortage of breath, and drowsiness. Besides these symptoms being an indicator for angina pectoris, Donald describes that starting a few hours ago, he additionally suffers from pain in his abdomen and changing paralysis of his right and left leg. Based on this description, the physician wants to ask for a second opinion and admits the patient to a hospital for further examination. The specialist who examines Donald in the hospital recognises some very specific clinical artifacts which raise his interest. Due to these symptoms, Donald has to undergo clinical as well as molecular genetic examinations, since this clinical fingerprint might be caused through a fibrillin-1 gene mutation. To find out more about Donald's potential genetic mutation, his clinical fingerprint is used as an input for a genotype/phenotype correlation. The quality and statement of such a correlation is highly influenced by the amount of data that can be processed.

Collaboration among various health care institutions, where data is made available by genotype/phenotype correlation services, is therefore of great importance. Luckily, the clinical fingerprint of Donald was indeed listed in the data set of a partnering hospital, connected to the grid and dynamically included in the search, and correlates with the Marfan–Syndrome.

An expensive molecular biological examination in which this genetic defect is confirmed is conducted. Therefore, in addition to the acute vascular operation he has to undergo because of his clinical symptoms, his family can be invited for genetic screening to avoid similar costly, high risk operations in the future. Using the approach described in this work, the correlation service does not only consider the in-house service of a single hospital. Rather, it is a self adaptive, virtual service that dynamically and in parallel calls all available genotype/ phenotype correlation services in the system, thereby jointly accessing the data sources of several health care institutions.

As a benefit of the architecture proposed, the client application as well as the genotype/phenotype correlation functionality does not have to be updated or rewritten to participate in or benefit from such a self adaptive environment.

Although the example is taken from eHealth digital libraries, the proposed architecture can of course be applied to other domains as well. Whenever it is appropriate to dynamically replace a single invocation of a service by multiple invocations, dynamic adaptation and parallelisation can be highly beneficial. The remainder of this extended abstract is organised as follows. We briefly describe the overall architecture and show the benefits of dynamic parallelisation for the application scenario. Finally, a conclusion and an outlook on future work are given.

OVERALL ARCHITECTURE

The goal of the architecture we propose is to improve the usability of a single service, as well as to facilitate faster and less error prone development for grid environments. This approach is based on the observation that, following the current proliferation of service-oriented architectures, the number of services and service providers in a grid will significantly increase. Especially services which are provider independent and are not bound to special resources can be distributed fast and widely in a grid environment or be deployed numerously on demand. Although the availability of many congruent services as well as the computational resources thereby offered seems to be within reach, adapting functionality for parallel execution is still necessary and tedious.

The task of partitioning request parameters and re-integrating results afterwards is highly application-specific and, from our perspective, cannot be solved in a generic way. Although we see the potential to identify classes of applications according to the mechanism they partition and re-integrate requests which allows to have pre-built splitter and merger services, an expert in the problem domain will be necessary to tailor them for the specific need or perform some additional, application domain specific work. We name a service, enriched with the capability to partition incoming requests and reintegrate partial results, a dynamic service.

Apart from that we introduce a Dynamiser component, which can be built generically and which is responsible for state management, failure handling, and service discovery. While the latter characteristic is independent concerning the twofold approach failure handling and state management differs. In case of a dynamic service aiming to leverage the result quality, the unexpected absence of a 'worker' service already in charge of a partial task does not hinder in producing a result. If partitioning the request of a computationally intensive task to gain better performance, the overall results rely on each sub task and the Dynamiser is responsible for compensating any failing 'worker' service.

The following logical units can be identified for dynamic services. The box in the center of the left side, labeled 'Payload Service', represents the actual service. It is responsible for providing application semantics, *e.g.*, a genotype/ phenotype correlation on a local database. This is usually a piece of business logic that has existed beforehand and is now supposed to be opened to the grid and enabled for parallel execution.

To achieve this goal, it is surrounded by another box, labeled 'Common Interface Wrapper', which encapsulates the 'Payload Service' and enhances it with a common interface.

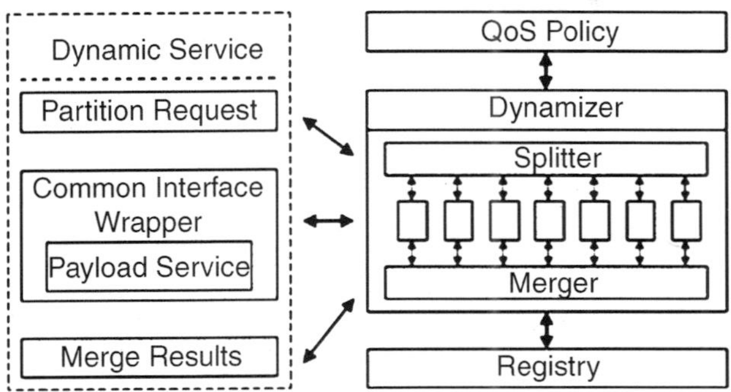

Fig. Overall Architecture

On top, 'Partition Request' encapsulates knowledge on how incoming parameters for the 'Payload Service' have to be partitioned, so that the original request can be decomposed into numerous new sub-requests. Each of these sub-requests can then be distributed on the grid and be processed by other instances of the originally targeted service.

The box at the bottom integrates results returned from the grid to provide the original service requester with a consolidated result. It can therefore be seen as the counter operation to the 'Partition Request' service.

The combination of these elements is referred to as 'Dynamic Service'. To find instances of the originally targeted service, a registry is used. This registry provides information on which services are available, how they can be accessed, and what their properties are. The 'Dynamiser', depicted on the right hand side, makes use of the services. It glues together the previously described services by making the parallel calls and coordinating incoming results. The 'Dynamiser' can interact with all services that adhere to a common interface, as ensured by the 'Common Interface Wrapper'.

It can be integrated in environments able to call and orchestrate services, or it can be packaged and deployed together with specific services. To make the best possible use of the 'Dynamiser', the user can send an optional description of the desired service quality along with the mandatory parameters needed to process the request. In this Quality of Service (QoS) policy, the user can, for example, describe whether the request should be optimised in terms of speed, in terms of bandwidth or if it should aim for best accuracy.

Since these specifications can be contradictory, adding preferences to rank the user's requirements is of importance. To better illustrate the mechanisms within the 'Dynamiser' regarding the user specified QoS policy, we consider the following example: the specialist from the previously introduced health care scenario specifies that he wants to use as many genotype/phenotype correlation information as possible and as affordable within a 300 Euro budget. The 'Dynamiser' finds 7 services with a total of 2 gigabytes of searchable data, each charging 60 Euros per query. Alternatively, there are 40 services available provided by smaller institutions, having just searchable amounts of data starting from 4 megabytes up to 30 megabytes and charging.50 per query. The algorithms on how to reconcile the user specifications, the details of the QoS description language and how to integrate this best with our existing implementation is currently investigated.

INFLUENCE OF REPLICATION ON AVAILABILITY WITHIN P2P SYSTEMS

Peer-to-peer (P2P) digital libraries are highly dynamic as they shall facilitate data sharing among users. The churn rate is high as their peers enter and leave the system frequently. Hence, the dependability of peers is worse than the corresponding characteristics of traditional servers. Particularly, current P2P systems employ *small-world topologies*, *cross-partition pointers*, *self-organisation* and *periodic description updates* to improve dependability. In summary, these means aim at maintaining the topology and communication among available peers in the presence of failing peers.

P2P systems offer services which are delivered by participating peers. The operation of a service requires access to resources, like databases. Usually, these resources are hosted by the peers who deliver the service. If the hosting peers fail, the service crashes jointly. Hence, means of retaining communication and topology do not suffice to improve dependability of P2P services. Means must address the resources hosted on peers as well. Replication and caching are suitable means to improve availability of resources. Digital library systems provide data and metadata.

Usually, caching is preferred to replication for data like audio and video files as this kind of content changes rarely. However, metadata is subject to replication, because it is updated by users frequently, *e.g.*, to rate content. For example, Kov´acs et al. describe a peer-to-peer digital library which caches content and replicates metadata. P2P systems differ from traditional distributed systems. For example, intermediate peers influence the dependability of communication, and fault characteristics of peers are worse than the corresponding attributes of traditional servers. Therefore, replication has to be investigated specifically for P2P contexts, because solutions for traditional distributed systems may not be appropriate. Our work addresses this issue for the voting-based replication strategies *Read-One- Write-All* (ROWA) and *Majority Consensus* as a first step. Particularly, we explore the availability of read and write operations on replicated resources compared to non-replicated resources.

RELATED WORK

Vanthournot et al. propose small-world topologies, self-organisation, and cross partition pointers as means of fault-tolerance within P2P systems. They simulate P2P systems to investigate the resulting dependability. They focus on failures of peers and connections, but omit the issue of resources on peers. Replication based on rumour spreading is proposed for P-Grid. These algorithms ease consistency conditions to improve availability and performance. They focus on analysing the communication overhead.

THE XPEER ARCHITECTURE

P2P systems which are required to be highly dependable in the presence of frequent updates under a sequential consistency model come into question for voting-based replication. Our current work includes the XPeer architecture for data integration within such systems. XPeer is a logical super-peer architecture which is well suited for digital libraries. It addresses the issue of querying distributed data in a large scale context by realising an integrated schema.

This schema is formed from heterogeneous information sources by classifying data sources into domains and creating user profiles for query optimisations. Information sources are integrated using XPeer's novel concept of super-peer application in a database environment. Super-peers are used to integrate information sources from clusters of interest or similarity. However, these sources are prone to disappear in a P2P architecture, causing problems for the query service and the optimisation process. The Replication Service described here is used to extend the original architecture.

METHOD

The availability of reading a replicated resource must be considered separately from the availability of writing, because the behaviour of replication control strategies may differ for reading and writing. We evaluated the resulting values by discrete event-simulation of scenarios. We developed a simulation model of peers following real-world implementations like Freenet and incorporated techniques of replication.

A scenario consists of a P2P system with specific peers, connections, and their availabilities, a replication strategy and a distribution of replicas to peers. The set of all possible scenarios is infinite. We restrict ourselves to a subset of scenario classes for the investigation. The set of all scenarios can be characterised along five main dimensions: P2P architecture, P2P instantiation, faults, replication architecture, and replication deployment.

The P2P architecture describes the conceptual layout of a P2P system. The dimension is subdivided into degree of centralisation, structure, and style of communication. The degree of centralisation determines whether a system may have centralised elements, *e.g.*, index servers. The topology of P2P systems may be structured, *e.g.*, to a ring or small-world topology. The style of communication describes whether peers are able to communicate indirectly by relaying and forwarding messages. A P2P instantiation is a derivation of an actual P2P system from architecture. It describes how many peers participate in the system and how they are connected.

The faults dimension specifies the fault characteristics of peers and connections. We assume an exponential distribution of faults. For our purposes, the mean time to failure and the mean time to repair suffice, because the availability and reliability of peers and connections can be derived from these values. The replication architecture describes the conceptual behaviour of replicas. Several classifications of replication are known. The replication instantiation specifies the actual number and distribution of replicas to peers.

RESULTS

We derived 36 scenarios classes from the dimensions above. We chose decentralised and super-peer architectures with unstructured, mesh-like, and small-world topologies and indirect communication. The mesh-like topology is a special type of a structured topology, whereby each peer is connected to four neighbours to form a net. A small-world topology is characterised by short paths of intermediate peers between any pair of peers. The number of peers is fixed to 49 for each scenario. The connections are chosen depending on the demands of the topology. The range of mean times to failure and mean times to repair is derived from observations of a real-world system. Two simple types of weighted voting are considered for the replication architecture: Read-One-Write-All (ROWA) and Majority Consensus.

The number of replicas is fixed to five for deployment. Their distribution to peers is managed in two ways: They are located on peers with best fault characteristics or are allocated according to a normal distribution. Each scenario class is simulated with a single read or a single write access to acquire the resulting availability. Additionally, each obtained P2P system is simulated with a non-replicated resource to be able to evaluate the relative influence of ROWA and Majority Consensus. The results of the simulations for each scenario class are presented in table. The relative influence of the replication techniques compared to the corresponding scenario classes without replication is illustrated in figure.

The ROWA strategy requires access to a single replica for reading. We expected that the strategy heavily improves the availability of reading. It has its best influence for availability of reading for scenario class 12 with about 4.25 per sent. The worst influence occurs for scenario class 5 where no influence was measured at all. Not surprisingly, it improves reading for most scenarios. However, for some scenario classes the influence is negligible.

The ROWA strategy requires access to all replicas for writing. Hence, all hosting peers must be available for executing a write operation successfully. We expected that the strategy heavily decreases availability of writing, which was confirmed with relative influences ranging from '32.89 per sent to 0.15 per sent. The Majority Consensus strategy requires access to more than half of the replicas for reading and writing.

Resulting Availability for Reading		Replication Control Strategy					
		None		Read-One-Write-All		Majority Consensus	
		Replica Distribution		Replica Distribution		Replica Distribution	
Structure		Best Peers	Normal Distr.	Best Peers	Normal Distr.	Best Peers	Normal Distr.
Unstructured / Fault Distribution	Uniform Good	0.9993		0.9997		0.9995	
	Uniform Medium	0.9762		0.9871		0.9879	
	Normal Distr.	0.9470	0.9468	0.9775	0.9758	0.9781	0.9752
Mesh-Like / Fault Distribution	Uniform Good	0.9998		0.9998		0.9996	
	Uniform Medium	0.9752		0.9886		0.9858	
	Normal Distr.	0.9692	0.9387	0.9740	0.9747	0.9780	0.9732
Super Peer / Fault Distribution	Uniform Good	0.9994		0.9997		0.9997	
	Uniform Medium	0.9628		0.9785		0.9761	
	Normal Distr.	0.9209	0.9099	0.9493	0.9486	0.9470	0.9299

Resulting Availability For Writing				Replication Control Strategy					
				None		Read-One=-Write-All		Majority Consensus	
				Replica Distribution		Replica Distribution		Replica Distribution	
				Best Peers	Normal Distr.	Best Peers	Normal Distr.	Best Peers	Normal Distr.
Structure	Unstructured	Fault Distribution	Uniform Good	0.9992		0.9989		0.9995	
			Uniform Medium	0.9763		0.9296		0.9879	
			Normal Distr.	0.9470	0.9467	0.9499	0.6382	0.9781	0.9753
	Mesk Like	Fault Distribution	Uniform Good	0.9996		0.9981		0.9998	
			Uniform Medium	0.9750		0.9271		0.9858	
			Normal Distr.	0.9690	0.9388	0.9220	0.6359	0.9778	0.9730
	Super-Peer	Fault Distribution	Uniform Good	0.9994		0.9983		0.9999	
			Uniform Medium	0.9627		0.9627		0.9760	
			Normal Distr	0.9207	0.9098	0.6612	0.6106	0.9471	0.9297

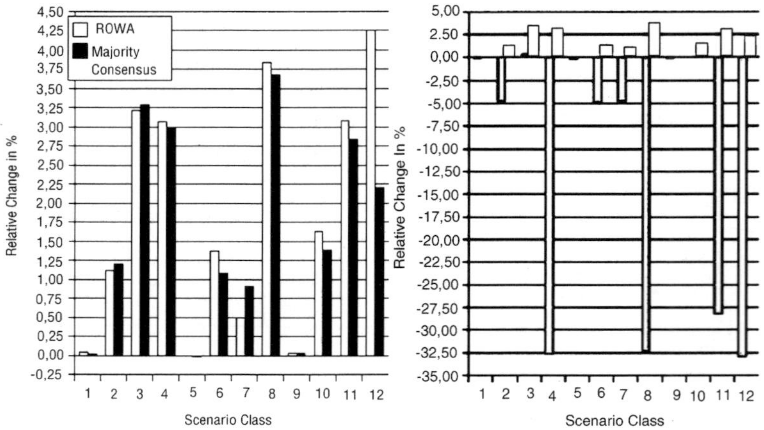

Fig. Relative Change Reading/ Writing

We expected that the strategy improves both availabilities. The influence for reading was expected to be worse than the influence of ROWA, because access to more than one replica is required. It has its best influence for scenario class 8 with a relative improvement of about 3.68 per sent. The worst influence occurs for class 5 where its influence is negligible. In general our expectation was confirmed as the strategy improves availability for reading and writing. The influence for read operations was worse than the influence of ROWA. However, it exceeds ROWA for the scenario classes 2, 3, and 7. It is interesting to see that it does not decrease availability significantly for any scenario class we chose. A broader generalisation of the simulation results is a topic for future work. Even small changes to the scenario may have high impact on the resulting values. However, our results already indicate at this stage that voting-based replication strategies are a favourable replication technique for P2P systems when high consistency is required. Even if the peers of the scenario classes had fault characteristics worse than traditional servers, Majority Consensus improves availability of reading and writing.

ADAPTIVE REPLICATION STRATEGIES AND SOFTWARE ARCHITECTURES FOR PEER-TO-PEER SYSTEMS

The use of replication techniques for data in distributed information systems aims at improving non-functional properties of these systems. Particularly, availability, reliability, and performance should be increased. When considering heterogeneous, autonomy-preserving systems such as distributed digital libraries, the replication techniques employed should be able to adapt to varying proper- ties of the individual systems at run-time. Adaptive replication strategies need to be realised by a software architecture which provides the context for their implementation.

Digital library systems, whose information providers are organisationally closely related, for example under the umbrella of a single institution, should be tightly coupled, in order to allow for a high degree of consistency to be maintained. Other digital libraries, such as those of separate publishers, should be coupled less tightly, to allow for retaining their autonomy. This can be realised by a replication strategy based on peer-to-peer (P2P) techniques which combines intra-institutional and inter- institutional replication strategies. The overall replication strategy is evaluated and optimised at run-time, such that domain-specific requirements are incorporated into a multi-dimensional problem model.

DATA REPLICATION STRATEGIES

Data replication aims at increasing availability, reliability and performance of data accesses by storing data redundantly. A copy of a replicated data object is called a replica. Replication ensures that all replicas of one data object are automatically updated when one of its replicas is modified. Replication involves conflicting goals with respect to guaranteeing consistency, availability and performance. An improvement of one of these properties usually implies a degradation of the others. Replication in a distributed system is realised by a replication strategy, which is often controlled by replication managers. The quality of a strategy can be measured by the correctness criterion it safeguards. The strictest criterion is that of one-copy-serializability: The concurrent execution of a set of distributed transactions is one-copy serialisable, if its effect is equivalent to the sequential execution of the transactions on a non-replicated database.

Besides this criterion a number of other correctness criteria have been defined, which are less strict and thus easier to fulfill. Replication can be performed in an eager or lazy way. In the case of eager replication, when one replica is modified by a transaction, the other replicas of the concerned data object are updated within the original database transaction, as opposed to lazy replication where only the originally accessed replica is updated within the original transaction, while the other replicas are updated in separate transactions. The classification into synchronous and asynchronous replication strategies is essentially equivalent to this classification. Combinations of synchronous and asynchronous replication have also been studied. The concept of an adaptive replication manager was first proposed in. Its goal is to achieve an optimal trade-of between tight and loose coupling of in- formation systems, which is realised by dynamically switching participating systems between being synchronously and asynchronously updated.

PEER-TO-PEER SYSTEMS

Peer-to-peer systems are distributed systems that follow a communication model of equal nodes which communicate directly with each other. In the following we introduce deferent styles of peer-to-peer architectures before we describe the specific benefits of replication within peer-to-peer architectures.

Styles of Peer-to-Peer Architectures

The class of peer-to-peer architectures can roughly be divided into pure and hybrid peer-to-peer architectures. Pure peer-to-peer architectures are completely decentralised. Each peer in the network is equipped with both client and server functionality and the architecture does not contain any central servers at all. Hybrid peer-to-peer architectures combine characteristics of pure peer-to-peer architectures and client/server architectures. Some services are offered by servers and are therefore centralised, whereas other services are based on the peer-to- peer communication model.

Hybrid architectures can further be subdivided into centralised architectures and super-peer architectures. In centralised architectures there are nodes with pure server functionality which offer exclusive services. Super-peer architectures are also called hierarchical architectures and combine the concepts of decentralised and centralised architectures. A super-peer is a peer which acts as a server for a set of ordinary peers and usually interacts with other super-peers. Ordinary peers are typically organised in clusters together with a single super-peer. Super-peer architectures are particularly suited to support both intra- and inter-institutional cooperation because they allow for representing the structures of an institution within the super-peers' clusters as well as the structures among different institutions by connecting the different super-peers accordingly.

Peer-to-Peer Replication

Today's replication strategies often depend on centralised solutions. Replicating heterogeneous, autonomy-preserving information systems, however, requires flexible and well-coordinated approaches. Intra- and inter-institutional replication should be addressed by an integrated approach, where institutions are coupled via a suitable peer-to-peer infrastructure.

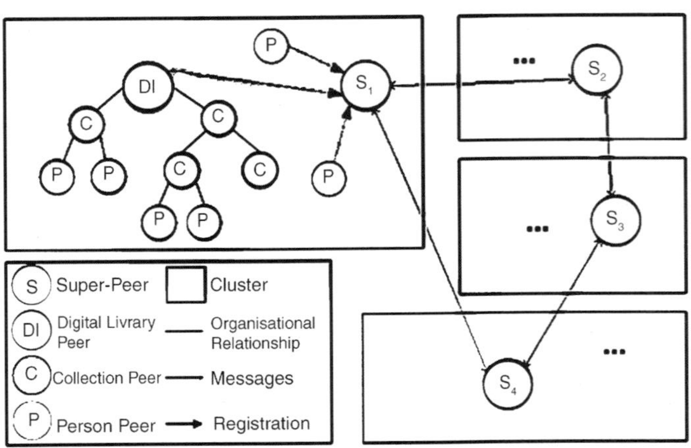

Fig. Organisation-oriented Super-peer Architecture for Digital Libraries

A super-peer architecture reflecting the requirements of different cooperative digital library systems is shown. We have chosen a super-peer approach because it allows structuring the logical network in accordance with the organisational structure. This architecture is one example of how to model specific organisational requirements by extending peer-to-peer architectures by an additional layer which provides information on the organisational context. The architecture forms a basis for intra- and inter-institutional integration and replication of distributed data resources and services.

Digital libraries together with specialised sub collections as well as individual users are represented by different types of peers. The connections among these peers as shown in the upper right of figure are only one example of how a library may be organisationally structured. Other, non-hierarchical structures are also sup- ported. Documents and also services may be controlled by the digital library as super ordinate institution, by single collections and also by single person peers who *e.g.* can offer their individual metadata or link lists to interesting web documents. The intra-institutional structure is complemented by an inter-institutional coupling with the help of super-peers. The super-peers impose a partition into clusters of organisationally closely related peers, where one cluster may comprise one or more institutions. Super-peers have more responsibilities than ordinary peers. A super-peer stores metadata concerning the structure of the institutions under its auspices and of the data resources and services it provides. Thus, its main task is to mediate between the different clusters.

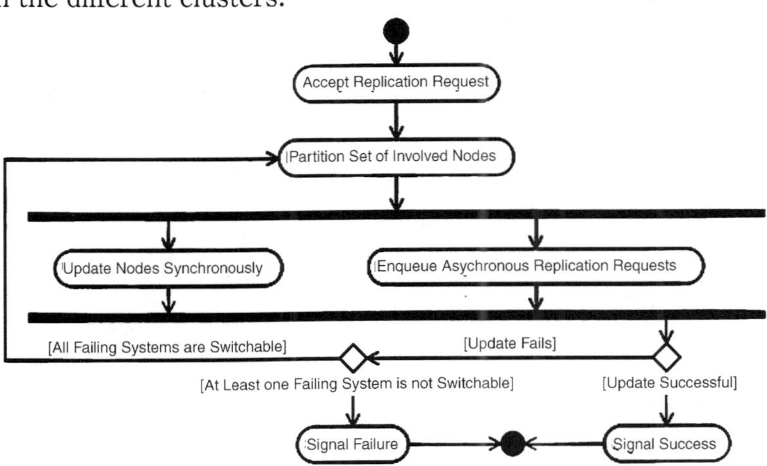

Fig. Adaptive Replication Strategy

The structure given by an organisation-oriented super-peer network can serve as foundation for the realisation of adaptive intra- and inter-institutional replication strategies. Within a single institution the overall information system is usually composed of multiple component information systems, which must replicate data permanently due to high availability requirements. An advanced replication strategy is required to facilitate both high consistency and autonomy of the component information systems, each of which must not be vitally impaired when other systems fail. An optimal trade-of between these conflicting requirements can be reached by combining synchronous and asynchronous replication into an adaptive replication strategy. Each system may be replicated either synchronously or asynchronously at any time. Switching between synchronous and asynchronous replication should be configurable and adaptive with respect to the current network configuration status. The configuration is performed using a system of rules, which is continuously evaluated at run-time to ensure adaptivity. The correctness criterion of the replication strategy is evaluated by means of an appropriate consistency measure, *i.e.* a measure of the probability of consistent accesses. A transaction that modifies a replicated data object is called a replication request. It is initiated by any node connected to the peer-to-peer network and is sent to its replication manager: One possibility to determine the replication manager is to use the digital library peer as intra-institutional replication manager, if the initiating node is contained within an institution. If the replication request is not confined to the originating institution, or if the initiating peer is not assigned to an institutional digital library peer, its super peer is used as an inter-institutional replication manager. The process realising an adaptive replication strategy is illustrated for one replication request.

By evaluating the system of rules, the involved nodes are split into two groups, those that are to be updated synchronously and asynchronously, respectively. After that, both groups of nodes are processed. The nodes in the synchronous group are directly updated, while the update requests for the nodes in the asynchronous group are enquired into a message queue. All node updates are performed in parallel within one transaction.

If all synchronous updates were successful, the processing of the replication request is completed and positively acknowledged. If a synchronous update fails, the replication manager checks whether the failing systems may be switched to asynchronous update mode. If this is the case, the corresponding systems are switched and the processing of the replication request is restarted. If some system could not be switched, the replication request fails. Asynchronous replication requests in the message queue are continuously processed in an independent thread of execution. If a system to be updated is not available, the corresponding request stays in the queue until the update has successfully been performed.

PEER-TO-PEER REPLICATION FOR DIGITAL LIBRARIES

Today's digital library systems cooperate in manifold ways. They exhibit a varying internal organisational structure, *e.g.* given by the introduction of specialised sub-collections or by extraction of project-specific reference libraries. Furthermore, different business models also including the ability to count the cost of library access have to be taken into account. Against this background, the ability to map intra- and inter-institutional requirements to the underlying digital library system as presented is of paramount importance. Libraries including resources other than traditional library documents like *e.g.* resource collections in e-science or health information systems emerge. This calls for the determination of detailed strategies not only for searching these collections but also for replication of both resources and services.

DIGITAL LIBRARIES OF THE FUTURE AND THE ROLE OF LIBRARIES

Research on digital library (DL) systems started in Europe in the mid-nineties. At that time DLs were seen essentially as repositories of digital texts accessible through a search service which was operating by indexing information stored in a centralised metadata catalogue. The construction of a DL was very resourceconsuming since, for each new DL, both the content and the software providing the DL functionality were built from scratch. As a result of this development approach, only powerful user communities or user communities with in-house computer science technical skills could afford the building up of DLs. These DLs were created to serve end-users only as consumers of information. They did not provide any functionality for submitting the documents.

The submission was usually performed either by the author or by a librarian operator by means of specific procedures residing outside the DL. Today, the requirements imposed on DLs are very different from that early time. A novel notion of DLs, also referred to as "knowledge commons" has recently emerged, whose fulfilment requires new technologies and new organisational models. This paper focuses on such new DLs by first discussing the motivations for their introduction, then presenting an innovative DL technology, called DILIGENT, and, finally, illustrating the role that libraries can play in this new scenario.

2

Libraries – An Investment in Our Future

Libraries provide the physical and virtual spaces that are an integral part of an overarching system that provides continuous opportunities for learning from birth to senior age. By offering all New Yorkers the opportunity to acquire the knowledge they need to be informed and engaged participants in an open democracy, libraries empower individuals. Library "profit" is demonstrated through both the promotion of economic enterprise and the social return on investment. Libraries continue to undergo tremendous transition as they move to virtual services in response to changes in technology and the expectations of their patrons, and as they facilitate not only the use of existing information, but also production of new information through online communities and efforts to preserve local history.

One significant change is the increasing convergence among traditionally different types of libraries in the services they offer. Such convergence includes online access to digital resources, the re-tasking of library space, the need for staff skilled in virtual librarianship and collaborative learning, as well as more customary types of service. Because of the continuing centrality, complexity and diversity of today's knowledge creation and information distribution environments, it is important that our students and residents be equipped with both print and digital literacy skills — how to find, evaluate, and effectively use information from a variety of sources and formats.

Literacy – and in particular digital literacy — lies at the heart of the mission of all libraries. Regardless of the many levels of technological change, libraries remain the embodiment of Americans' "right to educate themselves", a critical necessity in a knowledge economy where everyone must relentlessly improve their skills throughout their lifetime.

The library is what makes lifelong learning for *all* residents both possible and practical, including, and perhaps especially, for those with special challenges such as the disabled, homeless and economically disadvantaged. People unable to respond to new challenges and invest in their own abilities are likely to become an economic liability, unable to participate fully in society. Libraries continue to represent a community investment in a vision of a better tomorrow through sharing information, knowledge and, hopefully, wisdom. They are the repositories for the collective memory of our communities, our state, and our nation, and offer us an institution that reflects the American dream of self-help and equity. Today's libraries are busier and more vibrant than ever because of, not in spite of, the dramatic impact of digital technology. But even though they have a well established and well respected brand, libraries suffer from outdated public attitudes based on misperceptions that are limited to their traditional roles, stereotypes and the constant assault of competing commercial information providers.

UNIVERSAL RECOMMENDATIONS –FOR ALL LIBRARIES

The themes of Access, Information Literacy and Sustainability are woven through all libraries in our state and nation. Though each serves its unique community, all share these values.

MODELS FOR SUCCESS

Over six decades ago the State of New York outlined its vision for universal access to information for all residents through its creation of library systems. This remarkably successful model has evolved to embrace nearly all the libraries within our state, creating a framework and foundation for the fulfillment of this dream. The notion that any and every child or adult may follow their curiosity to its fullest extent, accessing resources from around the world, is today a reality for most, but not all, of our state's residents. Vibrant libraries of all types, enjoying the robust support of their community or constituency and working in partnership with their library system and its collaborative systems are able to bring these resources into their communities. We have the potential to fulfill this vision for all.

RECOMMENDATIONS

To assure that tomorrow's libraries continue to be a vibrant and vital part of all New Yorkers' lifelong learning experience, all libraries must:

- Improve the marketing of library services to all clientele and communities by rebranding libraries while addressing the erroneous perceptions about the need for libraries in a digital world.
- Develop better tools for advocacy, and identify library champions at all levels of governance: university and school boards, town and city management, State Education Department, Board of Regents, New York State Legislature and Executive branch.
- Collaborate to integrate services and collections of all types of libraries while developing a transparent and seamless world of library services that are ubiquitous and instantaneous, yet personalised and flexible, serving all ages and needs.

- Seek operational and cost efficiencies in light of technological opportunities, energy efficient facilities, and online service delivery methods.
- Develop economic justifications for the investments that governments, communities, individuals and philanthropic organisations are asked to make in libraries, and enhance the role of libraries as economic drivers for their communities.
- Recruit technologically savvy staff and train current staff in virtual librarianship while influencing higher education to appropriately educate tomorrow's service providers.
- Function at the front lines of e-resources (including e-books) purchasing, licensing, digital rights management, digital curation, resource-sharing, and preservation; and advocate for the delivery of open content as embodied in initiatives such as the Digital Public Library of America or the Berlin Declaration on Open Access to Knowledge in the Sciences and Humanities.
- Actively address issues concerning the privatisation of information and its impact on traditional models of library services, defending residents' rights to free access, free lending and the intersharing of materials among libraries.
- Create collaborative partnerships with all cultural and educational organisations in the state to offer our residents the most comprehensive educational opportunities available anywhere in the world.

SCHOOL LIBRARIES (P-12)

School libraries are deeply engaged in the implementation of the New York State P-12 Common Core Learning Standards. There is a well documented connection between student achievement and effective school libraries. The role of school librarians is evolving as they teach students information literacy to be savvy information consumers, producers and judges of appropriate content in all formats. School librarians increasingly collaborate with teachers in designing curricula, developing learning experiences, and providing technical infrastructure that are ideally placed to support differentiated instruction and facilitate special programmes for the gifted as well as students with special needs. The school librarian is unique in that he/she addresses the depth and breadth of the entire curriculum, and leads in teaching a 21st Century curriculum of enquiry, problem solving and content creation.

MODELS FOR SUCCESS

The best school libraries are fully integrated into the P-12 learning experience and are at the hub of each campus, reaching into every classroom as well as into students' homes. Based on the research findings of the recent Information Brief: The Impact of School Libraries on Student Achievement published by the NY Comprehensive Center, it is clear that with the shift to the Common Core Standards and a commitment to five key elements of the Regents reform agenda, school libraries with certified school librarians play an important role in student achievement, curriculum development and instruction. Information and digital literacy is recognised as a critical aspect of each student's education. The school librarian is a true educational partner with every teacher and administrator in providing the best possible learning experience for each child.

RECOMMENDATIONS

The Board of Regents and State Education Department should formulate policy and regulation that will:

- Adopt and implement a statewide information fluency curriculum framework, aligned with the New York State P-12 Common Core Learning Standards, which, through certified school librarians and a strong library programme, will provide equitable access to information and digital literacy instruction and tools. Such a framework will further the schools' ultimate goal of preparing students, beginning at the elementary level, with the literacy and digital skills and knowledge needed for career or college.
- Expand the existing Commissioner's Regulations to require a certified elementary school librarian in every school to strengthen instructional leadership in meeting the P-12 Common Core Learning Standards, and enforce library staffing regulations in all public schools.
- Create incentives to encourage school districts to actively expand and promote access to the school library collection of online resources, e-books, and Web 2.0 tools, available 24/7, to create learning and enrichment opportunities that reach beyond the school day and encourage yearround learning.
- Create incentives to encourage school districts to adopt flexible scheduling to support full academic day access to school librarians, school library resources and information and digital literacy instruction.
- Create incentives for school libraries to collaborate with other libraries and communities to result in full-time, full-year access to information that will further opportunities for all students.

TRAINING AND SUPPORT TO USERS

The importance of the library as a resource centre and the endeavor of the management to exploit the resources gathered over the years with a lot of investment, need not be over emphasised. However, it has been the experience of many a library, especially those attached to organisations, the use of their resources appear to be little compared to the efforts put in building up the resources. As such there appears to be a constant need to initiate outreach programmes in order to enhance the usage of the library to the maximum extent. Library is looked upon as a centre for learning. The Library has to strive to repackage the material that is received in the library in the form of Alerts, reviews, digests, abstracts and databases to enhance library utilisation and improve readership.

Also, in view of the rapid developments in Information and Communication Technologies, the role of a librarian is not like what it used to be a few decades ago. Added to IT, satellite communication systems, networking, Internet and intellectual property rights, have all made the library environment more complex.

Further, the budgetary constraints, inadequate infrastructure, falling standards in human resources are all compelling the librarian to change his attitude from a mere custodian of information to that of a facilitator. As the library is a service institution there should be close interaction between the information providers, processors and users to enhance the effectivity of any resource centre Keeping in view the factors, National Institute of Rural Development (NIRD) conducted a learning programme on. This programme provided a forum for the users of information and the library personnel to come together, to understand each others way of dealing with information and how the information barriers can be overcome and what best practices are to be adopted to increase the utilisation of the resources of the Library through various training programmes.

LIBRARY UTILISATION AND READERSHIP ENHANCEMENT (LURE)

When CORD conducted the one-day programme LURE I in 1991, had a modest goal to find out the ways and means to increase the library utilisation by adopting innovative methods to lure the readers. This was based on a feeling that we have been investing in the library huge amounts of money year after year, trying to equip the library with more relevant reading material and also recruit trained personnel to make the resources more useful. While we are trying to build up a tempo, we had a feeling somewhere along the line that the readers or users are still not coming along with us. This feeling lead us to an introspection which gave rise to the impetus for conducting a programme for the first time on LURE in 1991.

As stated earlier, the learning programme provided an opportunity for interaction between the library professionals and our own users in understanding the lacunae in promoting exploitation of library resources. In the first workshop on LURE in 1991 several issues were thrown up such as the following.

ISSUES FOR CONSIDERATION

As the reader is reluctant to come to library, it may be necessary that the library has to go to the reader. Naturally, that situation will determine the kind of services that are planned or envisaged to enhance the usage of the library. The issues that influence the usage hinge upon how the information needs are gauged and the methods that are adopted to identify those needs.

Some of the other major issues identified are:

- Focus of the parent organisation.
- Information collection.
- Information processing.
- Information search in the Internet era.
- Information dissemination and;
- Information barriers.

The workshop offered a set of simple but effective steps to increase the library use with suggestions like involvement of users in procurement of literature, client based services, etc.

The other major recommendations include:

- The book selection and acquisition are both important and modalities like participatory practices have to be followed;
- User education and user services have to be frequently conducted by the library to improve the interaction between users and the library personnel;
- A brochure on the library highlighting the library collection, cataloging and classification system followed and the services offered would be more useful;
- Immediate computerisation of all activities of library;
- Creation of new services like abstracting, alerting service, reference and making digests on specific topics, etc.
- Augmentation of facilities for document supply and other physical facilities like proper sign boards, stools to reach higher shelves, etc., and
- Strengthening of the resource sharing at the local level.

These recommendations were taken seriously as they were particularly important in the over all development of the library utilisation. Fortunately, most of the suggestions would be implemented with a telling effect on the positive response of the readers.

LURE – II

After a gap of nearly two years, CORD thought of again reviewing the library utilisation with the completion of library automation. In 1993 a second programme on LURE was conducted. This time with a difference. The impetus came from the management of parent organisation. There was a constant refrain from the management that with automation is there any improvement in the utilisation of library resources? How many faculty are visiting the library? What is the ratio between faculty and participants of various training programmes that visit the library? What special arrangements were made to familiarise the participants with the new automation, etc.

These were a few of the questions that were bothering the management. Also, with computerisation of library procedures, a new barrier is likely to be perceived by the users.

Such 'Automation anxiety' may have to be taken into consideration in designing training programmes on library initiation. The participants were chosen from not only the users of the library but also the participants of the then running courses, besides other librarians of neighbouring institutions. The programme was conducted in 3 sessions.

In these sessions several papers based on cases illustrating the circulation facility, visitors register, pattern of usage of library on different dates and use of various information products of CORD were presented. These studies provided a picture of the pattern of library usage after the automation which appeared to be promising and provided the guidance as to how to increase awareness and access to information.

Several suggestions emerged based on the discussions and some of which are as follows:—

- Information Products:
  - The coverage of indexing and abstracting services done through CORD Index and CORD Abstracts is found to be satisfactory. However, emphasis may have to be given to the immediate interest of the faculty members depending on their research and training programmes.
  - The journals that are covered in CORD Alerts may have to be displayed at a designed place for their immediate location and identification of articles given in the service.
- Maintenance:
  - Upkeep and maintenance of various sections will provide the necessary incentive for the users to browse.
  - Library staff should be trained and motivated to assist the readers.
- User Studies:
  - Though the faculty members are patronising the library, there is a scope for improvement.
  - Visitors to the Library are not always recording their visits in the prescribed register and so it did not reflect the total visits made by the academic staff in comparison with non-academic staff. A strict vigil on the visitors register may have to be maintained to satisfy the management.

The other major recommendations include:

- Promotion of library with a professional image is essential;
- Library staff should be trained in inter-personnel communication skills;
- There is a need to display current journals in more attractive and useful manner like displaying latest issues at a prominent place, rearranging of primary journals in alphabetical sequence, etc.
- NIRD publications should be displayed prominently for outside visitors.
- A marketing approach to its library and information products is essential. For this purpose Library counters and surrounding areas should be used for display of not only for acquired publications but also NIRD publications.
- There are about 3000 participants in a year coming to NIRD to participate in the training programmes, who should be given orientation tour to the library for better appreciation of the resources. Also, a session on information resources, and information management relevant to the theme of any course wherever possible should be arranged apart from display of the publications pertaining to the training programme.
- A faculty directory, user manual, training of staff on information technology, etc., are other suggestions that emerged from the programme.

After LURE-II in 1993 there was marked improvement in the appreciation of library services, the physical facilities and the environment in the library. Non-book material like CD-ROMS, videos, electronic journal have slowly started to show their presence.

In the mid 90s internet opened gates to the Information sources world wide, and made possible access to information from a remote location. As a result it has become more important to look into the problems of transforming a traditional library into an information clearinghouse.

LURE – III

Against this backdrop a 3rd LURE programme was conducted in the year 1998 after a gap of 5 years. This learning programme was made into a National Workshop inviting papers from all over India on various themes such as library utilisation; techniques of readership enhancement; evaluation of library services; internet and changing role of the librarian, etc., Participants from several parts of the country made their presentations based on their own back-home experience in user education and identification of user needs. This workshop revealed various kinds of experiments that are on-going in several parts of the country by innovative librarians and demystifying the Internet for the librarian and the user. Information search in the Internet era has totally changed the way the readers look for information. Searching Internet should become a matter of routine in any special library, to make the expression "Internet is Librarianship" truly applicable.

Some of the other major recommendations of the workshop were:

- Continuous study of user needs.
- Development of communication skills of the library personnel.
- Role of parent organisation in recognising the contribution of their libraries and supporting their activity.
- Design and update of user manual in the fast changing information technology environment.
- Change of attitude of librarians to the market driven economy and interact with the users more closely and make users appreciate the library services.
- A thematic approach to all the library services have to be, *i.e.*, the information products of the library like CORD INDEX, CORD ABSTRACTS should follow the themes identified for the research and training of the institute.
- The Selective Dissemination of Information (SDI) service can perhaps be concentrated on a faculty or a discipline at a time. Once a faculty is studied for a period of 6 months or so as a focussed group the impact on the group and its activities perhaps be quantitatively measured.

CORD is giving continuous training to the Library staff in the areas in order to serve the clientele for effective use of Library Resources. They are also deputing the staff to other training programmes to get trained in these as well as new emerging areas. Simultaneously providing training and support to the users for better utiliztion of the resources without any barriers. Thus a new era emerged where information driven activities gained importance which will hopefully energise the users as well as information specialists to come together and work for the better uilisation of information following the best practices in information dissemination through regular training programmes.

USE OF PUBLIC LIBRARY SERVICES

Expert assessment of the nation's health care system suggests that it is slow in translating knowledge into practice and that patient care is not keeping abreast of advances in basic research. The American Medical Informatics Association recently proposed a plan for improving health care delivery. The plan focusses on clinical decision support, which "encompasses a variety of approaches for providing clinicians, staff, patients or other individuals with timely, relevant information that can improve decision making, prevent errors, and enhance health and health care."

The National Library of Medicine (NLM) can make a substantial contribution to improving national health by making a wide range of biomedical resources readily accessible to advanced information technology. There is a large, and growing, amount of online health-related information. Some resources are in the form of text readily accessible only to humans; examples include MEDLINE/PubMed and ClinicalTrials.gov. Other information is structured and includes biomedical vocabularies, clinical and molecular biology knowledge bases, and model organism annotation databases. Within NLM, examples include the Unified Medical Language System and Entrez Gene.

There are also several specialised biomedical databases, for example the BIND database and PharmGKB, as well as commercially curated drug databases, such as Micromedex DRUGDEX and DrugDigest. The growth of online information resources for biomedicine is outstripping access applications that could allow users to maximally exploit those resources. In order to take full advantage of available resources, the Library needs to provide services beyond traditional information retrieval.

Emerging research provides the underpinnings for developing applications that accommodate the growth in online information. Advanced applications manipulate information, not just text, and provide visualisation of results and interconnections among multiple sources. Some research concentrates on extracting information from text. Other emerging systems focus on using the information extracted; examples include automatic summarisation, question answering, and knowledge discovery.

METHODS AND PROCEDURES

We discuss issues involved in constructing a Biomedical Knowledge Repository and illustrate an emerging Web application that exploits a preliminary version. The SemRep and Sem Gen natural language processing systems will be used to extract information in the form of semantic predications consisting of arguments and a predicate that represent relations between concepts asserted in text. Information in biomedical structured resources will be converted into a common format and all information will be integrated into the repository. Finally, a significant aspect of this project is the development of applications that exploit the Biomedical Knowledge Repository.

Extracting Predications from Text

Two programmes developed at LHNCBC will initially be used to extract semantic predications from ClinicalTrials.gov narrative and MEDLINE/PubMed citations for the repository. SemRep was devised to apply to the clinically oriented research literature, while SemGen addresses the genetic etiology of disease.

SemRep

SemRep is a rule-based symbolic natural language processing system developed for the biomedical research literature. As the first step in identifying semantic predications, SemRep produces an underspecified syntactic analysis based on the SPECIALIST Lexicon and the MedPost part-of-speech tagger. The most important aspect of this processing is the identification of simple noun phrases. In the next step, these are mapped to concepts in the Metathesaurus using MetaMap. Syntactic analysis in table, for example, contains Metathesaurus concepts and semantic types for the sentence in table.

Table. SemRep Analysis

Sentence	Phenytoin induced gingival hyperplasia	(1)
Syntactic analysis	[[head(noun(phenytoin)), metaconc('Phenytoin' :[orch,phsu]))], [verb(induced)], head(noun(['gingival hyperplasia')), metaconc(' Gingival Hyperplasia':[dsyn]))]]	(2)
Semantic Network	'Pharmacological Substance' CAUSES 'Disease or Syndrome'	(3)
Semantic Predication	Phenytoin CAUSES Gingival Hyperplasia	(4)

SemRep relies on structures to translate syntactic structures into semantic predications. One aspect of this processing is 'indicator' rules which map syntactic elements to predicates in the Semantic Network. Argument identification rules then find syntactically allowable noun phrases to serve as arguments for indicators. If an indicator and the noun phrases serving as its syntactic arguments can be interpreted as a semantic predication, the following condition must be met:

The semantic types of the Metathe-saurus concepts for the noun phrases must match the semantic types serving as arguments of the indicated predicate in the Semantic Network.

For example, in the structure given in table, the indicator *induced* maps to the Semantic Network relation in table. The concepts corresponding to the noun phrases *phenytoin* and *gingival hyperplasia* can serve as arguments because their semantic types match those in the Semantic Network relation. In the semantic predication produced as output, the Metathesaurus concepts from the noun phrases are substituted for the semantic types in the Semantic Network relation.

SemGen

SemGen was adapted from SemRep in order to identify semantic predications on the genetic etiology of disease. The main consideration in creating SemGen was the identification of gene and protein names as well as related genomic phenomena. For this SemGen relies on ABGene, in addition to MetaMap and the Metathesaurus. Since, the UMLS Semantic Network does not cover molecular genetics, ontological semantic relations for this domain were created for Sem Gen. The allowable relations were defined in two classes: gene-disease interactions and gene-gene interactions.

Other Systems

The information submitted to the repository by SemRep and SemGen could be supplemented with output from other natural language processing technologies that produce relationships. Phenotypic information from clinical narrative could be made accessible with the NLP system described by Friedman *et al.*. For molecular biology phenomena, several systems use syntactic templates and shallow parsing to produce a variety of relations, including gene and protein functions, protein interactions, and protein modifications such as phosphorylation. Friedman *et al.* use extensive linguistic processing for relations on molecular pathways, while Lussier *et al.* use a similar approach to identify phenotypic context for genetic phenomena.

Converting Structured Data into a Common Format

Since, relations in structured resources are already represented in some kind of formalism, their conversion to a common format is somewhat easier than extraction from text. However, the challenges in normalising such knowledge are not unlike those encountered with textual data. In both cases, knowledge extraction involves syntactic issues and semantic issues.

Various formalisms are used to represent structured data, including relational databases, tables, graphs, etc. Currently, no universal conversion mechanism is available. Moreover, the semantics of the data is often implicit or limited, for example, to short column names in a database schema. The objective of the conversion is the creation of 'normalised knowledge'. This effort, in the context of knowledge management, is somewhat equivalent to term normalisation. Knowledge normalisation ensures that the same entity referred to in different resources is ultimately identified in such a way that it is recognised as a unique thing. Knowledge normalisation forms the basis for information and data integration.

Description of Resources

Over the past twenty years, NLM has developed many knowledge resources, from various perspectives. Terminological resources such as the *Unified Medical Language System* (UMLS) result from the integration of many existing terminologies and ontologies, represented in a common formalism–UMLS' Rich Release Format—and partially normalised. While synonymous terms are grouped together as names for a given concept, synonymous relationships are typically not identified as such.

Nevertheless, with some 8 million relations, the UMLS Metathesaurus constitutes an important resource, providing mostly hierarchical relations and co-occurrence relations. Another source of structured knowledge is represented by the many databases available under the umbrella of the NCBI's Entrez system. While some databases such as MEDLINE/PubMed and *Online Mendelian Inheritance in Man* (OMIM) are mostly textual resources, many other NCBI databases contain predominantly structured information.

Entrez Gene, for example, is a gene-centric resource in which a record provides gene properties such as names, associated diseases, function, sequence, etc. While numerous links have been created across the resources in the Entrez system for navigation purposes, such links typically require human interpretation and therefore cannot be used for knowledge discovery purposes in high-throughput systems. Finally, structured databases and knowledge bases are also available outside NLM.

One example of large, publicly available genomic resource is represented by the genome annotations for the major model organisms. Here, the existence of a controlled vocabulary—the Gene Ontology—has contributed to developing unified functional annotations, integrated in systems such as the Mouse Genome Database and the Saccharomyces Genome Database. In the clinical domain, the various knowledge bases of drug information constitute important resources about drug-drug interactions, drug kinetics and metabolism, and indications and contraindications. DRUGDEX, produced by Micromedex, is an example of such a resource.

Representing Normalised Knowledge

One of the strengths of the World Wide Web is that it relies on textual information, easily created and interpreted by humans. This is also one of its principal limitations. The absence of explicit semantics prevents agents from being able to make sense of the information on the Web. This is the motivation of the Semantic Web, which aims at creating a vast collections of integrated and interoperable resources.

There is an obvious parallel between the Semantic Web and the Biomedical Knowledge Repository we propose to create. The technologies developed for the Semantic Web offer possible solutions to some of the challenges we face, including selecting a formalism for normalised biomedical knowledge and identification issues for biomedical entities. It is worth noting that some of these issues are still actively being debated in the Semantic Web community, especially in the Semantic Web Health Care and Life Sciences Interest Group.

Formalism

Many of the resources produced by NLM and other organisations are available in XML, the eXtensible Markup Language. However, the semantics of XML is limited. In addition to XML, the World Wide Web Consortium (W3C) has produced the specifications of other formalisms for representing resources.

Collectively know as Semantic Web technologies, these specifications define the building blocks of the Semantic Web. Of particular interest to us is the Resource Description Framework. RDF extends the capabilities of the extensible markup language XML as it enables many-to-many relationships between resources and data. The resulting structure is a graph in which the nodes are resources or data and the edges are relationships.

The basic unit in RDF is therefore the equivalent of a triple, similar to a relation in the UMLS Metathesaurus or a predication extracted by SemRep. RDF integrates limited inference rules, enabling, for example, the definition of subclasses and subproperties.

Some extensive resources such as UniProt have already been converted to RDF. The BioRDF task force of the W3C Semantic Web Health Care and Life Sciences Interest Group currently investigates methods whereby existing biomedical resources can be converted to RDF.

Such methods include XSLT, GRDDL and DB2RDF, among others. The *eXtensible Stylesheet Language Transformation* (XSLT) uses a stylesheet approach to converting XML to RDF. GRDDL specifies associations between markup languages–including XLM–and RDF. Finally, DB2RDF is used to convert databases to RDF.

Identification Issues

In order for RDF triples to form a graph–and for integrated knowledge to be interoperable-entities and relationships must be identified consistently and unambiguously. For example, if the disease *Neurofibromatosis 2* is identified by the code *SNOMEDCT:92503002* in one resource and by the code *MESH:D016518* in another, the RDF triples involving *SNOMEDCT:92503002* and *MESH:D016518* will not come together as expected unless both resource are converted to the other annotation system or mappings are created between the two systems.

For example, the UMLS Metathesaurus could be used to convert or bridge between MeSH and SNOMED CT, in this case through the concept *C0027832*. The predications extracted from the literature by SemRep already use UMLS codes to identify biomedical entities. From a technical perspective, several technologies have been developed by various communities to implement identification mechanisms for RDF.

There are three major identification mechanisms:

- LSID (Life Science Identifier), promoted by the Life Sciences community. Examples of applications using LSID include Taverna and resources created by the BioPathways Consortium;
- Solutions based on the HTTP protocol, promoted by the W3C; and
- ARK (Archive Resource Key), promoted by the Digital Library community.

There are important differences among three mechanisms regarding location independence, backward compatibility, resolution mechanism and versioning. It is unclear at this time what mechanism would suit our needs best.

Pilot Project: Converting Entrez Gene to RDF

As a proof of concept, we converted the Entrez Gene database into RDF. The entire Gene database in its native ASN.1 format was downloaded by FTP from the NCBI web site and later converted to XML using the programme gene2xml provided by NCBI. Using the *eXtensible Stylesheet Language Transformation* (XSLT) approach, we mapped the element tags of the XML representation to more intuitive relationship names manually, and used them during the automatic conversion to RDF. Finally, we stored this RDF version of Entrez Gene in the Oracle 10g relational database management system, which provides support for storing and querying native RDF data. The conversion process is illustrated in figure.

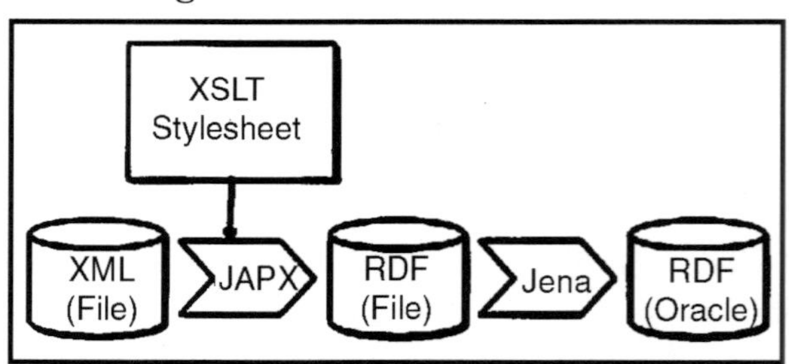

Fig. Overview of the Conversion of Enrez Gene from XML to RDF

Mapping XML Element Tags to RDF Properties

While XML data can be mechanically converted to RDF, the resulting RDF graph would be of limited interest because the semantics of the properties is most often implicit in XML and needs to be made explicit. Starting from one typical Entrez Gene record, we identified all its XML element tags, corresponding to the properties of the gene, as described in the Gene record.

Examples of such properties include *<Genetrack_geneid>* and *<Genetrack_update-date>*, indicating the identifier and the update date of the gene record, respectively. A total of 124 unique elements tags were identified. Because XML element tags represent gene properties, they were transformed into predicates in RDF. For example, *<Genetrack_geneid>* becomes *has_unique_geneid* and relates the gene record to its unique identifier in the Gene database. Note that the RDF property now conveys the notion–implicit in the XML representation–that the identifier is a unique identifier, corresponding to a primary key in a relational database. Converting XML elements to RDF properties requires familiarity with the structure and content of the original record structure and is a key component to the mapping process. After eliminating redundant and superfluous XML element tags, 106 unique RDF properties were created. The mapping of Entrez gene XML element tags to RDF properties is specified formally using the XPath language and constitutes a stylesheet. This stylesheet is specific to the conversion of the Entrez Gene database.

Converting XML to RDF through XSLT

Once the stylesheet is created, it can serve as an auxiliary file for existing programmes realising the XML to RDF conversion. In other words, the major interest of this approach is that no specific code is required for the conversion, because the transformation logic resides entirely in the stylesheet. We used JAXP, the Java *Application Programming Interface* (API) to XML, to implement the conversion. The resulting 411 million RDF triples were then loaded in a store using Oracle 10g using the Jena API.

Lessons Learned, Issues and Challenges

This experiment confirmed the feasibility of converting a large resource from XML to RDF. It also showed that the issues are not technical, but rather lie in the necessity of making explicit the relationships represented implicitly by element tags in XML. This step requires the manual intervention of a domain expert. In our experience, it took less than a week for one person familiar with both bioinformatics and stylesheets to formalise the mapping between XML element tags and RDF properties.

Although the stylesheet created is specific to the Entrez Gene database, it is expected that part of the expertise acquired during this transformation can be applied to transforming other NCBI resources. The major unresolved issue concerns entity identification. If the RDF graph resulting from the conversion of Entrez Gene is to be integrated with clinical or bibliographic information, the diseases associated with genes must be represented not as literals as they currently are, but by their identifiers in the corresponding clinical and bibliographic controlled vocabularies, or with the *concept unique identifier* (CUI) in the UMLS Metathesaurus. Only after such mapping will the RDF graph integrating Entrez Gene and, say, the Metathesaurus, support queries such as *Find all genes associated with neurodegenerative diseases*. The knowledge required in this cases comes in part from Entrez gene and from UMLS.

INTEGRATING PREDICATIONS: BIOMEDICAL KNOWLEDGE REPOSITORY

The Biomedical Knowledge Repository can be understood as a specialised version of the Semantic Web. It consists of an extensive collection of predications, represented in a common format, processable by computers.

Biomedical terminologies and ontologies provide the concepts involved in the facts. Logical reasoners extend the capabilities of the repository by inferring new knowledge. Each fact in the repository is annotated with metainformation regarding its origin, making it possible for applications exploiting the repository to select facts of interest in a given context and for a particular task. Once it is fully populated, the Biomedical Knowledge Repository is expected to comprise several hundred million facts, collected from hundreds of sources.

ORIGIN OF THE PREDICATIONS

The Biomedical Knowledge Repository (BKR) comprises predications form three major sources: extracted from the biomedical literature by NLP programmes such as SemRep, converted from existing structured knowledge bases, and contributed by users. In our vision of the BKR, NLM not only contributes to populating the BKR, but also makes it available to the community as a framework for researchers to deposit their predications.

Predications resulting from experiments, from alternative processing of the literature, and inferred from other predictions, for example, can be contributed by members of the community and made available to others. One measure of success of the BKR would be for it to become a standard repository for the knowledge created through biomedical research experiments. In order to maintain the consistency and integrity of the BKR, its developers would have to follow guidelines regarding formalism of the predications and identification mechanism for biomedical entities.

Metainformation Associated with the Predications

Just as few users need all the vocabularies in the UMLS Metathesaurus for a given purpose, it is unlikely that all predications will be equally useful for a given task, such as question answering. Instead, a mechanism supporting the selection of relevant sets of predications is needed.

The metainformation associated with each predication enables this selection and may include the source of the predication, the method of extraction, the date of extraction, in addition to the usual metadata associated with MEDLINE/PubMed citations for predications extracted from the literature. Researchers contributing predications to the BKR will be requested to annotate them with similar metainformation. Another form of contribution to the repository is to provide not predications, but annotations to existing predications. Such a contribution represents a form of collaborative curation of the repository by the community, similar to the framework developed by the SWAN project for the Alzheimer research community.

Storing the Predications

Several technological solutions, called RDF stores, have been developed for storing information in RDF format, generally implemented on top of some storage system. One such open source RDF database is Sesame. More recently, traditional database management systems have started offering direct support for native RDF triples. For example, version 10g of the Oracle system supports RDF in addition to the relational model. Since, we need to store large amounts of both RDF and traditional information, we started experimenting with Oracle 10g while converting Entrez Gene to RDF last summer. Preliminary results are encouraging although we might face optimisation issues.

Querying the Predications

Analogous to SQL for relational databases, SPARQL is the language for querying RDF. Like SQL, SPAQRL queries have a SELECT and a WHERE clause. However, in a SPARQL query, the WHERE clause follows the pattern of a RDF triple in which at least one element of the triple is replaced by a variable. In the BKR, the predications to be queried would first be selected based on their annotations. For example, a typical query supporting multidocument summarisation would be as follows.

Select all predications from MEDLINE/PubMed returned by a PubMed query on *metabolic syndrome*, restricted to citations from *JAMA*, *Am J Cardiol.* and *J Hypertens.*, published between 2004 and 2005. Additionally, select those predications from the UMLS Metathesaurus and Entrez Gene having at least one node in common with those from the literature.

Integrating Predications

The query example presented above illustrates the interest of integrating knowledge under a unique framework. First, there is a unique namespace for all knowledge in the BKR. As suggested, largely rely on the UMLS for identifying biomedical entities.

Second, once integrated into a graph, the predications can serve as a basis for inferencing, creating additional knowledge along the way. This represents an advantage over traditional database and information retrieval approaches. Finally, complex rules can be written to implement additional reasoning. For example, it is possible to restrict queries to those redundant predications asserted in more than 2 sources and for which the frequency of occurrence is above a certain threshold.

Estimated Size of the Repository

Once fully instantiated, the Biomedical Knowledge Repository is expected to comprise several hundred million predications extracted from the literature, terminological resources and structured knowledge bases. Assuming an average of ten predications is extracted from the title and abstract of each MEDLINE/PubMed citation, we can expect about 150 million predications from MEDLINE/PubMed.

The UMLS Metathesaurus records about 9 million relations, either symbolic or statistical. Some seven million functional annotations for the major model organism databases are recorded in the Gene Ontology database. Finally, our conversion experiment with Entrez Gene yielded over 400 million RDF triples. In this experiment, the objective was to systematically represent in RDF all the information present in the original XML file. In fact, part of this information would become metainformation in the context of the BKR, resulting in a significantly smaller number of triples to be actually contributed to the repository.

Exploiting the Repository: Semantic Medline Web Portal

As a pilot project to exploit a preliminary version of the Biomedical Knowledge Repository, we are developing a Web portal, called Semantic Medline, for managing the results of PubMed searches. The portal is designed as a Java-based Web application that seamlessly integrates PubMed, SemRep processing of the results of the search, automatic summarisation, and, finally, visualisation of the results, with links to the underlying citations and relevant additional knowledge in the UMLS Metathesaurus, the Genetics Home Reference, and Entrez Gene. Realtime access is achieved by pre-processing text from MEDLINE/PubMed abstracts and other sources with SemRep/SemGen and storing the results in a database.

Background

Several recent systems visualise the results of information identified in text as a way of providing users with enhanced access to the information retrieved. Results are often represented as a graph of interrelated relationships. The Telemakus project is based on relationships identified by hand and is meant to enable knowledge discovery through interactive visual maps of linked concepts among documents. Jensen *et al.* constructed literature networks of genes found relevant in gene expression data analysis.

Analysis is based on co-occurrence of genes in MEDLINE/PubMed abstracts. Van der Eijk *et al.* use various relations for literature-based discovery. The relationships represent co-occurrence of MeSH headings associated with MEDLINE/PubMed citations by a mapping programme. Feldman represent several gene-related relations in a graph. The relations were extracted with a type of underspecified natural language processing. Finally, Tao *et al.* visualise genomic information across both structured and textual databases.

Implementation

Semantic Medline is implemented as a three-tier, Java EE-based Web application. The three-tier architecture allows for the separation of user interface, application logic and data storage, providing improved performance, easier maintenance and scalability. We leverage mature open-source technologies in the development to the extent possible. The prototype runs in a Tomcat servlet container on an Apache Web server. It has been developed using the Apache Struts Web application framework. This framework encourages the use of *Model-View- Controller* (MVC) paradigm to provide a clean separation of application model, navigational code, and page design code through the use of Java Servlet API.

The controller is a Java servlet that mediates the application flow; the model comprises Java classes that represent the functionality of the semantic tools and the view is JSP pages that contain dynamic content. A MySQL database is used to store Semantic Medline data, which includes semantic predications extracted from MEDLINE/PubMed abstracts and ClinicalTrials.gov clinical study texts as well as a subset of UMLS Metathesaurus data. The database tables are prepopulated from plain text files that contain SemRep/SemGen output and Metathesaurus data using Perl scripts. Hibernate *object/relational mapping* (ORM) tool is used to programmatically access the database. We use such Hibernate features as database connection pooling and query caching for increased performance.

Using Semantic Medline

MEDLINE/PubMed contains more than 16 million citations drawn from nearly 4,600 journals with biomedical relevance. Searches often retrieve large numbers of items. For example, the query 'diabetes' returns 207,997 citations. Although users can restrict searches by language, date and publication type, results can still be large. For example, a query for treatment for diabetes, limited to articles published in 2003 and having an abstract in English finds 3,621 items; limiting this further to articles describing clinical trials still returns 390 citations. It is difficult for a user to effectively exploit the information in this many citations. Semantic Medline addresses this difficulty by allowing users to summarise the results of searches focused on one of several points of view, including diagnosis and treatment of disorders, drug interactions and adverse events, genetic basis of disease, and pharmacogenomics.

A clinical scenario based on a summary focused on drug interactions illustrates the potential use of Semantic Medline for taking advantage of the research literature in clinical practice. In a hypothetical situation, a patient presents with peptic ulcer and tests positive for *Helicobacter pylori*. The clinician has tried several standard regimens including two different triple regimens: and; however, the patient still tests positive for *H. pylori*.

In order to gain insight from recent research, the physician uses Semantic Medline to issue a PubMed search for lansoprazole. SemRep extracts 5,971 predications from 564 citations returned by this search, and automatic summarisation for drug interactions involving lansoprazole condenses the final list of predications to 182, which are visualised by the system as the interactive graph in figure. Figure provides an informative overview of recent research on lansoprazole represented as predications asserting INTERACTS_WITH. Each predication is linked to the MEDLINE/PubMed citation that generated it.

Of interest for this case are two predications in the graph: 'Lansoprazole INTERACTS_WITH Famotidine' and 'Famotidine INTERACTS_WITH CYPC19 Enzyme.' SemRep extracted the first predication from a citation with title seen in the first line of table and the second from a citation with in the second line.

Table. MEDLINE/PubMed Citations

PMID	Title
15963082	Effect of concomitant dosing of famotidine with lansoprazole on gastric acid secretion in relation to CYP2C19 genotype status
15710002	Concomitant dosing of famotidine with a triple therapy increases the cure rates of Helicobacter pylori infections in patients with the homozygous extensive metaboliser genotype of CYP2C19

Both citations discuss the salutary effect of combining famotidine with lansoprazole. In the second citation, which reports on a randomised controlled trial, the authors realised between 63 per cent to 100 per cent eradication of *H. pylori* with the addition of famotidine to a standard triple therapy and conclude that this is a promising option for patients who phenotypically are extensive metabolisers. If the patient in this hypothetical scenario falls under this category, it would be a potentially valuable regimen to pursue.

EVALUATION PLAN

We intend to follow a multifaceted evaluation plan, focusing evaluation activities on specific aspects of the project.

Evaluating Extraction

For this project, effectiveness of information extracted from text crucially depends on the accuracy of SemRep and SemGen. We have performed linguistic evaluation across a wide variety of predicates that includes the clinical as well as the genetic domain.

Among the predicates evaluated were Treats, Prevents, Location_of, Causes, Isa, Interacts_ With, Affects, Disrupts, Process_of, Part_of, Manifestation_ of, Associated_With, Inhibits, Stimulates and PREDISPOSES. Recall on the extraction of semantic propositions with these predicates has ranged from 41 per cent to 74 per cent and precision from 68 per cent to 84 per cent. Previous evaluations have been reported in and as suggested, continue this evaluation paradigm.

The framework for evaluating knowledge extraction from terminological and structured knowledge bases is not as well established as the evaluation of relation extraction from text. However, several aspects are particularly important. The rules used for the conversion need to be reviewed independently by several experts for a given knowledge base and integrated across databases in order to ensure consistency of the extraction of the relationships. Key to the consistency of the graph is also the mapping of literals to concepts–the nodes in the RDF graph and their consistent representation by identifiers from authoritative sources.

Evaluating Integration

Ideally, the graph resulting from integrating knowledge from several sources is consistent both structurally and semantically. Therefore structural techniques based on graph theory and semantic approaches similar to reasoning services created for description logics are expected to play a central role in evaluating the quality of knowledge integration in the repository.

However, the UMLS Metathesaurus, while resulting from the integration of a much smaller body of terminological knowledge, is already not always structurally or semantically consistent. Like the Metathesaurus, the Biomedical Knowledge Repository will allow contradictory predications to be represented as long as they occur in the original information sources. However, consistency is expected to be found at both structural and semantic levels on limited subsets of the repository.

Evaluating Applications

When evaluating applications such as automatic summarisation, it is useful to compare results against curated resources. Standard measures of performance can be calculated with respect to the reference standard chosen. For treatment of disease, the British Medical Journal clinical evidence concise is one alternative. For drug interactions and adverse events, Micromedex DRUGDEX, DrugDigest, and the First DataBank's National Drug Data File can be used. A more ambitious method, requiring human experts, is task-based evaluation. Ultimately, user-centred evaluations such as the one described by McKeown must be considered.

PROJECT SCHEDULE

- *Year 1:* Pilot study, processing all of MEDLINE/PubMed, integrating Entrez Gene
- *Year 2:* Integrating UMLS and other NCBI resources
- *Year 3:* Annotating predications, opening the BKR to collaborative development and use
- *Year 4:* Fully integrated ALS system available

PROJECT RESOURCES

This project relies on a range of existing competencies and resources and has the potential to federate research energies throughout the Lister Hill

Center. In addition to the efforts of the two core component projects, Semantic Knowledge Representation and Medical Ontology Research, the success of this project relies on collaboration with the Indexing Initiative, the Lexical Systems Project, and ClinicalTrials.gov. The effectiveness of applications drawing on the repository could be strengthened by providing links to Visible Human images where appropriate. In order to accomplish the goals of this project additional staff and equipment are required: staff for creating and populating the repository and servers for providing effective access to the repository. Initially, PubMed and ClinicalTrials.gov will be processed by SemRep and SemGen and the predications extracted will be stored in the repository. Dedicated servers are required to process PubMed for this project.

TECHNOLOGY AND THE INFORMATION MARKET PLACE

While library collections may have gone far past the tipping point between physical and virtual by 2020, libraries themselves will continue to evolve as community centers for both technology and intellectual pursuits. Many digital resources, including e-books, are leased, not owned. To counter this, shared cloud or virtual libraries, such as those under development by the Hathi Trust and Digital Public Library of America should be developed to serve as surrogate research libraries. The research community must make sure that valuable content is not locked up by commercial interests. There must be greater attention paid to the development of affordable statewide digital platforms, negotiated statewide licenses for electronic books, periodicals, research databases, and similar materials. NOVELNY or a similar initiative must continue to grow, and libraries of all kinds must digitise local content.

RECOMMENDATIONS

The Board of Regents and State Education Department should formulate policy and support initiatives that will:

- Address copyright, licensing, and digital rights management with one firm voice.
- Encourage the growth of NOVELNY or a similar initiative by adding more e-resources of all kinds for statewide access.
- Identify the current costs of e-resources from all public funds to best determine economies of shared acquisition and use across all schools, libraries, public universities, and state government agencies.
- Foster the development of a common statewide e-book platform and address the particularly high costs of *STEM* (Science, Technology, Engineering and Mathematics) online electronic resources.
- Encourage branding of all e-content to demonstrate libraries' value to remain visible and relevant to end users, wherever they may be.

- Encourage all libraries and library systems to anticipate and participate in the development of a single, digital library with rich functionality that serves all.

SUSTAINING OUR LIBRARIES

This plan, with its sixty recommendations, many based on successful models already operational, makes it clear that libraries - as educational institutions and community centers - are central to the well-being and economic development of the state. While it is difficult to establish priorities for funding when there is so little available, it makes sense to develop those resources – like libraries and library systems – that are part of the solution to the problems we face as a state and as a nation. The genesis of this planning document was the recognition that significant new state aid for libraries was not imminent. However, it is hoped that this report to the Board of Regents makes it clear that libraries and library systems cannot be sustained and continue to be responsive to the needs of our state's residents without increases in financial support.

The visible and vocal support of the Board of Regents is essential to the success of this effort. As a starting point, the Board of Regents should support full restoration of library funding as outlined in the Education Law. Before it is too late, and libraries are forced to cut even more staff and hours - or close altogether – fair funding for new programmes and services as outlined in this Plan is needed. These recommendations should serve as the basis for specific legislative proposals from the Board of Regents and library advocacy organisations to build a foundation of success for our libraries over the next decade.

SAVING LIBRARIES WITH TECHNOLOGY

There has never been a harder time for libraries: unprecedented public funding cuts, required to cope with a deep economic downturn; the challenge of keeping abreast of rapid change in the technologies of content and search and discovery; and the quiet but insistent questioning of what role there is for public libraries in the modern world. Responses have been varied but predictable. In one camp are those people who cling to the values which led to the development of the modern library service – books, education, self-advancement and personal development – and in the other those bureaucrats who argue that if money has to be saved libraries must be sacrificed in order to divert funds to more pressing social problems. Of course not everyone takes such extreme views, and many feel there is a middle way to be found which protects the best of the library tradition, exploits the existing network of buildings, and doesn't put pressure on rapidly dwindling funds.

Book Industry Communication (BIC) is firmly of this view. BIC is partially a creature of the library sector, having been set up in 1991 by the British Library, the – then – Library Association, the Booksellers Association and the Publishers Association to develop and promote standards for electronic communication in what we now call the supply chain. Its first chairman was Tony Hall, managing director of what is now Capita Software Services but was then BLCMP and subsequently Talis. Its original focus was to bring EDI (electronic data interchange) to the wider book world, but it quickly broadened its outlook to include bar code technology, product metadata, identification standards and subject classification. Much of the book trade – and a significant part of the library supply chain – runs on standards that BIC has developed over the past twenty years.

We believe that, unlike the book trade, the library sector has never been able to leverage available technology sufficiently to gain real cost savings from its deployment. The savings are there to be had, but only a comparatively small number of libraries have taken advantage of the opportunities. There are various reasons for this. One is the lack of the commercial drivers which galvanise interest from the book trade. Another is the lack of technical expertise in libraries themselves. Another is the huge diversity that comes from multiple library authorities making independent investment decisions on the basis of their own needs.

Perhaps the most telling, though, is the fact that the companies which exist to serve the library sector – LMS providers, RFID suppliers, stock suppliers and others – have made too good a living from the non-standard environment which these other factors have allowed to develop. Stock suppliers have made their money from servicing books to the specific needs of their customers rather than from the books themselves; LMS and RFID suppliers have been only too glad to tailor systems to individual needs rather than sell a standard product. These are the costs which BIC believes can be saved; and we are encouraged in this by the growing realisation by the companies involved that better delivery of standard products is in the end a more realistic and appropriate policy to adopt.

BIC's remit is about standards, collaboration and consensus. We believe there are huge wins to be made from eliminating waste in the library supply chain, by using technology and standards in a judicious way to cut away at the cost structures that have been allowed to exist in the public library sector because of its fragmented structure.

WHAT ARE THE KEY COMPONENTS OF THIS STRATEGY

EDI is one. Though the BIC standards are widely adopted by libraries and their suppliers, only a minority of libraries has implemented the full cycle of EDI messages – quotes, orders, delivery notes, invoices – and reaped the benefits of error avoidance, once-only keying and paperless transactions. Fewer still have been able or willing to create electronic links between library and corporate finance offices, so that invoices can flow electronically between approval and payment. EDI may be a little complicated to set up, but all the major library suppliers have invested heavily in standards-based electronic communication, and transaction costs are a fraction of any alternative and repay the investment many times over when it is in place.

RFID is another. This technology is hardly new, having been widely adopted by libraries, primarily as a more sophisticated alternative to bar codes for self-service applications, and where it has been implemented it has been universally acclaimed as a way to enable the more productive deployment of staff, facilitate longer opening hours, and provide a more welcoming environment for users. Now, with the help of the BIC/CILIP RFID in Libraries Group and its support for the new ISO 28560 standard, RFID is expanding its potential beyond self-service to stock management and other functions in the library, reducing workloads and providing ongoing cost reductions.

What is more, the standard enables libraries to invest in the technology, confident that they are not locked in to any specific vendor's software or hardware. BIC has published a UK profile for the standard, which has the acceptance and support of all the major RFID suppliers.

The work BIC has done on RFID has spawned other things too. For many years the required communication between self-service devices and LMSs has been handled by 3M's SIP2 protocol. In response to growing dissatisfaction from LMS providers, BIC has commissioned an entirely new communication framework which both extends the functionality of SIP2 but also defines web services as a mechanism for the transfer of information.

PUBLISH/SUBSCRIBE FUNCTIONALITIES FOR FUTURE DIGITAL LIBRARIES

We are interested in the problem of *distributed resource sharing* in future digital libraries. We adopt a pure P2P architecture but our ideas can be easily modified to work in the case of hierarchical P2P networks, as in. *Information providers* (DLs) and *information consumers* (users) are both represented by peers participating in a peer-to-peer (P2P) overlay network. There are two kinds of basic functionality that we expect this architecture to offer: *information retrieval (IR)* and *publish/subscribe*. In an IR scenario a user poses a *query* and the system returns information about matching resources.

In a pub/sub scenario a user posts a *subscription* to the system to receive notifications whenever certain events of interest take place. In this extended abstract we concentrate on the latter kind of functionality and sketch how to provide it by extending the distributed hash table Chord. *Distributed Hash Tables (DHTs)* are the second generation *structured* P2P overlay networks devised as a remedy for the known limitations of earlier P2P networks such as Napster and Gnutella.

We present a set of protocols, collectively called *DHTrie*, that extend the Chord protocols with pub/sub functionality. We assume that resources are annotated using a well-understood attribute- value model called *AWPS* in. Thus publications and subscriptions will also be expressed in *AWPS*. *AWPS* is based on *named attributes* with value *free text* interpreted under the Boolean and vector space (VSM) models. The query language of *AWPS* allows Boolean combinations of comparisons *A op v*, where *A* is an attribute, *v* is a text value and *op* is one of the operators 'equals', 'contains' or 'similar'. The following is an example of a publication in *AWPS*:

{ (*AUTHOR*, *"John Smith"*), (*TITLE*, *"Information dissemination in P2P ..."*), (*ABSTRACT*, *"In this paper we show that ..."*) }

The following is an example of a query:

$(AUTHOR = \text{"John Smith"}) \wedge (TITLE \sqsupseteq P2P \wedge (information \prec_{[0,0]} alert)) \wedge (ABSTRACT \sim_{0.7} \text{"P2P architectures have been..."})$

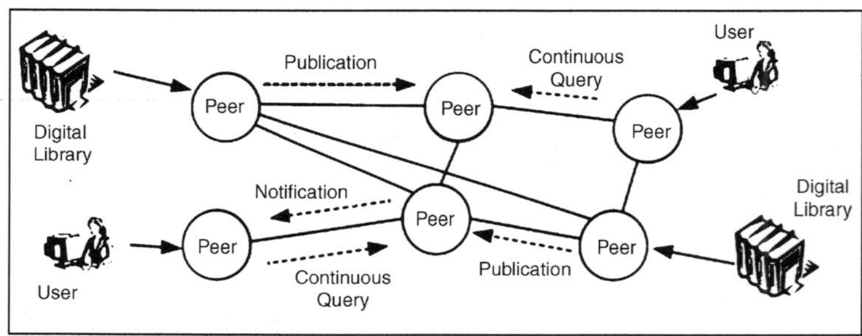

Fig. Distributed Resources Sharing in Future DLs

This query requests resources that have *John Smith* as their author, and their title contains the word *P2P* and a word pattern where the word *information* is immediately followed by the word *alert*. Additionally, the resources should have an abstract similar to the text value *'P2P architectures have been...'* with similarity greater than 0:7. The contributions of this abstract are the following.

The research presented in this abstract is a continuation of our previous work on the DL information alert architecture DIAS and the system P2P-DIET. The main contribution of our current work is that our protocols are extensions of DHTs and achieve much better scalability, robustness, fault-tolerance and load balancing. The rest of this extended abstract is as follows.

THE DHTRIE PROTOCOLS

We implement pub/sub functionality by a set of protocols called the *DHTrie protocols*. The DHTrie protocols use *two levels of indexing* to store queries submitted by clients. The first level corresponds to the partitioning of the global query index to different nodes using DHTs as the underlying infrastructure. Each node is responsible for a fraction of the submitted user queries through a mapping of attribute values to node identifiers. The DHT infrastructure is used to define the mapping scheme and also manages the routing of messages between different nodes. We use an extension of the Chord DHT to implement our network. The second level of our indexing mechanism is managed locally by each node and is used for indexing the user queries the node is responsible for. In this level, each node uses a hash table to index all the atomic queries contained in a query by using their attribute name as the key. For each atomic Boolean query the hash table points to a *trie*-like structure that exploits *common words* and a hash table that indexes text values in equalities as in. Additionally for atomic VSM queries an inverted index for the most 'significant' query words is used as in. In this abstract as suggested, focus on the first level of indexing and present the sub- scription, publication and notification protocols that regulate node interactions. Protocols for query updating and removal are omitted due to space. The local indexing algorithms we use and their experimental evaluation are thoroughly discussed in.

The Notification Protocol

When a message FwdResource containing a publication *p* of a resource arrives at a node *P*, the queries matching *p* are found by utilising its local index structures and using the algorithms. Once all the matching queries have been retrieved from the database, *P* creates notification messages of the form notification and contacts all the nodes that their queries where matched against *p* using their IP address associated with the query they submitted. If a node *P0* is not online when *P* tries to notify it about the published resource, the notification message is sent to the *successor*. In this way *P0* will be notified the next time it logs on the network. The modifications to the join and leave protocols of Chord to achieve this functionality originally presented in the non-DHT system P2P-DIET are omitted due to space considerations. To utilise the network in a more efficient way, notifications can also be batched and sent to the subscribers when traffic is expected to be low.

Frequency Cache

In this part, we introduce an additional routing table that is maintained in each node. This table, called *frequency cache* is used to reduce the cost of publishing a resource by storing the IP addresses of the nodes responsible for frequent words contained in published documents. FCache is a hash table used to associate each word that appears in a published document with a node IP address. FCache uses a word *w* as a key, and each FCache entry is a data structure that holds an IP address. Thus, whenever *P* needs to contact another node *P0* that is responsible for queries containing *w*, it searches its FCache. If FCache contains an entry for *w*, *P* can directly contact *P0* using the IP stored in its FCache. If *w* is not contained in FCache, *P* uses the standard DHT lookup protocol to locate *P0* and stores contact information in FCache for further reference. Using FCache the cost of processing a published resource *p* is reduced to $O(v + (h - v) \log N)$, where v is the number of words of p contained in FCache. FCache entries are populated as follows. Each time a resource p is published at a node P, P contacts the nodes responsible for storing queries with words contained in p. After this process is over, P knows the contact information of those nodes, and stores it to FCache along with the word each node is responsible for. After that, for each publication taking place at P, P maintains this routing information for the most frequent words contained in resources published to it. Notice that the construction and maintenance of FCache is based only on local information and that the only extra cost involved is FCache misses and the routing information discovered is also cached for further reference).

BRIEF PRESENTATION OF EXPERIMENTAL RESULTS

We have evaluated DHTrie experimentally in a distributed digital library scenario with hundreds of thousands of nodes and millions of user profiles. For our experiments we used 10426 documents downloaded from CiteSeer and also used in. The documents are research papers in the area of Neural Networks and as suggested, refer to them as the NN corpus. Because no database of queries was available to us, our queries are synthetically generated by exploiting 2000 documents of the corpus. The remaining 8426 documents are used to generate publications. Our experiments show that the DHTrie protocols are *scalable*: the number of messages it takes to publish a document and notify interested subscribers remains almost constant as the network grows. Moreover, the increase in message traffic shows little sensitivity to increase in document size.

We demonstrate that simple data structures with only local information can make a big difference in a DHT environment: the routing table FCache manages to reduce network traffic by a factor of 4 in all the alternative methods we have studied. Since probability distributions associated with publication and query elements are expected to be skewed in typical pub/sub scenarios, achieving a *balanced load* is an important problem. We have studied an important case of load balancing for DHTrie and present a new algorithm which is also applicable to the standard DHT look-up problem.

3

Library Information Technology on Information Professionals

INTRODUCTION

As quoted by Matson, new technology is, of course, very powerful and brings in 'an imperialistic thrust' not only into librarianship, but into everyday life. Not surprisingly, the new roles created by the changing technology have commanded attention and have made up a large part of recent literature about librarians. He added the resulting proliferation of online catalogs, librarian have been spurred by technological developments to become more efficient organisers and planners. They have, in short, brought their traditional skills to the service of the new technologies. As claimed by Hyams, the role of the New Information Professionals (NIP) in the learning environments is likely to be much more global. It is a call for librarians to rethink their job functions and the future of the academic library as center of technology. The change that's happening isn't at all like the automation change the librarian went through. It is a fundamental kind of change: 'To Who We Are and What We Do."

NEW ROLES, NEW SKILLS AND NEW PEOPLE

Researcher argue that library jobs and jobs for information professionals are changing at the same—or even greater as experienced in other parts of our economy and society. Are librarians, new and old, keeping pace with these changes? Are they stuck in a traditional mind-set about their jobs and the settings for those jobs? What are some of the new horizons available to librarians willing to 'think outside the box" as far as their careers are concerned? What prepares the librarian for these emerging jobs? The struggle of librarians in academic libraries to cope with the dynamic changes brought by technology is real. The new roles and skills include:

As Library Webmaster

The single most significant factor in the changing information jobs has been the Internet. It has changed everyone's job, some people's job descriptions', and the job market itself, example as Webmaster.

Definition of Webmaster

The essential assignment of the Webmaster as defined by Richmond is:

- "... a person who manages a Web; a mediator between Web authors and system administrator—ensures that applicable standards such as HTML validity and link liveliness are met; optimises the Web architecture for navigability; takes editorial responsibility for the content, quality and styles of the site; finds, creates and installs tools to create Web content and check consistency; develops and enforces the house style; liaises with graphic artist; provides first level user support..."

From this definition, it is clear that Webmasters must be responsible for several roles in their day to day activities.

Task Analysis of the Webmaster

Van der Walt strongly believe that Webmasters were originally depicted as members of an organisation who were early adopters of Internet and Web technologies and who saw the need to educate the rest of the library users in using those technologies. His statement is strongly supported by the researchers who claimed that an area where early Web expertise could be found was the *academic,* and specifically *university,* environment.

Vander Walt listed several responsibilities of the Webmaster such as:

- Administration and daily management of a Web site such as home page design, Web-based online searching, searching Web sites, Intranets and Internal database publishing
- Understand the broad purpose and potential of a Web site—that is, what the site can accomplish and what it may be able to do in future
- Possess a thorough understanding of the organisation and have a background in marketing, familiarity with the Internet
- A solid understanding of programming languages and technology
- Keep up with and also recognise the significance of emerging technologies and business models, and be able to inform and educate the rest of the organisation
- Experiment with unproven technology to develop WWW sites and the Webmaster is a solo space explorer, often looking at way-out-in-front technology'
- A person with the necessary technical talent in user interfaces and a good knowledge of operating systems, as well as creative skills in graphic design, marketing, advertising, copy writing and event planning

The Growing Importance of the Webmaster

These basic responsibilities are slowly being enhanced. Today the Webmaster has become an integral part of an education venture vital to the entire strategic planning of the library. As a newcomer in the information retrieval field, the Webmaster forms an essential part of the online presence of any organisation, as it is he or she who leads the Web site development team in managing an effective and efficient Web site.

The value of librarians as webmasters in the university as claimed by Stover is for a number of reasons:

- First, to support the scholarly communication process because disseminating information is a function that traditionally been associated with librarians
- Second, librarians have a certain measure of expertise in the area of organising and providing access to information. What better way to share their skills with the academic community than by turning Web documents into one-stop-shopping malls that offer the end user subject access to a document along with the full-text of the document itself?
- Third, Web publishing gives us a higher profile on campus, which is an important asset these days because of the changing nature of higher education and changing role of librarians
- Fourth, the Web provides unique access to scholarly information because of its serendipitous nature, its immediacy, its hypertext structure, and its universal appeal. Why wouldn't librarians want to be involved with this exciting technology at the publishing level?
- Fifth, it provides our parent institutions a positive reputation in the national and international academic communities. This is more important ever given the current climate of declining enrollments that many colleges and universities face today.
- Sixth, Web publishing allows us to bypass the profit-based system of print publishing that has tormented librarians for years by gouging out huge chunks of money from their budget.

As claimed by Van der Walt, many Web sites are now becoming mission critical in the sense that they are seen as a marketing tool for the university and also as a support tool for the end-user or library customers. The Internet and World Wide Web are both essential elements in the IT infrastructure of any organisation. Thus the Webmaster can play an important role in managing the library assets according to the information center's strategic planning.

As Systems Librarian

Shearer describes the term Systems librarians as:

- "Individuals who are responsible of designing, supporting and developing systems to enhance access to and management of the library's collection. Ensuring that the computer-based systems are essential to the library's work at all times."

Responsibilities

- Evaluation, planning, implementation and maintenance of library automation and Internet access, network maintenance as well as web page design and maintenance.
- Evaluation and selection of databases and software and staff training.
- Maintains computer security and hardware.

Skills

- Knowledge of networking, Internet and software applications.
- Ability to master new computer hardware and software.
- Ability to diagnose and solve hardware, software and networking problems.
- Ability to communicate technology to the uninitiated.
- Ability to work in a dynamic and changing environment.

Electronic Access to What and by Whom

Selecting academic information resources requires a broader view. For any library, the determination of which databases to provide and who will access them has become an ever more complex due to the number of databases that are now available has grown by leaps and bounds over the past few years. Today's systems librarian is often involved in the decision of which database service to supply to end-user desktops. There are myriad choices of general topic and specialty products available online, on the Intranet, on CD-ROM, and via the Web, at all price points. In today's academic setting, the librarian not only has to take into account the resource for the library's own collection but has to weigh offering the database to a wider user base against what end users within the university are already accessing by way of their own desktops.

Thus the systems librarian must weigh the type of access to provide against questions of:

- Timeliness,
- System capabilities, and
- Client expectations of good service.

Access Policies

Schuhnan quote that once the library decides which databases to select, it must determine how to deploy them and who will have access to them. As electronic access to external databases becomes more prevalent throughout all academic areas, the systems librarian's budget and equipment come under greater pressure. Whenever contemplating the addition of a new database resource it's also a good opportunity to review internal corporate access policies. As quickly as events dictate change in resource selections, policy revisions will naturally be carefully thought about more frequently. Decisions such as supplying access to information for those with a 'need to know' are undergoing modification.

Increasingly, those with a 'need to know' occupy expanding outward circles within organisations. Schulman added, smart organisations are extending information resources access to more employees as competitors become more aggressive and move more quickly. They are finding that providing more employees with timely access to competitive information allows an organisation to respond to competitive threats more quickly.

As the system librarian continuously evaluate databases and the provision of access to them, here is a series of questions to ask each time considering a new source:

- Is this source unique or does it duplicate an existing resource.
- If it's a close duplicate, is it less expensive, easier to use, or unique in another beneficial way.
- How does this database fit in with the corporate mission.
- Who within the university will benefit from this database—all users, faculty members and university community.
- What is the cost-benefit ratio.
- What critical element does this database supply that overcomes a poor cost-benefit ratio.
- Does this resource fit within our existing budget.
- Does another resource have to be eliminated to bring on this resource, and, if so, what impact will that have to the budget and to those who depend on the resource under consideration for elimination.
- Will this resource improve service to our clients/customers? How?
- In what format will we purchase the database.
- How will this database be integrated into our other resources.
- What changes have to be made to the hardware/software configuration to accept this new database and how will this impact our budget? How will it impact access to other resources?
- How will we provide access to this resource?
- Who in which departments and at which levels within the university will have access to this resource? Directly? Indirectly.
- Will end-user training have to be provided?
- Will additional staff be required?
- What other departments should be involved in this decision?
- How much time and effort is involved in implementing access to this resource?
- When will the corporation see a return on investment?

Thus by using this list as a guideline and foundation for decision making should help the system librarian to revise the questions as the mission, budget, environmental influences changes and stay ahead of the game.

As In-House Content Providers

The meaning of In-house Content Provider refers to:

- "one who was interested in exploring the balance between making its content freely available on the Internet while protecting its print-based revenue stream."

Funke provide a comprehensive comment on the new role of the Information Professionals as an In-House Content Providers. He claimed that along with the new technologies comes interacting with different groups within an organisation such as the MIS people, an information professional must have the ability to effectively 'bring content to the table" and work effectively with MIS as a team to make this content readily available. In order for information professionals to effectively do this, they must keep up with the latest technologies related to text retrieval, content organisation, search technologies, and knowledge management.

Bringing Content to the Table

Making MIS people understand the importance and expertise of people who know content and how clients will use it can be a constant uphill battle. Many programmers in this situation view another 'player' either as a threat or someone who doesn't have their background. Unfortunately, the onus lies on the information professional to make programmers understand what we can contribute, the value we can provide.

For starters, before you can integrate content into a Web site, you must understand:

- The overall requirements of the current Web site, including servers,
- Their ability to handle various indexes; search engine capability; and
- How the parser is set up to integrate content.

The Information Professional can provide expertise on how to organise content on a site; how users might search for the content; and the search requirements needed to access the content.

Metadata

Many information professionals have taken courses such as cataloging and indexing. These courses can serve as a foundation for the resource-organising activities on the Internet involving metadata. Metadata provides document information on and from Web sites, producing an index or directory to the resource. With the tremendous growth of content on the Web, there is a need to standardise the organisation of the information.

As metadata standards are further defined and organisations embrace these new standards, many questions will need answering such as:

- What will be worth cataloging?
- How detailed should the descriptions of various resources be?

Information Professionals can play a major role in helping answer these questions.

Search Engines

Researcher added, the evaluation and use of search engines is a 'product' that Information Professionals should manage within their organisations because they:

- Understand and know how to use Boolean logic.
- Can evaluate search engines from the user perspective?
- Know how to implement effective user searching of content.

Some of the major Intranet search engines available these days include Fulcrum Surfboard, Verity, Microsoft Index Server, and Excalibur. Thus, when implementing the Boolean logic features of these search engines, most programmers, will say that users cannot grasp Boolean logic or that such control is unnecessary as long as the search engines do relevancy rankings of documents retrieved. Users can go beyond basic Boolean operators such as AND, OR, NOT, which programmers usually dictate for them, and take advantage of proximity operators such as NEAR and NEARIN.

From experience, when one explains the differences in search results to users, *e.g.*, the effect of using the Boolean operators and NEAR, end-user searchers understand and respond positively right away. Programmers may support their positions by doing a query to see how many searches were performed using each Boolean operator. Information Professionals should try search queries for this type of data, too. Request the tools to perform this kind of query. What some programmers find difficult to understand is that you just can't implement a feature without some user education. Information Professionals can play an important role by providing this guidance within their organisations.

Information Retrieval Agents

Making sense of the overwhelming amount of indexed information constitutes one of the biggest challenges of the Web. To help, we see a rising use of Web robots, called information retrieval agents. These agents know where to look for relevant information based on user direction, advanced search algorithms, and learned behaviour. Major players in this area include NewsBot, Agent ware, and Wise Wire. As organisations move towards managing knowledge, intelligent information retrieval agent software tools will playa major role and will require people with the ability to manage and evaluate these tools. Search agents work when a user sets up search queries to 'train the documents,' whereby the agents learn from human behaviour and use pattern recognition to find relevant information to automate the retrieval process.

Information Professionals with expertise in searching and content analysis can help manage and evaluate these tools. Note that several of the traditional electronic publishers have already begun exploring this technology, *e.g.*, LEXIS-NEXIS and UMI with WiseWire Professional, an agent technology that evaluates user's viewing habits. Like it or not, new technologies are changing the information professional's role and the opportunities to enhance one's role have become boundless. To take advantage of the opportunities, Information Professionals must keep up with the emerging technologies, recognise the opportunities to utilise our skill sets, and work with MIS to effectively implement change. At times it can be frustrating and overwhelming, but the opportunities to grow and learn outweigh any negatives.

AS KNOWLEDGE MANAGER

Peter Drucker has predicted that the most important profession in the next century will be knowledge worker, and knowledge workers are not the same as computer systems specialists. He claimed that the most competent ones are likely to be reference librarians using sophisticated hardware and software, tools which the end user does not know how to use. Certainly, those who have exploited the almost unlimited opportunity to provide more information have taken advantage of this development.

Still, Drucker assumed that this deluge of knowledge would drown us and force us to seek people to manage that knowledge. Knowledge workers would assess knowledge on behalf of those who had neither the time nor the inclination to do so. The concept of knowledge management embraces the need to organise large data files, and to link and integrate different but related files and databases to one another so that users can move between and among related resources efficiently.

Thus, Church believe the transformation from librarian to knowledge manager is clearly underway; however, a deeper look at the direction that the Internet is taking business reveals the possibility of more far-reaching changes. As many library services processes move to the Internet, the use of information will become integrated with these processes. In this environment, information as a distinct function or resource may no longer exist.

Changing Roles and Responsibilities

The information transfer cycle is directly affected by Internet use. They should "embrace the entire new information transfer cycle, from the creation, restructuring and representation of information to its dissemination and use." They have an important and valuable role to tell users what users ought to see and read. It is to protect library clients from drowning in the information overflow and help them work smarter.

How their role as knowledge managers would evolve within the next few years, Church outline five key functions:

1. *Consultant:* Their role would involve less 'doing' and more consultation. This role would require remote support to endusers within the organisation. In effect, 'foot traffic' would be replaced by remote consultation for complex search strategies.
2. *Analyst:* Some information professional felt that their role would require increased value-added in the form of analysing and interpreting information that is presented to end-users.
3. *Intranet content manager:* With the integration of external data into corporate Intranets, a key function of the information services professional will be to source and manage the content which is accessible through the system.
4. *Product planner and marketer:* Data integration also forces information professionals to become product developers and planners, with responsibility for packaging information and marketing products, services and delivery strategies to internal audiences.
5. *Corporate knowledge manager:* Increased recognition of knowledge as a valuable strategic resource could heighten the importance of the information professional. It foresee a merger of all information functions into a single department or function. Being the Knowledge Manager just means that they create value to my organisation by facilitating access to high quality information and by networking people and their ideas together using the technological infrastructure.

These new responsibilities imply a totally different skill set. The emphasis will shift from:

- Technical skills in the library to communication,
- Facilitation, training and management skills.
- Interact with IT staff and managers beyond Knowledge Management (KM).

To adjust to these more far-reaching changes, information professionals must search beyond current bounds and think in terms of benefits to their organisations.

Right now, information can be used to enhance competitiveness and productivity. These same benefits will remain in the future, no matter what the role involves.

If information is to be seamlessly integrated with transaction processes, then someone must scope out work-related behaviours to ensure that it is done in the most efficient and effective manner. And, if equal information and technology is available to everyone, then competition rests on the ability to interpret and apply these tools. Clearly the impending shift to knowledge management represents an exciting change for academic librarians. However, it's an opportunity that requires a great deal of preparation, and a new way of thinking.

AS COLLABORATORS/PARTNERSHIPS

All organisations are in the period of transformation including academic libraries and librarians should use this period of change to establish, refocus and strengthen partnerships with other professionals groups within their institutions.

There are two significant groups with which library professionals should establish strong collaborative relationships:

1. Faculty and
2. Technologists.

Creth suggest in order for a real partnership to succeed, librarians need to see themselves as part of the teaching and research endeavor, and participate as an active and integral member of the education team. He added, for some librarians this idea of a partnership with faculty may require incorporating a different concept of their importance in relation to the faculty and developing new expectations and different behaviour. In the most general sense, librarians need to be certain that their commitment to service does not display itself through behaviour that is like of a servant.

Library professionals also need to reshape and strengthen their relationships with the computer specialists in the university with reasons such as:

- To eliminate much of the waste that occurs in most organisations where computer and information technology remains untapped or barely utilised because the learning curve is too steep for so many people and because the design of the equipment and software is so often far from intuitive.
- The New Information Professionals can provide constant feedback to designers and programmers about what works, what does not work, what new functions are needed.
- They can become the voice of the inexpert user, the typical person who is not technically inclined but strongly needs the service that the technology promises to deliver.
- They are both dealing with changing and chaotic times, and their activities are centered around information technology, so they should naturally consider themselves partners in addressing the many challenges that exist.
- They need to be willing, to share the act of discovery, to be able to identify shared goals, and to work together as peers.

If, librarians are to be prepared to absorb and even help shape the magnitude of predicted change into this 21st century, then it will be important for librarians to realign their relationships within the university so that strong partnerships exist to provide us with necessary support as well as knowledge for meeting the challenges ahead.

AS EDUCATOR

Anderson emphasised that librarians have always played a key role in education. They have formed relationships with subject specialists to build library collections to support instruction in the classroom and provided instruction in the form of classes on library skills and have conducted library instructional orientations sessions to assist students doing research in their classes. Today, in the digital age, librarians can no longer be simply information providers or the 'keepers of knowledge'.

The changes in technology using electronically stored and retrieved information has changed the way patrons and students are able to access, retrieve and use information. The instantaneous access of information through the Internet has made vast amounts of information and data available to anyone with a computer, a modem and a provider. Digital information is changing the role of librarians from "a person who students ask for assistance in finding information to someone who needs to provide services and instruction regardless of place, time or format." But how do we make important and valid information available to our faculty and students that may appear on the Web tomorrow?

Big Six Information Skills

As educators, Eisenberg have suggested that librarians must acquire these skills; the ability to:

- Define the task,
- Information seeking strategies,
- Location and access,
- Use of information,
- Synthesis,
- Evaluation.

The librarian's role too has:

- Expanded with a much broader instructional and participatory role in the instructional process. This role can be one of actively participating in the building of on-line courses by providing assistance in finding current and valid information for instructors delivering instruction on the Internet.
- Extend into the area of providing instruction and librarians must be involved in creating independent thinkers.
- Enhanced their roles to knowledge navigators and instructors teaching the discipline called information literacy.
- Be one of teaching critical thinking and resource-based learning.

New vocabulary in education such as: living curriculum, critical literacy, information power, information literacy, and information problem solving mandate that we re-examine our roles as professional information providers and educators. Students need to acquire the skills of evaluating information. This new vocabulary is bringing new challenges in library instruction. Changes in education such as the infusion of instructional technology and the use the Internet to deliver instruction has also changed how libraries and librarians can provide and assist instructors in teaching in the digital age.

New Trends in Instruction—Web Based Course Delivery

The trend in education towards distance learning and web-based courses is providing new challenges for information professionals as service providers as well as instructors. We are required to provide access to quality and valid information to support on-line instruction as well as provide on-line instruction both indirectly in the form of guides and on-line tutorials as well as directly in the form on courses to teach information literacy. Universities are recognising the necessity of requiring an information literacy course as part of the curriculum in the digital age.

As educators, the librarians are using a variety of tools and teaching techniques to assist students such as:

- *Provide instruction through learning guides and on-line tutorials:* Finding quality information is the biggest challenge our faculty and students are faced in the research and instructional process. With the advent of distance delivery of instruction and web-based pages for libraries using the vast amounts of information available on the Internet, it is essential that independent learners are skilled in locating information. Students can access these tutorials and guides from home or from the computers in the library and walk through self-paced instruction on any topic from "What is the Internet? To How do I do research?"
- *Provide access to guides to recommended search engines for the Internet:* Using search engines effectively and choosing the best search engines for your specific needs may be the most challenging skill that learners need to master. Guides to recommend search engines that introduce and compare search engines in a standard format are an invaluable tool for independent learners. Students can readily compare the different features of several search engines and access the search engines directly from your library's page.
- *Provide instruction in the area of Information Literacy:* Teaching Information Literacy in the electronic environment is a new and exciting role for librarians. Creating courses and formal instruction in the discipline of information literacy with the purpose of encouraging independent learners and critical thinkers to meet the challenges of the new information age is the role of the future for librarians. In today's workplace, employees are not only expected to

work well with others, communicate well, find creative solutions to problems; they will also be expected to use the Internet and electronic information effectively to solve problems and conduct business. More and more businesses are moving towards conducting business on the Web for advertising, delivering services and products as well as using the Internet as a communication tool. Librarians must be involved in creating valuable employees with the current skills required to be successful on the job.

Librarians are the most appropriate professionals to lead the team of people in finding the answers to the challenges we are facing in the digital environments of electronic information and the Internet. They have always been the experts at teaching people how to use the tools to locate that information regardless of format. They are the most effective searchers and researchers and their basic role of teaching those skills has not changed. Thus, in this fast and ever-changing information environment, librarians need to make full use of information and multimedia technology to support a greatly expanded teaching venture. The technology and varied format of information is changing and making new demands on their profession. In this fast-paced world it is important that they change with the changing roles and challenges.

AS MANAGERS

Researcher address how change has affect everyone in the organisations from leaders to employees and clients—the needs to shift his or her mind-sets, seeing the organisation and their established and new roles sometimes highly threatening and unfamiliar activities. Thus he added, employees need emotional support to adapt to change; support in learning new ways of working and relating. Linda claimed that information technology has changed a librarian's jobs; they have to readjust to new situation and develop new skills of managing the investments of an organisation—in people, technologies, and collections. As managers, they need to look for outcomes rather than just thinking about managing a resource at the resource level. The human resource in any organisation is the key to its success or failure.

Changes in Library Management

We have seen that the major external force that is technology had affected libraries; that means the library managers must use new structures in their management. *Strategic planning—strategic thinking*—should be a fundamental concept that librarians incorporate into their daily activities. Overall they need to give greater attention to strategic planning at the organisation and departmental level, and then integrating these strategic plans into the goals and activities of individual professionals. With a shifting organisational environment and culture, managers should shift their responsibilities and approach to one that is more consultative and supportive rather than one of authority and control.

The role of the manager should focus on:

- Coaching and mentoring staff.
- Development of staff.
- Developing shared values and vision among staff.
- Providing resources within framework of cost-benefit assessment.
- Taking pride in the accomplishments of others,
- Providing incentives to team work.

Library staff who are struggling to keep up with the demands in today's work environment require, indeed deserve, new ways for accomplishing their work. The redesign of the library organisation is imperative if we are to move rapidly and with an entrepreneurial spirit in the delivery of services in the current interactive high- speed communication environment.

Thus to be successful, libraries must reshape the prevailing corporate culture and build into their organisational structures and their approaches to work.

As managers, researcher stress that they must possess:

- The ability to identify, anticipate, and quickly respond to constantly changing customer needs.
- Capable of leaps forward and breakthrough performance.
- Must be ready to abandon formerly successful approaches to work, strategies, processing systems and services.
- Good communication at all levels, staff participation and training.

The librarians in transition that want to consciously manage their change efforts need to help their staff understand the change process and how they can positively participate. Creating an overall framework that shows the considered changes are a natural evolution from current practices, assessing that the organisation has the expertise and climate to implement the proposed changes.

Instead of organising personnel around how librarians do their work, librarians must:

- Organise around customers and how they do their work.
- Reduce hierarchy, flatten the organisation, and eliminate redundancy in order to be more responsive to changing needs and new opportunities and developments.
- Give up their need for control and their desire to create stability.

We Live in a Time of Change

The information has change our profession and library managers today have to pick up new skills to adjust to changes and to be able to survive in the future.

INFORMATION TECHNOLOGY IN LIBRARIES

The application of information technology in libraries results in increased operational efficiency. The IT increases productivity of library staff. It relieves professional staff from mundane jobs that involves a lot of duplication so that they can be fruitfully used for user-oriented library services.

It improves quality of services rendered by the library. Use of information technology ensures ease of functioning, accuracy and economy in human labour with greater speed. The exponential growth of information has made manual system redundant giving way to computerised information storage and retrieval tools.

Effective and efficient handling of huge quantum of information is only possible by using computers, which have the added advantage of being highly accurate and efficient that adds value to information. Moreover, the technology also helps in rendering services that were hitherto not possible using traditional means. The new information technology facilitates improved management of physical and financial resources. The advances in technology and its availability at lower cost, has also raised expectations of users from librarians and libraries.

The new information technology, on one hand, facilitate wider access to information for the library users, on other hand, it facilitates wider dissemination of information products and services generated by the library. The availability of networks facilitates resource sharing and high-speed communication with other libraries.

DEVELOPMENTS IN COMPUTER AND MICROPROCESSOR TECHNOLOGY

Dramatic reductions in the size and cost of computer components and equally impressive gains in the speed, storage capacity and reliability of hardware components have expanded their use rapidly in all activities and functions of a library and information centre. Notable reductions in the size of microprocessors combined with dramatically enhanced capacity have added new dimensions to the computer new hardware technology.

Initially, small silicon chips contained only few components and circuits, but the average number of components has doubled each year Since, 1965. Early small-scale integration efforts first gave way to large-scale integration (LSI) chips that contained thousands of components, very large-scale integration (VLSI) chips that contained hundreds of thousands of components and circuits, and now ultra large-scale integration (ULSI) chips come with millions of components and circuits.

A microprocessor, also known as Central Processing Unit (CPU) of a computer, is a complete computation engine that is fabricated on a single chip. Microprocessors are manufactured by different companies like Intel, Advanced Micro Divices (AMD), Motorola,etc. However, most widely-used microprocessors are manufactured by Intel. The first microprocessor used in a PC was Intel 8080. Introduced in 1974, it was a complete 8-bit microprocessor on a single chip. Intel 8088 used in the IBM PC in 1979, was the first microprocessor that made its presence felt in the market.

The PC market moved from the 8088, 80286, 80386, 80486, Pentium, Pentium-II, III, IV and now to Intel Dual Core and Quad Core. The new Intel Dual Core can execute any piece of code that ran on the original 8088, but the Dual Core runs about 3,000 times faster. The capacity of a microprocessor is measured in terms of the number of bits it can send or receive and the number of bits it can process internally.

The 8088 was an 8/16 bit processor, indicating that it can send or receive 8 bits of data and internally process 16 bits of data at a time. The 80286 was a 16/16 bit processor and 80386 chip had a 32-bit processor with a 32-bit data path and, as a result, was much faster than either the 8088 or the 80286 chip. The 80486 chip, introduced by Intel in late 1989, had a 32- bit processor.

It has architectural enhancements, Hence, it performed better than the 80386 chip. The Pentium is a 32-bit processor with a 32-bit data path. It is three times faster than the 80486. The Pentium II and III had a 32-bit processor with a 64-bit data path. It was three times faster than the Pentium. The Pentium IV is a 32-bit processor with a 64-bit data path, and was introduced in 2000.

It is four times faster than the Pentium. Currently, PCs and laptops are equipped with Dual Core which is a 64-bit processor with 64-bit data path and processing speed of 3.0 Ghz. Like microprocessor technology, digital storage devices have also witnessed notable reductions in its size and cost with dramatically enhancement in capacity of storage.

There are two types of data storage devices, *i.e.*, removable data storage devices and Non-removable data storage devices. The data storage devices come in many sizes and shapes. The storage devices can also be categorised based on media used for storage, for example magnetic storage media, optical storage media, metal-oxide semiconductors or flash memory devices (popularly known as Pen drives or USB drives). Magnetic storage media are commonly used for large volumes of data (*e.g.*, video, image, or remote sensing data). Large amounts of data are stored through tape drives because the capacity on the drives is huge - three billion (or three gigabits) of data per square inch can fit on a single magnetic disk.

Hard discs, floppies, tapes, cartridges, etc., are example of magnetic media. CD-ROMs and DVD ROMs are example of optical storage media which can again be of two types, *i.e.*, i) write-once, read-many: data once written cannot be erased; and ii) Rewritable: the data that is once written can be erased completely and the same storage device can be used again for storing different data. A typical disc used in a computer-based CD drive stores 650 MB.

Digital Versatile Disk or DVD, initially stood for Digital Video Disc. Like a CD, DVD is an optical storage system for read-only, recordable and rewritable applications. The DVD format provides several configurations of data layers, moving from 2D storage to 3D storage. Each configuration is designed to provide additional storage capacity. The similarity between the DVD and the CD gets smaller with each upgraded configuration, however, DVDs in contrast to CDs has storage capacity of 4.7 GB.

Metal-oxide semiconductors-based storage devices, popularly known as pen drives or USB drives or flash memory devices, is Non-volatile computer memory that can be electrically erased and reprogrammed. It is a technology that is primarily used in memory cards and USB flash drives for general storage and transfer of data between computers and other digital products. Flash memory stores information in an array of memory cells made from floating-gate transistors.

In traditional single-level cell (SLC) devices, each cell stores only one bit of information. Some newer flash memory, known as multi-level cell (MLC) devices, can store more than one bit per cell by choosing between multiple levels of electrical charge to apply to the floating gates of its cells. Flash drives are now available with 8 GB storage capacity. Digital collections that are too large to store entirely on a disk use hierarchical storage mechanisms (HSM). In an HSM, the most frequently used data is kept on fast disks while less frequently used data is kept in nearline such as an automated (robotic) tape library.

An HSM can automatically migrate data from tape to disk and vice-versa as required. Intelligent storage networks and snap-servers are now available in which the physical storage devices are intelligently controlled and made available to a number of servers.

A number of RAID (Redundant Array of Inexpensive Disks) models are also available for greater security and performance. The RAID technology distributes the data across a number of disks in a way that even if one or more disks fail, the system would still function while the failed component is replaced.

DEVELOPMENTS IN COMMUNICATION AND NETWORK TECHNOLOGY

Communication technology, with its ability to transmit data and information from one location to another, serve as a tool to exploit potentials and ability of computer to store and process vast amount of information. A computer communica-tion network is an interconnection of a collection of several computers from which the user can select the service required and communicate with any computer as a local user.

A computer communication networks can be viewed as a collection of nodes with computing resources and nodal-switching computers that facilitate communication through a set of transmission links. Developments in communication technology have made it possible to interconnect geographically dispersed computing resources of different kinds and makes.

Users can access the network through PCs and terminals attached to a node and messages traverse these networks through the switching nodes. Since, computer communicates using digitised signals instead of electric signals, it requires different transmission facilities than those used for transmitting analogue electrical signals. It is, however, a common practice to use conventional telecommunication links for data transmission by converting digital signals into analogue signals using a process called 'Modulation' and the device that performs the conversion is called the MODEM (MOdulator - DEModulator).

Currently, terrestrial, satellite-based data networks, Integrated Service Digital Network (ISDN) and wireless networks are available that can handle all kinds of communication requirements (, *i.e.,* voice, data, telemetry, facsimile and video) without discrimination.

The computer networks can be grouped into four categories based on geographical locations of its computer terminals, *i.e.*,

- *Local Area Network (LAN)*: interconnection of many computers within a given local area, more often premises of a single organisation building. A very high speed of data transmission can be attained within a limited geographic area. LANs are typically configured in a star, bus or ring. Low speed LANs use telephone wires or copper cables, optical fibre cables are used to achieve high-speed transmission of data.
- *Wide Area Network (WAN)*: WAN is used to interconnect a number of widely dispersed computers in various cities of a country or different countries. WANs use communication media maintained by telegraph or telephone companies. These networks usually have land telephone lines, underground coaxial cables, microwave communication and satellite communications.
- *Metropolitan Area Network (MAN)*: MAN refers to inter- connection within geographical limits of a city or town.
- *Gateways*: Gateways consist of software and hardware that are required to interconnect networks amongst themselves. Gateways contend with any differences in packet sizes, protocols and addressing methods between the two networks it connect. Gateways are also used to connect LANs to WANs and WANs, in turn, can be linked through gateways to create national and international data communication networks.

The communications networks can be grouped into the following three categories based on the technology and communication media used by them:

- *Public Switched Telephone Network*: PSTN are managed by common carriers usually telephone companies/departments the world over. The PSTN generally provide two basic services, the normal dial-up connections to the subscribers and permanent leased connection between two subscriber's points. The permanent leased connections provide single traceable line between two subscriber points. The leased lines are generally less prone to noise than dial-up lines.

- *Public Data Network*: Analogous to the public telephone network, many domestic common carriers provide data communications services via a specialised network called a Public Data Network (PDN). Most Internet Service Providers (ISPs) use combination of PDN and PSTN for providing Internet connectivity.
- *Integrated Services Digital Networks* (ISDN): An ISDN is a network that provides end-to-end digital connectivity to support a wide range of services, including voice and Non-voice services.

Computer networks use physical channels through which information is transmitted between computers in a network. Media may be classified as bounded, *i.e.,* wires (twisted pair telephone wires or UTP CAT 5), cables (co-axial) and optical fibres; or unbounded, *i.e.,* radio waves or microwaves. Data communication is an integral part of the modern information storage and retrieval systems in terms of their online access. Today, network technology works on client server architecture with middleware used for connecting software components or applications on clients and servers.

Technique of packet switching, evolved in 1960s, is used for transferring data between computer systems with an objective to facilitate networked computers to communicate seamlessly across multiple, geographically dispersed locations. The Transmission Control Protocol (TCP) and Internet Protocol (IP), called TCP/ IP suite, is the backbone of Internet and other TCP/ IP based networks.

With developments in communication technology, institutions have options to set-up fibre optic-based gigabit LAN or wireless LAN. Depending on the geographical location, institutions have options to buy terrestrial or satellite-based Internet bandwidth its combinations from a number of Internet Service Providers (ISPs).

A CONCEPTUAL SCHEMA OF INFORMATION ACCESS

We characterise the space of information access by the following, orthogonal dimensions:

- The information access model, which establishes the basic terms of the system/user interaction;
- The information access mode, which establishes the role of the user and that of the system during their interaction.

INFORMATION ACCESS MODELS

Similarly to an information retrieval model, an information access model specifies:

- A representation of the objects to be accessed;
- A representation of the user information needs; and

- A function associating a set of objects to each user information need.

Information access models can be categorised according to the options available on each one of their dimensions. For object representation, following we distinguish between simple objects and composite objects.

Simple objects cannot be further decomposed, and can be represented along the following dimensions:

- *Content abstractions*: These are representations used to access objects via IR techniques. They are created by IR indexers in an automatic way, by extracting low-level features from objects, such as the number of word occurrences in a text, or the energy level in a certain region of an image); content abstractions retain that part of the information originally present in the object content that is considered sufficient to characterise the object for access purposes;
- *Content representations*: These are symbolic representations of the meaning of documents, that is descriptions formulated in some suitable knowledge representation language, spelling out the truth conditions of the object. Content representations can be constructed manually, sometimes with the assistance of some knowledge extraction tool, or automatically, for instance via object classification methods. They can be precise or uncertain, depending on whether or not the content representation formulas are expressed in an un- certain logic, such as fuzzy or probabilistic logic.

Composite objects are structured set of simple objects, thus they are typically represented as mathematical *structures*, reflecting their internal organisation. Finally, objects, whether simple or composite, can have a *profile*, that is an attribute-based description of their external properties, such as the author and the publisher of a book, or the data and time at which an image has been taken, and the like.

In the context of digital libraries, the 4 dimensions of object representation reduce to 3 only, since content representations and profiles are typically grouped together under the label of discovery metadata. The metadata associated to a DL object can therefore vary from simple records typically adhering to some standardised schema to very complex representations expressed in some knowledge representation language which must be coupled with a representation of the underlying domain of discourse, in order to be properly used for, *e.g.* information access.

In summary, as suggested, therefore consider object representation as being categorised as:

- Content,
- Metadata, and
- Structure.

For information need representation, we have 2 options: formal language queries or natural language queries. For the retrieval function, we have 2 options: exact match or best match. Not all combinations of these options give rise to meaningful information access models.

Considering the object representation options we have the following:

- Content is typically addressed via IR techniques, based on natural language queries and best-match retrieval function. For instance, users access the con- tent of an image base by providing as a query an image itself In so doing, users are implicitly asking the system to retrieve images which 'looks' similar to the image query, at least as far as the system can tell. For this reason, methods providing access by content are often called '*similarity-based*' access methods. An analogous pattern is found in access models for textual or for audio content. Notice that in some models of this kind, the query may not be expressed in the same medium as the sought objects. For instance, when accessing by content a video database, users may provide an image as a query, and the system is expected to retrieve the scenes sharing visual similarity with the provided image. Similarity-based access models are medium-dependent, in that different media require different techniques, and the possibility of using the same or a similar technique across different media is very limited. In addition, experience has shown that even within the same medium, the effectiveness of techniques is application-dependent: for example, retrieving by similarity sport images requires different techniques from those necessary to establish the similarity of X-ray images.
- Metadata is typically addressed via formal language queries, thus we are in the realm of databases or knowledge representation, depending from the degree of sophisticatedness of the involved representations. For instance, to query a Dublin Core scheme, one needs a very simple language allowing to state basic relational conditions on simple numeric- or string-based attribute values; instead, to query an OWL representation the ability to state conditions involving taxonomies and navigation of graph structures is required. In general, a query to metadata takes the form of a logical formula, and an exact match retrieval function is employed for query evaluation, grounded in some logical theory. We call these models *semantic* access models. Some retrieval engines allow to exploit information retrieval techniques when accessing objects via their metadata records. This is achieved by seeing metadata records as pieces of text whose words are the attribute values. Such a text is treated in the same way as textual content, and matched against a natural language query as in a similarity-based textual access method. This kind of access model is widely employed on bibliographic records, as it frees users from the necessity of knowing the meaning of meta- data attributes.

- Also object structure can be queried in two different ways:
- Via exact match retrieval functions, such as the one underlying the query language XPath. In this case, the structural query is mostly embedded into a larger query addressing either content or metadata. We do not have therefore separate classes of access models but sophistications of similarity-based or semantic access models allowing also the specification of structural clauses in queries.
- Via best match retrieval functions, which express in a quantitative way the degree of similarity between the structure of each object and a user provided structure class. These models have been investigated in the con- text of XML, and are a structural variation of similarity-based models. We call the models falling in this class 'similar structure-based access models'.

In summary, we have the following information access model categories:

- Similarity-based access models, possibly with structural conditions;
- Semantic access models, possibly with structural conditions; and
- Similar structure-based access models.

INFORMATION ACCESS MODES

Independently from the access model, the information access modes establishes the role of the system and that of the user. Each of these two can be either passive or active.

Excluding the case in which they are both passive, we have the following 3 types of information access systems:

- *Query-answering systems*: in this case the user is active, that is, poses a query, while the system is passive, that is it just evaluates the user query and returns the result.
- *Filtering systems*: In which the user is passive, that is, does not pose any query, and the system is active, that is it selects on a stream of incoming objects, those that are deemed as relevant for the user; the relevance assessment is performed by relying on a user profile.
- *Personalised query-answering systems*: in which the user is active, that is, poses a query, and the system is active too, in that it alters the query evaluation process by taking into account the user preferences, represented as a profile. Recommendation systems also fall into this category, since they propose recommendations along with the answer to the query.

DISTRIBUTED SEARCH ACROSS IN DIGITAL LIBRARIES

The peer-to-peer (P2P) approach allows handling huge amounts of data of digital libraries in a distributed and self-organising way. These characteristics offer enormous potential benefit for search capabilities powerful in terms of scalability, efficiency, and resilience to failures and dynamics. Additionally, such a search engine can potentially benefit from the intellectual input of a large user community.

However, recent research on structured P2P architectures is typically limited to exact-match queries on keys. This is insufficient for text queries that consist of a variable number of keywords, and it is absolutely inappropriate for full-fledged Web search where keyword queries should return a ranked result list of the most relevant approximate matches. This stage builds upon the MINERVA system architecture presented in and brings current challenges to ultimatively making distributed search across digital libraries feasible.

MINERVA provides ranked search on data and an efficient query mechanism that adheres to reasonable space and bandwidth limits. Unlike the approach criticised in, we do not spread inverted lists across the directory, but use only pointers to promising digital libraries as compact metadata and utilise these pointers to efficiently answer multiple-keyword queries. We leverage the extensive local indexes to incorporate features that are impossible in the approach studied in, such as phrase matching or proximity searches. Our bandwidth requirements are well within the postulation that a query should send no more data than the size of the documents ultimatively retrieved.

RELATED WORK

Recent research on structured P2P systems, such as Chord, CAN, Pastry, or P-Grid is typically based on various forms of distributed hash tables (DHTs) and supports mappings from keys to locations in a decentralised manner such that routing scales well with the number of peers in the system. We briefly discuss some prior and ongoing projects towards P2P Web search. Galanx is a P2P search engine implemented using the Apache HTTP server and Berkeley DB.

The Web site servers are the peers of this architecture; pages are stored only where they originate from. PlanetP is a publish subscribe service for P2P communities, supporting content ranking search. PlanetP distinguishes local indexes and a global index to describe all peers and their shared information. The global index is replicated using a gossiping algorithm. The system appears to be limited to a few thousand peers. Odissea assumes a two-layered search engine architecture with a global index structure distributed over the nodes in the system. A single node holds the complete, Web-scale, index for a given text term. Query execution uses a distributed version of Fagin's threshold algorithm.

The system appears to cause high network traffic when posting document metadata into the network, and the presented query execution method seems limited to queries with at most two keywords. The paper actually advocates using a limited number of nodes, in the spirit of a server farm. The system outlined in uses a fully distributed inverted text index, in which every participant is responsible for a specific subset of terms and manages the respective index structures. Particular emphasis is put on minimising the bandwidth used during multi-keyword searches. considers content-based retrieval in hybrid P2P networks.

The peer selection for forwarding queries is based on the Kullback- Leibler divergence between peer-specific statistical models of term distributions. In addition to this recent work on P2P search, prior research on distributed IR and metasearch engines is also potentially relevant; see for overviews. However, their work has assumed a relatively small number of digital libraries or databases and a fairly static configuration.

DESCRIPTION OF THE SYSTEM DESIGN

As a detailed description of the system design has already been given in, we only present a brief overview here and refer the interested reader to this prior work. We view every library as autonomous. A conceptually global but physically distributed directory, which is layered on top of a Chord-style dynamic hash table (DHT), holds only very compact, aggregated information about the peers' local indexes and only to the extent that the individual peers are willing to disclose.

Every peer is responsible for a randomised subset of the global directory. The global directory consists of aggregated information (Posts) that contains contact information about the digital library who posted this summary together with statistics to calculate IR-style relevance measures that try to estimate the relevance of a particular digital library to a query.

These measures are used to support the peer selection process, *i.e.*, determining the most promising libraries for a particular query. If, at query time, the local query result is considered unsatisfactory by the user, a library retrieves a list of potentially useful libraries. Using collection selection methods from distributed IR and metasearch, a number of promising libraries for the complete query is computed from these PeerLists. In we have studied promising and efficient techniques for this purpose.

Subsequently, the query is forwarded to these libraries and executed based on their local indexes. The results from the various libraries are combined at the querying peer into a single result list; this step is referred to as result merging.

The goal of finding high-quality search results with respect to precision and recall cannot be easily reconciled with the design goal of unlimited scalability, as the best information retrieval techniques for query execution rely on large amounts of document metadata. Posting only compact, aggregated information about local indexes and using appropriate peer selection methods to limit the number of peers involved in a query keeps the global directory manageable and reduces network traffic. We expect this approach to scale very well as more and more peers jointly maintain the moderately growing global directory.

COLLABORATIVE SEARCH ACROSS DIGITAL LIBRARIES

Our work is driven by the question of how a collaborative search across digital libraries can benefit from the unique nature of the P2P paradigm. We want to address the shortcomings of centralised search engines and further benefit from the intellectual input of a large user community.

Democratic Community Search

To overcome the danger of the infiltration of a centralised index by (commercial) interest groups we leverage the indexes from potentially thousands of digital libraries, making it harder to bias the final query results.

Implicit User Feedback

Additionally, we want to incorporate the fact that every library has its own local index, *e.g.*, by executing all queries first locally at the initiating library and using implicit-feedback techniques for automated query expansion.

User Recommendations

We want to incorporate local user bookmarks into our query execution. Bookmarks represent strong recommendations for specific documents. Also, user bookmarks can be considered as compact samples of peer indexes that describe their fields of interest. Queries could be exclusively forwarded to thematically related libraries with similarly interested users, to improve the chances of finding subjectively relevant pages.

Replication

In order to achieve service levels comparable to today's search engines and in order to actually benefit from the infrastructural advantage of a distributed system, we are going to introduce a certain degree of replication to the directory. Currently, as dictated by the DHT-style maintenance approach, a peer gracefully leaving the system forwards its share of the global directory to another peer.

Analogously, a library entering the system asks for its appropriate share of the directory. While one approach to ensure a valid, complete, and up-todate directory is to simply rely on the libraries to regularly re-send their Posts to the directory, it is also necessary to replicate parts of the directory to avoid data loss as libraries ungracefully leave the system. Also, replication can serve as a load-balancing measure, relieving the burden from peers that host popular parts of the directory, and increases data availability. Adaptive, self-tuning strategies for choosing appropriate degrees of replication and placing replicas are an open issue in our ongoing work.

Caching and Proactive Dissemination

To further enhance query efficiency, statistical summaries and also the results of queries from across the network may be cached in a way that allows other peers not only to instantly benefit from the existing query results but also to benefit from click streamst that were recorded on the occasion of similar queries. Statistical summaries may also be disseminated proactively among thematically related peers. Finding good strategies to this end is a widely open issue.

Overlap-aware Query Routing

Peer selection has been a research issue for years. Most of the existing literature estimates the expected result quality of a collection, typically using pre-computed statistics, and ranks the collections accordingly. We believe that this is insufficient if the collections overlap, *e.g.*, in the scenario of digital libraries that share an arbitrarily large fraction of documents. We argue for the extension of existing quality measures using estimators of mutual overlap among collections. Preliminary experiments show that such a combination can outperform popular approaches based on quality estimation only, such as CORI. Taking overlap into account during collection selection in this scenario can drastically decrease the number of libraries that have to be contacted in order to reach a satisfactory level of recall, which is a great step towards the feasibility of distributed search across digital libraries.

Benefit/Cost Optimisation

Ultimatively, we want to introduce a sophisticated benefit/cost ratio when selecting remote libraries for query forwarding. For the benefit estimation, it is intuitive to consider such measures.

Defining a meaningful cost measure, however, is an even more challenging issue. While there are techniques for observing and inferring network bandwidth or other infrastructural information, expected response times are changing over time. One approach is to create a distributed Quality-of-Service directory that, for all peers, holds moving averages of recent response times.

DISTINGUISH COMPUTER TECHNOLOGY AND COMMUNICATIONS TECHNOLOGY

Computer Technology

You have certainly seen and, we would guess, used a computer. Nevertheless, let's define what it is. A *computer* is a programmable, multiuse machine that accepts data—raw facts and figures—and processes, or manipulates, it into information we can use, such as summaries, totals, or reports. Its purpose is to speed up problem solving and increase productivity.

Communications Technology

Unquestionably you've been using communications technology for years. *Communications technology*, also called *telecommunications technology*, consists of electromagnetic devices and systems for communicating over long distances. The principal examples are telephone, radio, broadcast television, and cable TV.

In more recent times, there has been the addition of communication among computers—which is what happens when people 'go online' on the internet. In this context, *online* means using a computer or some other information device, connected through a network, to access information and services from another computer or information device. A *network* is a communications system connecting two or more computers; the internet is the largest such network. Information technology is already affecting your life in exciting ways and will do so even more in the future. Let's consider how.

Information Technology and its Used in Education

In her sociology classes at Indiana University, professor Melissa Wilde uses a small wireless keypad linked to a computer to enable students to answer questions not by raising their hands but by pressing buttons, with the results appearing on a screen in the front of the room. Wilde has her students answer multiple-choice questions to see whether they understand her lecture points and to make necessary adjustments.

"I can instantly see that three-quarters of the class doesn't get it," she says. She also uses the technology to get students to answer questions about themselves—race, income, political affiliation—skewed, for example, Towards wealthier or poorer students, an event that fired up a half hour of excited class discussion. Maybe the classrooms at your school haven't reached this level of interactivity yet, but there's no question that information technology is universal on college campuses, and at lower levels the internet has penetrated 99 per cent of schools. Most college students have been exposed to computers Since, the lower grades; indeed, one-fifth of college students report they were using computers between ages 5 and 8, and all had begun using computers by the time they were 16–18 years old. At the college level, the great majority (85 per cent) of students have their own computers, and two-thirds use at least two e-mail addresses.

As you no doubt know, *e-mail* is 'electronic mail,' messages transmitted over a computer network, most often the internet. Three-quarters of college students use the internet 4 or more hours a week, and about onefifth use it 12 or more hours a week. About half are required to use e-mail in their classes. For academic purposes, most students use e-mail to set up appointments (62 per cent) with professors, discuss grades (58 per cent), or get clarification of an assignment (75 per cent). Besides using the internet to help in teaching, today's college instructors also use *presentation graphics software* such as PowerPoint to show their lecture outlines and other materials on classroom screens.

In addition, they use Blackboard, WebCT, and other *coursemanagement software* for administering online assignments, schedules, examinations, and grades. One of the most intriguing developments in education at all levels, however, is the rise of *distance learning,* or *e-learning,* the name given to online education Programmes, which has more than 3.2 million online students enrolled nationwide and grows more than 20 per cent a year. E-learning has had some interesting effects: for example, the home-schooling movement, whereby children are taught at home, usually by parents, has come of age thanks to internet resources. e-Learning has also propelled the rise of for-profit institutions, such as Devry and the University of Phoenix, which 8 per cent of full-time college students now attend.

More than a third of institutions of higher education—and 97 per cent of public universities—offer online courses, and many have attracted on-campus students, who say they like the flexibility of not having to attend their classes at a set time. e-learning has been put to such varied uses as bringing career and technical courses to high school students in remote prairie towns, pairing gifted science students with master teachers in other parts of the country, and helping busy professionals obtain further credentials outside business hours. But the reach of information technology into education has only begun.

In the future, as suggested, see software called 'intelligent tutoring systems' that gives students individualised instruction when personal attention is scarce—such as the software Cognitive Tutor, which not only helps high school students to improve their performance in math but also sparks them to enjoy a subject they might have once hated.

In colleges, more students may use interactive simulation games, such as McGraw- Hill's Business Strategy Game, to apply their knowledge to real-world kinds of problems. And employees in company training Programmes may find themselves engaged in mock conversations with *avatars*—computer depictions of humans, as are often found in online videogames—that represent imaginary customers and coworkers, combining the best parts of computer-based learning with face-to-face interaction.

HEALTH: HIGH TECH FOR WELLNESS

Computers Used in Health and Medicine

Viktor Yazykov, competing in the perilous Around Alone solo sailing competition, found himself in the stormy South Atlantic with a seriously infected arm that needed emergency surgery. So, with the help of step-bystep instructions sent by e-mail from Boston-based Dr. Daniel Carlin to his solar-powered laptop computer, Yazykov operated on his own arm. Yazykov's story is a dramatic example of *telemedicine*—medical care delivered via telecommunications. For some time, physicians in rural areas lacking local access to radiologists have used 'teleradiology' to exchange computerised images such as X-rays via telephone-linked networks with expert physicians in metropolitan areas.

Now telemedicine is moving to an exciting new level, as the use of digital cameras and sound, in effect, moves patients to doctors rather than the reverse. Already telemedicine is being embraced by administrators in the American prison system, where by law inmates are guaranteed medical treatment—and where the increase in prisoners every year has led to the need to control health costs.

Computer technology is also radically changing the tools of medicine. All medical information, including that generated by X-ray, lab test, and pulse monitor, can now be transmitted to a doctor in digital format. And image transfer technology allows radiologic images such as CT scans and MRIs to be immediately transmitted to electronic charts and physicians' offices. Patients in intensive care, who are usually monitored by nurses during offtimes, can also be watched over by doctors in remote 'control towers' miles away. Electronic medical records and other computerised tools enable heart attack patients to get follow-up drug treatment and diabetics to have their blood sugar measured. Software can compute a woman's breast cancer risk. Patients can use e-mail to query their doctors about their records.

Various *robots*—automatic devices that perform functions ordinarily performed by human beings, with names such as robo doc, RoboCart, TUG, and HelpMate—help free medical workers for more critical tasks; the four-armed da Vinci surgical robot, for instance, can do cuts and stitches deep inside the body, so that surgery is less traumatic and recovery time faster. Hydraulics and computers are being used to help artificial limbs get 'smarter.' And a patient paralysed by a stroke has received an implant that allows communication between his brain and a computer; as a result, he can move a cursor across a screen by brainpower and convey simple messages—as in *Star Trek.*

Want to calculate how long you will live? Want to go about gathering your family health history to see if you're at risk for particular inherited diseases? These are only two examples of health Web sites available to patients and health consumers. Although online health information can be misleading and even dangerous, many people now tap into health care databases, e-mail health professionals, or communicate with people who have similar conditions. For instance, hours after 10-year-old Robert Lord of San Diego fractured his spine in a fall from a tree, his father found an experimental drug on the internet, saving the boy from lifetime paralysis.

Often patients are already steeped in information about their conditions when they arrive in the offices of health care professionals. This represents a fundamental shift of knowledge, and therefore power, from physicians to patients. In addition, health care consumers are able to share experiences and information with one another. Young parents, for example, can find an online gathering spot at pediatrician Alan Greene's Web site.

MONEY: TOWARDS THE CASHLESS SOCIETY

Computers Affect and Financial Matters

"The future of money is increasingly digital, likely virtual, and possibly universal," says one writer. *Virtual* means that something is created, simulated, or carried on by means of a computer or a computer network, and we certainly have come a long way Towards becoming a cashless society. Indeed, the percentage of all financial transactions done electronically, both phone-initiated and computer-initiated, was projected to rise to 18.4 per cent in 2013, up from 0.9 per cent in 1993.

Besides currency, paper checks, and credit and debit cards, the things that serve as 'money' include cashvalue cards, automatic transfers, and digital money. Many readers of this book will probably already have engaged in online buying and selling, purchasing CDs and DVDs, books, airline tickets, or computers.

But what about groceries? After all, you can't exactly squeeze the cantaloupes through your keyboard. Even so, online groceries are expected to reach $7.5 billion in U.S., sales by 2012. To change decades of shopping habits, e-grocers keep their delivery charges low and delivery times convenient, and they take great pains in filling orders, knowing that a single bad piece of fruit will produce a devastating word-of-mouth backlash. Only about 46 per cent of U.S.,

workers have their paychecks electronically deposited into their bank accounts, but this is sure to change as Americans discover that direct deposit is actually safer and faster. Online bill paying is also picking up steam. For more than two decades, it has been possible to pay bills online, such as those from phone and utility companies, with special software and online connections to your bank. About 19 million American households do some bill paying online, and the number was expected to reach 61 million households in 2008.

Some banks and other businesses are backing an electronic-payment system that allows internet users to buy goods and services with *micropayments,* electronic payments of as little as 25 cents in transactions for which it is uneconomical to use a credit card. Micropayment, suggests futurist Paul Saffo, 'allows you to buy things by the sip rather than the gulp.' The success of Apple Computer's iTunes online music service, which sells songs for 99 cents each, suggests that micro sales are now feasible.

All kinds of businesses and organisations, from independent songwriters to comic book writers to the Legal Aid Society of Cleveland, now accept micropayments, using intermediaries such as BitPass and Peppercoin. Thus, you could set up your own small business simply by constructing a Web site and accepting micropay-ments.

LEISURE: INFOTECH IN ENTERTAINMENT AND THE ARTS

Leisure Activities be Affected by Information Technology

Information technology is being used for all kinds of entertainment, ranging from videogames to telegambling. It is also being used in the arts, from painting to photography. Let's consider just two examples, music and film. Computers, the internet, and the World Wide Web are standing the system of music recording and distribution on its head—and in the process are changing the financial underpinnings of the music industry. Because of their high overhead, major record labels typically need a band to sell half a million CDs in order to be profitable, but independent bands, using online marketing, can be reasonably successful selling 20,000 or 30,000 albums. Team Love, a small music label established in 2003, found it could promote its first two bands, Tilly and the Wall and Willy Mason, by offering songs online fRee for *downloading*—transferring data from a remote computer to one's own computer—so that people could listen to them before paying $12 for a CD. It also puts videos online for sharing and uses quirky Web sites to reach fans.

"There's something exponential going on," says one of Team Love's founders. "The more music that's downloaded, the more it sells." Many independent musicians are also using the internet to get their music heard, hoping that giving away songs will help them build audiences. The web also offers sources for instantly downloadable sheet music. One research engineer has devised a computerised scoring system for judging musical competitions that overcomes the traditional human-jury approach, which can be swayed by personalities and politics.

And a Spanish company, PolyphonicHMI, has created Hit Song Science software, which they say can analyse the hit potential of new songs by "reference to a finely parsed universe of attributes derived from millions of past songs." As for movies, now that blockbuster movies routinely meld live action and animation, computer artists are in big demand.

The 1999 film *Star Wars: Episode I*, for instance, had fully 1,965 digital shots out of about 2,200 shots.

Even when film was used, it was scanned into computers to be tweaked with animated effects, lighting, and the like. Entire beings were created on computers by artists working on designs developed by producer George Lucas and his chief artist. What is driving the demand for computer artists? One factor is that animation, though not cheap, looks more and more like a bargain, because hiring movie actors costs so much—some make $20 million a film. Moreover, special effects are readily understood by audiences in other countries, and major studios increasingly count on revenues from foreign markets to make a film profitable.

Digital manipulation also allows a crowd of extras to be multiplied into an army of thousands. It can also be used to create settings: in the film *Sky Captain and the World of Tomorrow,* the actors—Gwyneth Paltrow, Angelina Jolie, and Jude Law—shot all their scenes in front of a blue screen, and computer-generated imagery was then used to transport them into an imaginary world of 1939. Computer techniques have even been used to develop digitally created actors—called 'synthespians.' Actors ranging from the late James Dean to the late John Wayne, for instance, have been recruited for television commercials. And computerised animation is now so popular that Hollywood studios and movie directors are finding they can make as much money from creating videogames as from making movies.

But animation is not the only area in which computers are revolutionising movies. Digital editing has radically transformed the way films are assembled.

Whereas traditional film editing involved reeling and unreeling spools of film and cutting and gluing pieces of highly scratchable celluloid together, nearly burying the editor in film, today an editor can access 150 miles of film stored on a computer and instantly find any visual or audio moment, allowing hundreds of variations of a scene to be called up for review. Even Non-professionals can get into movie making as new computerrelated products come to market.

Now that digital video capture-and-edit systems are available for under $1,000, amateurs can turn home videos into digital data and edit them. Also, digital camcorders, which offer outstanding picture and sound quality, have steadily dropped in price.

TECHNOLOGY ACROSS THE CURRICULUM

If information technology skills are increasingly important in the world outside of higher education, then certainly educators need to examine the Programmes of study at their institution to see how they are preparing students to survive and thrive in the technology rich environment that has now permeated all areas of life. Information literacy, fluency in *information technology* (IT), technology across the curriculum, general education requirements, ubiquitous computing—there are many models for introducing technology into academic Programmes, but no silver bullet that meets the needs of every institution.

We are not attempting here to define one approach that every institution should take. Instead, we focus on factors that every institution needs to consider in successful curriculum development for fluency in information technology and information literacy, and we offer examples of strategies that can address these factors. Although we present these factors linearly, they are really recursive—consideration of any one factor may lead back to reconsideration of others.

In addition, although we focus here on curriculum development for undergraduate education, we recognise that the strategies we identify also have broader application to the design of continuing training Programmes for workforce development at the college or university level or in the work setting. The growing industry of IT-related training needs to be cognizant of the same range of factors as academic institutions in order to create successful Programmes. Supplying information technology workers and IT-enabled workers is a task that higher education shares with employers, and both sectors need carefully planned strategies to be effective in meeting that responsibility.

In our discussion, we have used examples from George Mason University's Technology Across the Curriculum (TAC) initiative because we are most familiar with it, but we would be the first to acknowledge that George Mason's Programme was designed to fit this institution's particular circumstances and is not necessarily appropriate at another institution.

PRELIMINARY DEFINITIONS

Information literacy and information technology fluency are overlapping but distinct competencies. They are complementary to each other—in today's world an information technology fluent person must also be information literate, and vice versa. In this context, the aim of *fluency* in information technology tends to focus on the technology itself; the goal of *literacy* is primarily concerned with the intellectual framework of dealing with information.

Both competencies, however, require development of a continuum of evolving skills that become possible through mastery of interrelated concepts and cultivation of broad intellectual capabilities. In Part One of this book, Herbert Lin gives an overview of what IT fluency consists of and comments upon its critical importance, drawing on the findings of a National Research Council study.

Mastery of the three types of knowledge characterises fluency in information technology, or FITness. These are the essential building blocks for acquiring knowledge of and sustaining the process of lifelong learning for FITness, bolstering a person's ability to succeed in the dynamic environment of information technology. Although the concept of FITness clearly goes well beyond the mechanical type of learning typically associated with computer literacy, its focus nevertheless remains information technology itself—hardware, software, networks, and so forth. In contrast, the central concern of information literacy "is an intellectual framework for understanding, finding, evaluating, and using information—activities which may be accomplished in part by fluency with information technology, in part by sound investigative methods, but most important, through critical discernment and reasoning". Development of information literacy focuses on information itself:

- Determining the nature and extent of information needed
- Finding and accessing needed information effectively and efficiently, whether it is available in the library, on the Web, from a government agency, in a book or journal, or in a map

- Critically evaluating information and its sources and using it effectively
- Understanding the ethical, legal, economic, and social uses of information

Like FITness, information literacy aims to develop, foster, and sustain lifelong learning. But unlike FITness, information literacy abilities are not exclusively or ultimately intertwined with or dependent on information technology.

KEYS TO A SUCCESSFUL PROGRAMME

In thinking about how to integrate either or both of the related concepts of IT fluency and information literacy into the curricula of an institution, we have identified ten factors as crucial elements in a successful Programme.

DETERMINE YOUR INSTITUTIONAL STAKEHOLDERS

An environmental scan is an important early step in addressing technology in the curriculum. Who cares, or might potentially care, about this issue? The list is certain to vary from institution to institution, but here are a few suggestions:

- Does your governing board take a strong interest in curriculum?
- Has your regional accrediting agency or state higher education board set guidelines for technology or information literacy competencies?
- Has the business community in your area expressed a need for employees with technology skills?
- Do some academic departments already offer technology-related courses?
- Are there faculty committees involved in curriculum development?
- How important is it to your students to develop their technology and information literacy skills?
- How do your alumni feel about an effort to include more technology skills in your institution's degree Programmes?

Don't overlook in your environmental scan academic support units such as the library, student services, and information technology—and even the public relations department, the development office, and institutional research staff.

The staff in these units are very likely to have not only an interest in the issue but the expertise to contribute to developing a successful initiative. Any or all of these groups can be a tremendous ally in developing a unified and coherent institutional approach to improving student technology and information literacy skills.

Conversely, they can also be a tremendous roadblock if they feel that their perspectives or interests in the issue are not being addressed by the proposed Programme. At the very least, your Programme will be deprived of their potential contributions of time, funding, or expertise if the Programme coordinators are unaware of their interest in the issue.

For George Mason's Programme, the governor and the state legislature turned out to be key players in initiating TAC. But the actual design and implementation required many participants within the institution. Not every group of stakeholders has the same strategic importance, of course, but institutional change being as difficult as it is, one supporter more or one resister less can make a difference in the success of the overall Programme.

ENGAGE YOUR STAKEHOLDERS

Having identified stakeholders or potential stakeholders in the issue of student technology and information literacy skills and their respective levels of strategic importance, you need to engage them appropriately. At a minimum, you can engage stakeholders by sharing information through a Web site, brochure, e-mail announcement, and the like.

At a higher level of engagement, you can actively solicit input on the project through a survey or focus group. For example, in designing TAC, faculty were surveyed quite early in the process to find out the degree to which they were already asking students to use technology in their courses and what kinds of technology they were using. By being able to give a big-picture view of what was already happening, we could show that our proposal aligned with a direction in which faculty were already moving.

We used focus groups both with faculty and members of our local business community to get ideas about exactly what technology skills students needed to succeed in an academic discipline and in a business environment. The high degree of overlap between the two groups helped faculty recognise that TAC had academic value and was not a vocational sellout to Non-academic concerns. Other levels of active engagement include membership on a working group or project team, a proposal review board, and an advisory group.

Whatever you can do to translate interest to participation and ultimately into ownership benefits the Programme. If it is seen as the work of only one or two people, it is much more difficult for the Programme to have long-term staying power, impact, and acceptance. The TAC Programme also uses showcases to continue engaging stakeholders. At our annual celebration of student learning, for example, TAC sponsors a prise for the learning project that demonstrates the best incorporation of technology in learning. We also have a prise sponsored by the university libraries for the best original student research to encourage development of information literacy skills. Hundreds of students and faculty visit the event and are impressed with what their colleagues are learning and doing with technology.

DEFINE YOUR TERMS

Now, with all these interested parties engaged in your Programme, there are a lot of ideas floating around about what the Programme should be. Multiple perspectives and a multitude of ideas can be healthy and helpful at some stages of development, but eventually the participants have to come to consensus on what the Programme really is and what they are actually buying into.

What would technology integrated into the curriculum look like at your institution? Does it mean every student takes a technology course? That every faculty member uses technology in delivering instruction? That every course requires students to use technology to complete the learning? That some courses or some students or some faculty use technology—and if so, which ones?

Perhaps more basically, what does 'technology' encompass? Are you focusing on office applications such as word processing and spreadsheets? Do you also include on-line search and research skills, information literacy skills broadly defined, multimedia skills? What about legal and ethical issues related to technology, such as privacy, security, and copyright?

Do you include use of such technology equipment as digital cameras and data projectors, computer operating systems, and programming languages? None of these possible definitions is necessarily the best for every type of institution. There can be excellent reasons for including or excluding certain features from your institutional approach. But to make the Programme work, everyone needs to know what is included and what is excluded so that the participants' energy is focused on the former. The strategies of engagement already mentioned also facilitate definition of terms and buy-in on the Programme definition. One cornerstone of TAC is a list of ten technology goals. It took almost a year of collaboration to come up with this list, but once it was established, we could work more easily with many groups to build a Programme around that set of skills.

Table. Technology Goals for George Mason University Students

Students will be Able to:	Essential (Examples)	Advanced (Examples)
1. Engage in electronic collaboration 'netiquette'	Send and receive e-mail; understand writing;	Participate in collaborative participate in an electronic conference
2. Use and create structured electronic documents automate repetitious tasks	Create, format, and edit a document using a word processing	Use templates, macros, and mail merge to Programme
3. Do technology-enhanced presentations	Use a presentation software package to create, format, and edit an electronic presentation their own	Modify standard tools and templates for presentations and develop

4. Use electronic tools for research and evaluation timeliness,	Understand and apply search strategies appropriate to the Web and on-line databases	Select databases and other resources according to discipline, and coverage
5. Use databases to manage information	Enter data into a Pre-existing database; conduct simple queries of a database	Set up a relational data-base of two or three tables: construct aquery for a simple rela-tional database
6. Use spreadsheets to manage information formulas	Enter data into a new or existing spreadsheet; format the layout of a spreadsheet	Use templates and macros to repetitious tasks: use statistical, logical, and financial
7. Use electronic tools for analysing qualitative and quantitative data	Use a statistical pack lage to enter data, name variables, and define variable values	Perform reliabi-lity and validity analyses
8. Use graphical and multimedia represen-tational technologies resize, crop change format)	Perform simple manipu-lations on existing images (download, lighting reverse, etc.)	Add special effects to an image (Colour,
9. Demonstrate familiarity with major issues legal, ethical, privacy, and security issues in information technology	Understand the basics of copyright and property law as they apply to electronic materials	Understand the ethical raised by artifi-cial intelligence, virtual reality, etc.
10. Have a working knowledge of hardware and software	Perform basic computer operations on at least one computer platform	Install basic peripheral devices (printer, scanner, etc.

IDENTIFY DESIRED OUTCOMES

Another important clarification for a successful Programme is identifying desired outcomes. This enables development of guidelines for participants about activities appropriate to the Programme, and it helps everyone know how you intend to measure the success of the Programme. Desired outcomes may include improvement of student technology skills, improved academic performance for students, more student satisfaction with academic Programmes, greater faculty use of technology, better job placement for graduates, or an enhanced reputation for the institution in an area of strategic importance to it.

Outcomes can also focus on building a specific partnership with the business community or with another college or university in the region or beyond. With TAC, George Mason's primary desired outcome is that every student graduates from the university with a range of technology skills based on the program's goals. As we revised those technology goals, we added specific performance descriptions so that faculty who were redesigning a course would know what kind of assignment—encompassing both technology fluency and information literacy as appropriate—they would need to build in.

Taking the domain of technology fluency as an example, the first definition of the technology goals indicated that graduates would be able to use a spreadsheet; in our revised version, we have specified more exactly what they need to be able to do with a spreadsheet in a beginning or general education course and what they need to be able to do with one in an advanced course in the major.

This focus on student achievement and student learning means that TAC does not fund proposals that focus on faculty delivery of instruction. At another institution, delivery of instruction may be an important step in achieving the goals of the Programme and thus well worth funding.

After three years, we reviewed and revised the list to reflect our changing understanding of the technology goals we wanted our students to achieve.

In the newest version, we have put more emphasis on being able to use representational technologies; consistent with the university's general education requirements, we have also explicitly identified information literacy skills as part of the desired goals.

IDENTIFY RESOURCES

Armed with understanding of exactly what you want to achieve, you must find existing resources or develop new ones that can help you meet your institution's goals. Take another look at that list of stakeholders and see what financial, personnel, or organisational resources they might have that can help build your proposed Programme. The more your program's goals align with the goals and interests of potential stakeholders, the more likely they are to share or contribute resources.

The availability of resources may determine priorities for implementing the Programme. In higher education, leveraging existing resources is an effective, time-honored strategy. If the provost, dean, department chair, chief librarian, head of student services, or development office supports your initiative, then you may be able to take advantage of funding already available for such purposes as curriculum development, faculty and staff development, workforce development, or even classroom renovation.

Or you may be able to use these funds to interest a business partner, state or local government, or a foundation in helping implement your project. If funds aren't available to accomplish everything you want, then target one part of the project whose success is assured and that is highly likely to engender additional funding.

In some institutions, technology enhancement may be considered to add value to the educational experience, so students and their parents pay an extra technology fee or buy a computer for student use. Likewise, the more the Programme can build on existing staff and existing organisational structures, the easier it is to implement. Is there an organisational or administrative structure in place at your institution that can manage this Programme? The goals of the Programme determine to a certain extent how elaborate a structure you need. If the Programme involves distributing money, then part of the administration has to be an institutional agent with fiscal authority. If the Programme is built as part of the regular faculty teaching load and no extra money is involved, then perhaps an existing academic committee structure at the departmental, school or college, or institutional level, as appropriate, can review and approve curricular changes that meet the Programme goals.

In implementing TAC, George Mason University did create a few new structures but as much as possible we used the existing resources and organisational structure of the College of Arts and Sciences and the Information Technology unit, the two principle partners in the initiative. When the university libraries began to restructure their instruction Programme with an information literacy focus, discussion began immediately to see how we could collaborate and help each other achieve mutual goals.

When the university added an IT proficiency component to its general education requirements, we worked closely with the universitywide general education committee to make sure that the TAC Programme was in harmony with general education goals and that the committee was aware of the TAC and library goals in planning its implementation.

CHECK YOUR TECHNOLOGY INFRASTRUCTURE

A Programme to enhance student technology learning needs technology resources and may flounder if they are not readily available. It can be extremely frustrating to plan new ways to get students and faculty to use technology, only to discover that there are few facilities on campus where they can learn or use these skills, or that the network or server capacity is insufficient to support your plans, or that the technology cannot be accessed when and where it is needed, or that insufficient networked digital scholarly resources are available. It is wise to start with an understanding of your institution's existing technology infrastructure and any plans already in place to enhance that infrastructure. Working with your IT staff and librarians, you may be able to target improvements in the areas most important to your Programme.

Besides looking at the existing structure, you should also take into account whatever increased demand for technology resources your Programme may generate. Once people start using certain kinds of technology in instruction, more faculty and students want to use them, and expectations grow. Not only do they want to do electronic presentations in every classroom; now they want electronic presentations with audio and video clips accessible over the network.

If there's no possibility that the institution can make that level of technology available, then you must manage expectations or else risk seeing your Programme labeled as a failure even as it succeeds. In the case of TAC, we had two major concerns about technology. Faculty wanted to be sure that students would be supported in learning technology skills outside of the classroom and that there would be enough technology-enhanced classrooms to allow faculty and students to demonstrate the targeted technology skills. We dedicated part of the IT staff to the task of mentoring students in technology skills; we focused our equipment funds on making more classroom technology available.

BUILD YOUR SUPPORT TEAM

New curricula using technology require planning on how you will support the students and the faculty who are to use that technology. Faculty support may include financial incentives or release time as well as student assistants, professional staff trained in instructional design and instructional technology, training classes in instructional technology, librarians to consult regarding research assignments and resources, printed and on-line resource materials, models of the kind of assignment or evaluation you want them to use, and peer mentors.

Students likewise need a range of support if they are expected to use technology in new ways as part of their learning process. Except for those in some technical disciplines, faculty generally do not want to dedicate class time for teaching technology skills or information literacy. So although they may expect students to be able to create an electronic presentation for class, they are not going to spend class time teaching this application.

Likewise, they may not devote instructional time to the process of conducting topical literature research and reporting of findings. Students who need it must be able to get the basics of these skills somewhere else. How will your institution facilitate this? Perhaps you can offer short training sessions through one of the technology-related academic departments. Perhaps you can include this kind of training in instructional sessions held by the library or IT staff.

In the TAC Programme, we made use of existing instructional support staff to work with faculty in developing and implementing course revision proposals. We also developed a new Programme to make available graduate and undergraduate student assistants for technology projects. In addition, we expanded an existing student technology facility to include a broader range of support and licensed on-line instructional modules for several hundred software applications.

DEVELOP AN ASSESSMENT PLAN

Assessment constitutes a key feature of educational endeavors. In practical terms, it helps you to keep on improving your Programme and assures your participants and funders that the Programme is doing what was intended. Therefore, think early on about how you will show that the Programme is achieving its outcomes.

Can you repurpose data that are already being collected at the institution, as through graduating senior or alumni surveys that ask about student use of technology during or after their educational experience? Or do you need to collect new sets of data? Perhaps you can work with admissions or student services to collect benchmark information about the technology and associated skills students bring with them to the institution. It is also important to work with the faculty who are teaching technology-enhanced courses so that they find ways to assess how students' skills change or how their learning changes as a result of introducing technology or information literacy skills development.

You may also want to look at specific tests of competency for all students or a random sample of students to demonstrate the impact of your Programme. The organisational structure of the Programme should include provision for how assessment data are collected and disseminated. Whoever is managing the Programme has to develop regular reports about how many students and faculty in which areas of the institution participate in the Programme, and collect data from faculty and other sources about its impact. In addition, thought should be given to how data are applied to improve the Programme.

Who is empowered to make adjustments to it? What are the processes for changing the Programme? In our TAC Programme, we began with a focus on the faculty who were redesigning the curriculum. Proposal guidelines called for inclusion of an assessment component. We didn't always get one, and we spent a lot of time helping faculty to develop that component, including recruiting the head of institutional assessment to give workshops in assessment strategies.

But we kept right on asking for those assessment plans and assessment reports until we got results. We also developed some programmatic strategies for tracking data, such as a grid of which courses included which technology skills; we published regular reports about the number of students, faculty, and departments participating in the Programme. The leadership of the Programme also had operational authority to implement change as a result of assessment information.

THINK PROGRAMMATICALLY

Curricular change is most effective when it is programmatic rather than episodic. If curricular change is left to each individual faculty member to implement, the institution is unlikely to be in a position to know if the end result matches the original intention. With technology fluency and information literacy skills in particular, it is critical to plan for building a range of skills across a number of courses; this can't happen unless there is programwide thinking about the connections between one set of skills and other more advanced ones.

Instead of asking individual faculty to think about technology in their individual courses, consider asking all faculty who teach a particular course to set technology or information literacy goals for the course. That way, every student who takes the course, no matter who teaches it, is working Towards the same outcomes as the other students are. If the faculty know, for example, that every first-year biology student uses spreadsheets to accomplish certain tasks, then faculty teaching more advanced courses can build on that to help students use spreadsheets for sophisticated data collection and analysis.

If use of spreadsheets in the first year is only hit-or-miss, depending on who is teaching the class, then it is difficult for faculty in other courses to build in advanced uses. Similarly, developing information literacy skills is a gradual and cumulative process. Abilities and skills acquired early on, beginning with introductory or general courses, serve students well in the courses of their chosen major.

George Mason's TAC Programme offered extra incentives for group and departmental proposals to encourage the broadest possible collaboration and development across an entire Programme of study. If your Programme is built around a single technology course for all students, then it is important that all faculty be aware of the skills introduced in that course so they can give students additional practice in using the skills in other courses later in their Programme of study. If there is no Programme for ensuring that students use a range of technology and information literacy skills, then they will probably be reintroduced to the same basic skills over and over—never having the opportunity to develop or use more advanced skills at all. In the TAC initiative, for example, we got many proposals for introducing students to Internet research and Web page design, but far fewer that focused on using spreadsheets or electronic presentations, making critical assessment of information and its sources and incorporating selected information in students' written projects, or understanding legal and ethical issues in technology use. We were able to use our tracking grid and our request for proposals to encourage course development across the whole range of skills that we wanted our students to learn.

THINK COLLABORATIVELY

Thinking collaboratively may be the most important strategy in working on your project. Terry O'Banion sets forth a model that is particularly relevant when applied to curriculum development: "Everyone employed in the learning college will be a learning facilitator, including categories formerly designated administration and support or clerical staff.... The goal is to have every employee... thinking about how his or her work facilitates the learning process". If the job of helping students develop interrelated technology fluency and information literacy is left to any one group—faculty, librarians, IT staff, career services—then many opportunities are lost. Understanding and using information and information technology is a multifaceted process that can be facilitated from many perspectives. The more the goal of helping students in that process pervades the institution, the more opportunities students have to learn and hone their skills in these areas.

Building as large a community of interest as possible brings more resources to bear and allows them to be used most productively. If an academic department can share instructional materials, directly or indirectly, then it can avoid duplicating work that is being done in other departments. For example, if many departments are introducing spreadsheets or electronic presentations into their courses, there is really no need for every one of them to develop independent tutorials, assignments, evaluation instruments, and so forth. The same holds true for courses incorporating assignments related to information literacy. At the least, if faculty members see what other colleagues have prepared, they can build on each other's work. At best, faculty from several departments might collaborate, assisted by librarians and instructional technologists, in building a library of assignments or tutorials or other instructional resources from which they all can draw. The TAC Programme builds on a collaborative relationship between the College of Arts and Sciences and the *Information Technology Unit* (ITU)—including increasingly the libraries, which are an administrative component of ITU—that involves shared goal setting, shared decisions about priorities and resource allocation, and shared commitment to student learning and success. Collaborative partnerships can also extend outside the institution—for example, with the business community—in developing internships that help students practice information and technology skills.

4

Library Information and Communications Technology

INTRODUCTION

Information and Communications Technology (ICT) have transformed Library and Information services globally. The Internet has provided universal access to information. Technological innovation has dramatically increased the rate of conversion of knowledge, information and data into electronic format. Developments in the software arena has generated powerful knowledge management software which has transformed the way knowledge is organised, stored, accessed and retrieved.

The digital revolution driven by ICT innovation has transformed academic libraries fundamentally. It has impacted on every sphere of academic library activity, *e.g.*, the form of the library, collection development strategies, library buildings and consortia. Information and communications technology have changed the academic library in a profound way. Computers and networked electronic resources had become an integral part of the academic library the past decade. This has been underscored by the phenomenon of knowledge or information commons in academic libraries, which refer to a specific environment in the library where a designated number of PC workstations, networked to databases and other e-resources, are made available to students. Every sphere of the academic library is being affected by ICT quite radically.

No longer is the library the untouchable custodian of information. It is being shaken to its very foundation, in fact its existence is being threatened. The academic libraries' traditional role of information custodian had been reduced to that of being one of many information providers. Of all the information and communication technologies the Internet and particularly the World Wide Web with its graphical user interface, has had the greatest impact on the information revolution. The number of electronic resources available on the Internet is growing at a phenomenal rate.

One of the major search engines Alta Vista has reported in 1996 that it has indexed 30 million Web pages. By 1998 the number of Web pages indexed by this search engine has leaped to 90 million. According to Farrow wide spread publicity has lead to assumptions that the Internet will meet all user information needs and that there will be no need for professional librarian intervention in future between user and information resources. Moyo states that student expectations that all their research needs will be met online are on the increase. Not only do students expect to find the information they need online, they also expect it to be available in full text. According to Tam and Robertson these assumptions have lead to a reluctance to use the physical library materials and to a decrease of visits to the library.

This phenomenon has fuelled fears of potential future job losses amongst librarians. Cheng explores the impact of information technology from an information ecological perspective. In information ecology the focus is not on information technology but on the human activities that are served. Cheng cites Nardi and O'day who draw a parallel between the explosive growth of information technology and the consequential Information explosion and a volcanic eruption. This eruption is impacting on everyone existing with the information ecosystem. Cheng emphasise the importance that we as academic librarians are clear about the challenges posed by this situation and also the opportunities offered.

Cheng highlights some of the changes that took place within the information ecology:

- The way we gather information, organise it, disseminate and use information has changed.
- The evolution of the Web has lead to availability of masses of information, electronic journals and databases.
- The way information is being published is evolving rapidly, *e.g.*, it is threatening current practices.
- New problems have come to the fore, *e.g.*, the issue of intellectual property rights of e-resources.
- User expectations have changed. Users expect full text delivery to the desktop.

Researchers are of the opinion that the changes that library and information services face are of an unknown and unpredictable nature. He states that it is impossible for library managers to predict future trends accurately. He feels traditional change management techniques are inadequate to deal with the changing environment that libraries are facing. For him it is a scenario where one has to brace oneself for whatever occurs. Under these conditions it is crucial that libraries make optimal use of the entire workforce.

It is of fundamental importance that customer service be given top priority. It is also essential that flexible organisational structures be created where workloads and responsibilities are shared and trust and responsibility are the norm rather than control. For library and information services in academic libraries to prevail under these conditions real leadership and real changes in management styles and organisational structures are necessary.

CONCEPTS DEFINED

Change

Robbins and Coulter defines change as any alterations in people, structure or technology. Change involves moving from the current state of things, the status quo, to a new state of things. It is therefore a process of moving from what is known to the unknown.

Information and Communications Technology (ICT)

Adeyoyin cites Bayode who defines ICT as "the acquisition, processing, storage, and dissemination of information by means of computers and other telecommuni-cation equipment." The Wikipedia free Internet encyclopaedia defines "information technology (IT) or information and communication(s) technology (ICT)" as the "technology required for information processing. In particular the use of electronic computers and computer software to convert, store, protect, process, transmit, and retrieve information".

From the definitions it is clear that the terms IT and ICT are used interchangeably and has the same meaning. According to Jimba information technology is rooted in three sectors namely information technology, telecommunications and the media and these sectors are converging on one another.

TYPES OF CHANGE

Researcher define change along a continuum ranging from low-scope to high-scope change.

Evolutionary Change

Evolutionary change is incremental by nature. Incremental change is smooth and happens gradually in an organised and predictable way. Incremental change tends to be small changes that lead to improvement but does not alter the operational structure of the academic library.

Strategic Change

Strategic, revolutionary or transformational change leads to radical transformation and often changes the general organisational structure. Transformational change tends to be very traumatic by nature. It can be generated as a response to a major crisis or a complete change in organisational strategy or purpose. The outcome of this type of change can lead to organisational transformation to the effect that the organisation might look completely different from what it used to be.

Discontinuous Change

The academic library is confronted with change that is unlike anything it has been exposed to before. Management theorists use the term discontinuous change. Pugh notes that discontinuous change is different from revolutionary change that is change undertaken to generate rapid results. Discontinuous change is unique in the sense that established management practices are inadequate to deal with it, in fact there is no model, paradigm or pool of experience that managers can fall back onto.

Researcher describes discontinuous change as turbulent, complex, traumatic, uncertain and of a revolutionary nature which requires different management skills to survive, supported by highly trained, motivated, flexible and multi-skilled staff that can be redeployed quickly and effectively if necessary. There is a stark contrast between the clearly defined boundaries of businesses in the 1960's and 1970's and the postindustrial era that is characterised by volatility, complexity and uncertainty. "This type of random, discontinuous change—which, by definition, is fast, traumatic, and revolutionary – requires very different management and leadership skills if the challenges it presents are to be handled innovatively and opportunistically." What organisations need in order to survive is highly committed, skilled, informed and trained staff which is willing to give their all.

Until 15 years ago change was incremental. One could build on lessons learned before. Since then change had become discontinuous. In this climate old management behaviours are inadequate. New ways of doing things are imperative which questions the practices that worked in the past. Information services in the academic library are driven by ICT with all its uncertainties and instability. Change is occurring at a greater dimension than ever before. The volume, pace and complexity of change is increasing at an unprecedented rate. A comparison between 1970 and to-day reveals that in 1970 only 5 per cent of change within organisations was of a continuous nature. Currently 75 per cent of all organisational change is of a continuous nature.

IMPACT OF ICT DEVELOPMENTS ON STAFF

Managers often introduce drastic change without considering its impact on people. People respond to change in a myriad of ways. Any significant change will impact on people's self-esteem, their motivation to do well, their status or the stress they experience be it positive or negative. It is of vital importance that managers do not overlook people when dealing with an ever-changing environment.

According to Morgan research suggests that 90 per cent of change initiatives fail because people are not taken into consideration. Change is good for academic libraries but its adoption requires tremendous input of physical, mental and emotional energy. After having to make intense inputs to accomplish change people expect to reach a plateau, a period for review and restoration of energy. The problem is that in the academic library this plateau had become non-existent because one peak follows after the other.

Phases People go through when Exposed to Radical Change

Elizabeth Kubler-Ross has identified 5 stages that patients experience when confronted with personal loss or death. These stages are denial, anger, bargaining, depression and acceptance.

Conner has used Kubler-Ross's 5 stages as a basis and extended it to 8 stages:

1. *Stability:* This is the phase just prior to change where everything is still normal.
2. *Immobilised:* When confronted with radical change people initially experience shock, confusion and become disoriented. During this phase people are out of touch with reality.
3. *Denial:* Conner defines denial as a refusal to accept reality. According to Fossum denial is a psychological defence mechanism that kicks in when individuals are confronted with radical change. It is a refusal to accept reality while the person's internal resources are being mobilised to eventually face a situation. To help staff to deal with this phase managers should use techniques designed to promote awareness that change has occurred or is in the process of occurring. The denial phase is a critical stage in the change process and people experience it differently. While some people are still dazed and out of touch with reality others may be ready to move on. Spending time on an individual bases with people struggling with this phase can be very useful.
4. *Anger:* During this phase people experience anger and outrage. They become emotional, irritated, frustrated and hurt and may often lash out at those supporting them.
5. *Bargaining:* This is a negotiation phase with a view to avoid the negative aspects of change. A typical example would be negotiating an extension of a deadline one is facing. This phase indicates the person is reaching a position where he or she can no longer avoid reality. This phase also demarcates the beginning of acceptance.
6. *Depression:* It is normal for people to become depressed when confronted with major change that affects them negatively. This is a very unpleasant phase but is an indication that the individual has come to complete realisation of the negative change being faced. It is an unpleasant phase but indicates another step towards acceptance.
7. *Testing:* At this point a sense of control is regained. A person might explore how to set new goals.
8. *Acceptance:* At this point people accept change. To go with an employee through the negative response model can be a costly

exercise because people need support at every step of the way. However the cost of an employee failing to go through the process can be more costly to an organisation.

Resistance

Managing change within the academic library is essentially about managing people since it is people that effect change. People who are such a critical factor in change implementation can also be a stumbling block to the change process by resisting change. Change initiatives are often shipwrecked because of resistance. Resistance leading to escalation in costs often delays change processes.

Resistance is such a central element in change management that it deserves serious attention in the change implementation process. Researcher states that one must neither fear resistance nor make efforts to avoid it. The inertia of systems which have relied on doing things as they have always been done and achieving objectives through well-tried methods is not to be underestimated. It is part of the organisational instinct for survival and as well as comfort and complacency and it breeds resistance.

The successful implementation of change in the academic library is by and large dependent on the attitudes of people to the change process. People respond in different ways to change. Whereas some people will experience change as an exiting and stimulating event others may find it frightening and intimidating and consequently resist change.

Causes of Resistance

Pendlebury identified the following causes of resistance:

- Lack of realisation of a problem.
- Not grasping the implementation of a solution.
- Outright rejection of a solution as it is seen as the incorrect option.
- Fear of the outcome of change.
- Lack of interest.

This kind of behaviour is often the result of a vision not clearly communicated or staff's unwillingness to face up to the demands of change.

Researcher identifies the following additional reasons why people resist change:

- *Security:* Fear of potential job losses.
- *Financial:* Fear of loss of income.
- *Pride and satisfaction:* Technological innovation might make jobs and skills redundant.
- *Freedom:* Structural changes might impact on freedom of decision-making.
- *Authority, responsibility and status:* Restructuring might lead to a loss of authority and respon-sibilities.

Resistance tends to manifest itself in many different ways. Conner distinguishes between overt and covert resistance. Overt resistance is open and can be constructive. Covert resistance is submerged and can gain momentum unobtrusively and ruin a project. Fossum describes covert resistance as a passive-aggressive form of resistance. It is difficult to manage because on the surface a person appears to do nothing but is often busy sabotaging a project through negative statements. In major change there will always be resistance. Creating an environment where people can openly express their fears will go a long way to minimize resistance. Managers need to be aware that resistance often manifests itself in an increase in absenteeism, reductions in quality, decreased productivity, strikes or slowdowns and increase in grievances.

STRATEGIES TO FACILITATE CHANGE WITHIN THE ACADEMIC LIBRARY

The prevailing organisational culture will determine how easy or complex it will be to communicate the need for change, share the vision and get people's opinions and participation. In an open culture communication is easiest. The leadership style, the trust people have in top management and the extent to which people are able to openly express themselves is of cardinal importance. Managers who have successfully implemented change understand that resistance is a natural reaction and would encourage it rather than suppress it. They would even reward people for open resistance in a constructive manner.

Fossum states that clear and open communication about pending change is crucial. Managers must not allow people to hear via rumours or the grapevine or the media about pending change. They should be open and upfront about pending change. Hearing from a third party will undermine trust and credibility. When communicating change it is important to send out positive and optimistic messages. Conner is of the opinion that effective leaders can change people's mindsets to a realisation that meaningful change is not only essential but also possible.

Morgan argues that buy-in is crucial in change management. If staff can take ownership of change, it will bolster commitment and assist in overcoming any obstacles. It is also crucial to involve staff in the decision making process. Participation will break the management versus staff syndrome. Instead of letting management do the problem solving it is useful to involve staff at all levels in this process. Managers must be careful not to make assumptions about the acceptance of change. It is better to get accurate feedback through interviews or surveys.

Techniques to Make Change Positive

Change creates conflict but the negative energy generated can be turned in constructive energy. Managers should realise that conflict in itself is not necessarily negative. It creates an opportunity to do creative problem solving with the staff. Conflict must never be taken personally. If people disagree managers should see it as an opportunity to find a more elegant solution that more staff members will find acceptable. People should be encouraged to be honest about how they feel and support one another. Managers should maintain their sense of humor. It is essential to cultivate an atmosphere that will transform negative issues of conflict into positive constructive energy.

Celebrate Success

It is important to sign-off change to ensure closure and enable people to move on. It need not be a celebration in the real sense. It could be a scenario where the team is thanked for their contribution. In that way they will see smaller change events as temporary unpleasant things to deal with and move on. If change events are seen as individual unrelated events it can lead to resistance.

ACADEMIC LIBRARY STRUCTURES

Organisational structure can be defined as "one of the interrelated components that define any organisation referring to the definition of individual jobs and their relationship to each other as depicted in organisational charts and job descriptions." It clarifies how information is distributed, and jobs are organised. For decades the hierarchical structure of management was regarded as the most efficient way of managing an organisation. This system worked well in and environment where the future was predictable and librarians were in the driving seat. Hierarchies were not designed to foster creativity and lead workers to self-fulfilment.

It is therefore very difficult to introduce fundamental change within hierarchical structures which are naturally resistant to change. In an effort to bring about reorganisation within organisations institutions try to either modify the existing hierarchical structure or replace it with something else. Deming as cited by Mullins states that management systems still prevalent today have had a destructive impact on people. According to Deming "people are born with intrinsic motivation, self-esteem, dignity, curiosity to learn... " Qualities such as these are undermined by a management style that reward top achievers and punish those that do worse. Managers that exhibit such management styles use disapproval as a negative control measure. This approach leads to a climate where staff performance is primarily directed at pleasing their superiors and that inevitably lead to average performance.

According to researcher managers have a natural tendency to maintain the status quo. They would instinctively fall back on models and practices that worked in the past. The volatile nature and unpredictability of information services is forcing managers to adopt new management styles. It is beginning to dawn on people that the bureaucratic way of management is becoming outdated and that change will be more effectively achieved through education, sharing, motivation, teamwork and coaching.

Moran states that unprecedented change has forced managers to re-evaluate structures. Customary practices designed to maintain organisational stability are being questioned. To cope with change, organisations have started flattening structures to induce more flexibility within those organisations. These new structures being adopted have decreased levels of hierarchy, increased flexibility and resulted in diminishing boundaries between departments.

Issues to Consider when Introducing New Structures

Management theorists are very reluctant to prescribe to a particular structural model but advise that structure should rather be designed to meet organisational needs and goals. Organisations should try and learn as much as possible from others who have implemented organisational change. They should never introduce a structure simply because it is being used elsewhere but always to meet specific organisational needs. Of cardinal importance is to determine how people within the organisation will adopt the new structure. Researcher shares the following points learnt from a process of restructuring:

Before implementing a process of restructuring it is important to have clear vision, goals and objectives with the focus on service delivery. It is useful to establish a core team to lead the restructuring process. It is vitally important that senior management support the process, *e.g.*, a deputy vice-chancellor. It is important to involve the entire staff component, listen to their inputs and concerns since ownership by the staff is vital for successful change implementation. Staff development programmes should be part of the process to prepare staff for new functions or roles they may be involved in.

After implementation it is important to critically analise the performance of the academic library within the new structure. Managers often do not adapt easily to the flatter less bureaucratic structures that are generally being adopted. Even staff members at lower levels experience this problem. Generally it is very difficult to introduce change that goes against prevailing organisational culture. Proper planning is needed to take the organisation from the existing structure to the new one.

Employee input in developing such a strategy is crucial. Research indicates that organisational transformation had been most successful in scenarios where employees had maximum input. Finally evaluation is necessary after change implementa-tion to determine its success. In reorganised libraries structures are always flatter resulting in manager's roles reverting from directing to coordinating. The prime purpose of reorganisation is to create a more effective organisation. Reorganisation results in academic libraries becoming learning organisations.

The learning organisation is characterised by staff empowerment, is team based, decentralised, practices participative management and information sharing. In the learning organisation the person closest to a problem has the responsibility and authority to deal with it. Tom Wilson as cited by Moran states that the academic library is in bad need of reconstruction. To Wilson academic libraries were essentially designed to manage physical artifacts. The rise of the Internet has completely transformed the way information is created, distributed and accessed.

The e-journal is a typical example. Johansen and Swigart as cited by Moran states "we had outlived the usefulness of models from the Industrial era but don't yet have robust organisational models for the information era". It is therefore of paramount importance that academic librarians continuously re-evaluate current structures and through an experimental process adopt new models. Moran states that for people who advocate restructuring there is good and bad news. The good news is that people understand that technological change will compel fundamental organisational change. The bad news is that there is a lack of urgency. Generally organisational change appears to be incremental rather than radical.

INTERNET-BASED COMMUNICATION SERVICES

Libraries use Internet-based communication system while attending their day-to-day routine works. An Internet-based communication system allows communication between computer users hooked into a network.

Internet-based communication system is used for com-munication between person-to-person, person-to-group and group-to-group. A document or message sent through electronic system may contain text, graphics, image, speech as well as other types of information.

INTERNET TECHNOLOGY AND ITS SERVICES

The Internet has revolutionised our society, our economy and our technological systems. Over the past century, important technological developments have created a global environment that is drawing people of the world closer and closer together. About fifteen years ago, most of the world knew little or nothing about the Internet. The Internet was then a private network accessible only to computer scientists and researchers who used it to interact with colleagues in their respective disciplines.

It is estimated that about 60 million host computers on the Internet today serve about 200 million users in over 200 countries and territories. Also, the total numbers of host computers and users have been growing at about 33 per cent every six months Since, 1988 – or roughly 80 per cent per year. The Internet has revolutionised the computer and communications world like nothing before. The invention of the telegraph, telephone, radio, and computer set the stage for this unprecedented integration of capabilities. The Internet is at once a world-wide broadcasting capability, a mechanism for information dissemination, and a medium for collaboration and interaction between individuals and their computers without barriers of geographic location. The Internet represents one of the most successful examples of the benefits of sustained investment and commitment to research and development of information infrastructure. Beginning with the early research in packet switching, the government, industry and academia have been partners in evolving and deploying this exciting new technology. Today, terms like 'Yahoo' and 'Google' are common part of our vocabulary. Internet-based communication services, content creation and delivery tools applicable in libraries.

Chat or Instant Messengers

Chat refers to any live discussions conducted using the Internet, usually between more than two persons using their keyboard to communicate. Chat Programmes allow users on the Internet to communicate with each other by typing in real time. It is a feature offered by many online services or Web sites that allows users to 'chat' by typing messages which are displayed almost instantly on the screens of other users who are using the chat room at a given time.

After entering a chat room, any user can type a message that will appear on the monitors of all the other users. Chatting is one of the most popular uses of the Internet. Generally the users remain anonymous by using nicknames or pseudonyms to identify themselves online. A variation of chat is the phenomenon of the instant messenger. Instant messaging can be used to communicate privately with friends, relatives or co-workers.

To send and receive instant messages, a user needs a connection to the Internet and instant messaging software such as Gmail Messenger, Yahoo Messenger and MSN Messenger. The instant messaging software enables a user to set up a list of contacts who also use the same Programme. Once this list is set up, one can see each contact as they come online. A chat session can be started with them quickly and easily. Most conversations are typed text messages that are sent back and forth, though more advanced users can exchange voice, video, files and more.

Electronic Mail (E-mail)

Electronic Mail, or e-mail, is a fast, easy and inexpensive way to communicate with other Internet users around the world. It is the most popular and widely used services of the Internet. E-mail is the term given to an electronic message, usually a form of simple text message that a user types at a computer system and is transmitted over some form of computer network to another user, who can read it.

E-mail offers speedy and economical transfer of messages anywhere in the world. Sending e-mail messages are virtually free even to long-distance destinations. Most integrated library system support e-mail-based communication to library users (for circulation and acquisitionrelated activities) and to the vendors/ publishers (for placing orders, reminders, cancellation, etc).

Listserv

Listservs are electronic groups that typically centre around broad topics such as Digital Libraries or Reference Service, etc. Listservers of IFLA with the name IFLA-l, Digilib-l LIBJOBS-l are good example of this. Every e-mail message sent to the listserv is distributed to all members of that listserv, which is potentially hundreds or thousands of people.

It does not cost anything to subscribe to a listserv, but simply requires that the user sends an e-mail message to the appropriate address with the message: subscribe (listserv) Firstname Lastname. Each Listserver has one address where a user sends requests to subscribe, un-subscribe, search the archives, etc., and another address to send actual questions or responses to the readers of the list. Apart from organising discussions, job announcements and conference announcements are popular usage of Listservs.

Conferencing

One of the most exciting features of Internet is to communicate, talk, and see groups of people in different locations around the world, without the expense of travel. Conferencing can take many forms, such as web chat, audio conferencing, video conferencing, multimedia conferencing, screen-sharing, etc. The conferencing Programmes, such as the popular CU-SeeMe, allow workgroups to use the Internet to see each others' faces in small windows on the computer screen and to hear their voices through computer speakers. One can use desktop video and audio simultaneously or audio can be used alone, or just use the screen-sharing capability without either audio or video.

Audio Conferencing or Internet Telephony

Internet telephony also called IP telephony is a combination of hardware and software that allows the Internet to be used as a telephone carrier. Internet telephony is the conversion of analogue speech signals used on current telephone systems into digital data, allowing calls to be sent over the Internet, bypassing long distance charges.

While the Internet was first devised as a way of transmitting data, it is now being used to make voice calls. Internet telephony is projected to explode as the costs plummet. After the costs of initial set-up and access to an Internet Service Provider, long-distance voice calls can be made via the Internet free of charge, but current quality of voice transmission over the Internet is not always as good as direct telephone service.

There are also PSTN/ Internet gateways that allow regular telephone callers to make Phoneto- Internet-to-Phone connections. There are PC-to-Phone connections and Phone-to-PC connections.

NetMeeting

Microsoft NetMeeting facilitates a new way of talking, meeting, working and sharing over the Internet. It uses Internet phone voice communications and conferencing standards to provide multi-user applications and data sharing over Intranets or the Internet.

Two or more users can work together and collaborate in reach time using application sharing, whiteboard, and chat functionality. NetMeeting can be used for common collaborative activities such as virtual meetings. It can also be used for customer service applications, telecommuting, distance learning, and technical support. The product is based on ITU (International Telecommunication Union) standards, so it is compatible with other products based on the same standards.

NetMeeting supports text chat, video shared whiteboard, transferring of files, directory of connected users. Files, such as documents or pictures, can be exchanged. One of the problems with net meeting is the break-up in audio that sometimes becomes inaudible when using it on the Internet, though it works fine over a high-speed company network.

Video Conferencing

Video conferencing is one of the most exciting areas of development in telecommunications, with applications ranging from business to government to education to home and family. Video conferencing involves sending video signals as well as audio and computer data signals. Conferencing can be done one-to-one, one-to-many (called multicast), and many-to-many (called multipoint). While video conferencing, one can talk as well as see the people sitting miles away as if all are discussing in one room facing each other.

One of the most popular applications is transmission on news from various locations by the TV news channels. It also has enormous potential for enhancing communications for small and mid-sized companies, as well as distance learning.

However, video conferencing requires sufficient bandwidth to transfer video files of acceptable quality. Desktop conferencing, therefore, is not yet widely implemented for business and educational use. As bandwidth increases, desktop video conferencing is expected to blossom. The PictureTel and Vtel are two of the largest companies that sell video conferencing equipment.

News Groups

Another Internet service similar to listservs is a newsgroup. News Groups are like an International bulletin board. Each group is a forum for a different subject, where a subscriber can post his/her questions or answers.

There are thousands of groups covering just about every area of interest. The difference between listserv and news group is that when a user joins a group, the mail is no longer automatically deposited into his mailbox. Instead a user is expected to go to the newsgroup himself to read it.

Some listservs can also be accessed as a newsgroup. A good analogy to a newsgroup is a bulletin board, *i.e.,* one can go to it, as opposed to having mail delivered to his/ her desk. The mails from newsgroup does not get cluttered and it can be easily regulate how often messages are read.

A drawback of a newsgroup lies in the fact that a user must remember to go out to the newsgroup to look for the information. There are hundreds of newsgroup communities. They centre around topics such as computing, news, recreation, social, and 'alternative' topics. There are newsgroups dealing with virtually every topic under the sun and new newsgroups appear every day.

THE COMMUNICATION PROCESS

Communication is the process of exchanging information by the use of words, letters, symbols, or non-verbal behaviour. Sending and receiving messages accurately is complex and difficult.

STEPS IN THE COMMUNICATION PROCESS

Two-way communication involves four major steps, and each step is subject to interference or noise:

- *Encoding the Message:* Encoding organizes ideas into a series of symbols, such as words and gestures, designed to communicate with the receiver.
- *Communication Media:* The message is sent over a communication medium such as voice, e-mail, instant message, Web log, or telephone.
- *Decoding the Message:* In decoding, the receiver interprets the message and translates it into mean-ingful information. Communication barriers are most likely to surface at the decoding step.
- *Feedback:* Without feedback, it is difficult to know whether a message has been received and under-stood. If the receiver takes action as intended by the sender, the message has been received satisfactorily.

Many missteps can occur between encoding and decoding a message. Noise, or unwanted interference, can distort or block the message

NON-VERBAL COMMUNICATION IN ORGANIZATIONS

A substantial amount of communication occurs through non-verbal communication, the transmission of messages by means other than words. Non-verbal communication supple-ments verbal communication; its purpose is to express the feeling behind a message.

Six categories of non-verbal communication are as follows:

- *Hand and Body Gestures:* Included here are frequent movements to express approval and palms spread outward to indicate perplexity. Gesturing should not be eliminated because it is a natural part of speech and thinking, and off loads some of the mental effort.
- *Facial Expressions and Movement:* A facial look and movements may show approval, disapproval, or disbelief.
- *Posture:* Posture can reveal attitude, such as leaning towards a person to shows a favourable attitude towards the message. Tilting your head and leaning in indicates you are concerned and engaged in the message.
- *Body Placement:* The placement of one's body in relation to someone else is widely used to transmit messages, such as moving close to indicate accep-tance. A speaking coach says that to effectively relate to an audience, you need a *kinesthetic connection*. This would include other forms of non-verbal communication as well as moving around effectively.
- *Voice Quality:* The way something is said can be more meaningful than what is said. Another aspect of voice quality is a person's accent. Regional accents can sometimes
- *Clothing, Dress, and Appearance:* Dress can communi-cate how willing an employee is to conform to organizational standards.

Another application of non-verbal communication is to assist in screening airline passengers who could be a security threat. Unusual behaviour and odd gestures might signal potential problems. Screening possible security threats by non-verbal communication rather than cultural stereotypes is much more acceptable to defenders of civil liberties. Many non-verbal signals are ambiguous, such as a smile indicating warmth or nervousness.

ORGANIZATIONAL CHANNELS AND DIRECTIONS OF COMMUNICATION

Messages travel over different channels and follow different directions.

FORMAL COMMUNICATION CHANNELS

Formal communication channels are the official pathways for sending information inside and outside the organization, usually revealed by the organization chart. With e-mail it has become easier for lower-ranking people to communicate with top management. Other formal channels include newsletters, meetings, and memos. Management by walking around could be classified as formal or informal.

INFORMAL COMMUNICATION CHANNELS

Informal communication channels are the unofficial networks used to supplement the formal channels, and usually rise out of work necessity:

- *Networks Created by Leaders:* Leaders make extensive use of informal networks to accomplish goals. *Operational networking* is aimed at doing one's assigned task more effectively. Some of this networ-king is part of the formal channel. *Personal networking* engages people from outside the organization in a person's effort to develop personally and advance. *Strategic networking* focuses networking on attaining business goals directly.
- *Chance Encounters:* Unscheduled and informal contact between managers and employees can be an efficient and effective informal communication channel. Spontaneous communication events may occur at many places on the work premises.
- *The Grapevine and Rumor Control:* The grapevine is the informal means by which information s trans-mitted in the organization. Rumors and gossip are the two major components of the grapevine. Rumors are typically about something people wish to happen, or dread. Gossip is part of the human condition, and is fueled by the need for affiliation. Information travels rapidly over the grapevine, and three-fourths of its information is true.

Rumors can also create productivity and morale problems. Good employees may leave in response to rumors about layoffs. Severe negative rumors, especially about product defects or poisonings, must be neutralized to prevent permanent damage. Rumors about the financial health of a company are also damaging. Rumors can be combated by enhancing formal communication because employees seek more information during times of intense rumors. For example, explain why you cannot comment or give full information.

COMMUNICATION DIRECTIONS

Messages in organizations travel in four directions: downward, upward, horizontally, and diagonally. A communication network is a pattern or flow of messages that traces the communication from start to finish. *Downward communication* is the flow of messages from one level to a lower one. *Upward communication* is the transmission of messages from lower to higher levels.

Companies have developed mechanisms to facilitate upward communication, including:

- The open-door policy,
- Town hall meetings,
- Complaint programmes and hotlines, and
- Web logs.

Horizontal communication is the sending of messages among people at the same organizational level. *Diagonal communication* is the transmission of messages to higher or lower organizational levels in different departments.

ORGANIZATIONAL LEARNING AS PART OF COMMUNICATION IN ORGANIZATIONS

An important output of communication channels is to transmit information to other workers so as to advance know-ledge and learning throughout the organization. A learning organization is skilled at creating, acquiring, and transferring knowledge. It also modifies its behaviour to reflect new knowledge and new insights. Managing knowledge and sharing information are also important. Knowledge management is the ways and means by which a company leverages its knowledge resources to generate business value. In addition to the specialized work of the *chief knowledge officer* in a learning organization, managers must also manage knowledge. A problem is that many workers jealously guard their best ideas.

BARRIERS TO COMMUNICATION

Barriers exist at every stage in the communication process, and they are considered to be noise or interference. Barriers are the *throughput* in the communication process.

Messages the most likely to be distorted are those that are complex, emotional, or clash with the receiver's mental set:

- *Low Motivation and Interest:* The most basic fact about communication is that the message must appeal to a need of the receiver.
- *Inappropriate Language:* Language can be inappropriate and can therefore create barriers for many reasons. Two factors of particular significance in a work setting are *semantics* and *difficulty level.* Contrary to popular sentiment, there are times when a low difficulty level is inappropriate. Jargon works well with insiders, and typically not well with outsiders.
- *Defensive Communication:* A general communication barrier is defensive communication—the tendency to receive messages in such a way that our self-esteem is protected. *Denial* of contrary information is part of defensive communication.
- *Insufficient Non-verbal Communication:* If verbal communication is not supplemented by non-verbal communication, messages may not be convincing.
- *Information Overload:* Information overload occurs when an individual receives so much information that he or she becomes overwhelmed. A message must have high impact to get around the overload problem. E-mail is exacerbating the problem of information overload. Many managers receive about 150 messages each day. Yet many workers at all levels are learning to manage e-mail better.
- *Poor Communication Skills:* Many messages fail to register because the sender lacks effective communi-cation skills. The plain language movement instructs workers in government, the sciences, business,

and the legal profession. Many messages left on voice mail systems are articulated so poorly that the receiver lacks enough information to act, including understanding the return phone number or electronic address. Poor listening is another communication problem.

- *Electronic Communication Problems:* Information tech-nology has created several new communication barriers, as exemplified by the impersonality of e-mail. Most managers use e-mail as a substitute for face-to-face interaction with group members. The nuances of human interaction are usually lost in e-mail exchanges. Computer graphic presentations can create communication barriers. It is important to maintain eye contact and not overwhelm the audience with a large number of detailed slides.

OVERCOMING BARRIERS TO COMMUNICATION

Most communication barriers are surmountable.

The general strategy is to be aware that such barriers exist, and to develop a specific tactic to deal with each one:

- *Understand the Receiver:* Understanding the receiver can help overcome every communication barrier. *Empathy* is needed to understand the receiver, and also helps build rapport.
- *Communicate Assertively and Directly:* If the sender explains explicitly and directly what he or she wants—and conveys feelings—the message is more likely to be received. An application of assertive communication is the informative confrontation, a technique of enquiring about discrepancies, conflicts, and mixed messages. It is helpful to repeat your message and use multiple channels. A *spin measure* is another form of indirect communication that might be converted into direct communication.
- *Use Two-Way Communication and Ask for Clarification:* Two-way communication reduces barriers because a dialogue helps reduce misunderstanding by commun-icating feelings as well as facts. Also, two-way communication allows for questions and answers. Two-way communication also helps build connections with people and is useful in obtaining clarification on what the other person means by a particular phrase. The telephone is making a comeback because it enhances two-way communication.
- *Elicit Verbal and Non-verbal Feedback:* The effective communicator asks for verbal feedback, and looks for non-verbal indicators of acceptance and under-standing.
- *Enhance Listening Skills:* Listening is a basic part of communication. A helpful technique is active listen-ing, which means listening for full meaning without making premature judgements or interpretations. Active listening includes listening for total meaning, and reflecting the

message back to the sender. An advanced skill for active listening is to ask questions instead of making statements. The receiver does not blurt out questions as soon as the other person is finished speaking.

- *Unite with a Common Vocabulary:* A management writer recommends that managers should first identify the core work of a business, and then describe it in a shared business vocabulary. In this way, the various functions would speak a common language. Business jargon can contribute to a common vocabulary but must be used cautiously to avoid misunderstanding.
- *Be Sensitive to Cultural Differences:* In order to overcome culturally based communication barriers:
  - Be sensitive to their presence,
  - Show respect for all workers,
  - Use straightforward language,
  - Be alert to cultural differences in customs and behaviour,
  - Be sensitive to non-verbal differences,
  - Do not be diverted by accent, grammar, or personal appearance, and
  - Be attentive to individual differences in appearance.
- *Engage in Metacommunications:* Many people make no particular effort to overcome communication barriers. Another possibility is to metacommunicate, or communicate about your communication to help overcome barriers or resolve a problem. In other words, talk about how well, or not well, the commu-nication is going.

HOW TO CONDUCT AN EFFECTIVE MEETING

Poorly conducted meetings are a productivity drain.
Group meetings can also be improved by such means as:

- Meeting only for valid reasons,
- Starting and stopping on time and offering refresh-ments,
- Keeping comments brief and to the point,
- Avoiding electronic distractions,
- Capitalize on technology when appropriate,
- Encouraging critical feedback and commentary,
- Striving for wide participation,
- Solving small issues ahead of time with e-mail, and
- Considering "huddling" when quick action is needed.

ORGANIZATIONAL POLITICS AND INTERPERSONAL COMMUNICATION

Politics is related to communication because so much inter-personal communication in organizations is politically motivated. Organizational politics refers to informal approaches to gaining power or other advantages through means other than merit or luck. In recent years, as managers have to rely more on personal influence and less on hierarchy, the meaning of organizational politics has become more favourable.

RELATIVELY ETHICAL POLITICAL TACTICS

A political tactic might be considered relatively ethical when it is used to gain advantage or power that serves a constructive organizational purpose.

Useful and relatively ethical political tactics are:

- Develop power contacts,
- Be courteous, pleasant, and positive,
- Create a positive image,
- Ask satisfied customers to contact your boss,
- Be politically correct, and
- Send thank-you notes to large numbers of people.

RELATIVELY UNETHICAL POLITICAL TACTICS

In reality, not all organizations are ideal and many people use negative political tactics to fight for political advantage.

Four widely practiced unethical political tactics are:

- *Back Stabbing:* You pretend to be nice, but all the while plan someone's demise. E-mail is widely used for back stabbing.
- *Setting up Another Person to Fail:* Give another person an assignment with the hopes that he or she will fail and therefore be discredited.
- *Playing Territorial Games:* Also referred to as *turf wars,* territorial games involve protecting and hoarding resources that give one power, such as information and authority.
- *Be Unpredictable:* Some particularly devious execu-tives behave unpredictably by design to keep people off guard.

EXERCISING CONTROL OF NEGATIVE ORGANIZATIONAL POLITICS

Carried to excess, organizational politics can damage productivity and morale, including hurting the careers of innocent people. *Being aware of the presence of organizational politics* leads to control. *Open communication* can also constrain the impact of political behaviour. *Avoiding favouritism* is a big help. Also, *managers should find a way to talk about territorial games.*

LIBRARY TECHNOLOGY: PLANNING FOR THE FUTURE

Whether public, private, or corporate, libraries are experiencing rapid changes as technology increasingly permeates their methodology and functionality. These technological changes affect all levels of librarianship, and management of new library resources and new expectations of staff must adapt accordingly.

As suggested, discuss management of resources and staff in today's fluctuating technological environment. In the first part, as suggested, use a systems development model to organize the discussion of resource management. In the second part, as suggested, turn our attention to issues that arise in the intersection between staff and technology by focusing on barriers to learning, online learning alternatives, and changes in staff development practices.

5

Library Information Science and Technology

INFORMATION SCIENCE

What is information science? The question, while seemingly simple, begs another, more complex one: *How is information science, or for that matter any field, to be defined?* This is a complex problem dealt with at length in philosophy and in other fields. Lexical definitions are necessary for providing a broad description and boundaries of the subjects covered by a field, but they cannot provide for a deeper understanding. Webster does not a field define. This is not to reject clear lexical definitions—not at all—just to establish their limitations.

In approaching the discussion of information science, I am taking the problem point of view as elaborated by Popper who argued that:

- [S]ubject matter or kind of things do not, I hold, constitute a basis for distinguishing disciplines. . . .*We are not students of some subject matter, but students of problems*. Any problem may cut right across the border of any subject matter or discipline.

Our emphasis is on problems addressed by information science. Although we provide definitions of information science and other fields in interdisciplinary relations with information science later in the chapter, we are doing this solely to advance the understanding of problems addressed by different fields and their relation to information science problems. Debates over the "proper" definition of information science, as of any field, are fruitless, and in expectations naive. Information science, as a science and as a profession, is defined by the problems it has addressed and the methods it has used for their solutions over time.

Any advances in information science depend on whether the field is indeed progressing in relation to problems addressed and methods used. Any "fixing," if in order, will have to be approached by redefining or refocusing either the problems addressed, or the methods for their solutions, or both. Information science has three general characteristics that are the leitmotif of its evolution and existence. These are shared with many modern fields.

They can also be viewed as problem areas with which infor-mation science has to deal on a general level:

- First, information science is interdisciplinary in nature; however, the relations with various disciplines are changing. The interdisciplinary evolution is far from over.
- Second, information science is inexorably connected to information technology. A technological imperative is compelling and constraining the evolution of information science, as is the evolution of a number of other fields, and moreover, of the information society as a whole.
- Third, information science is, with many other fields, an active participant in the evolution of the infor-mation society. Information science has a strong social and human dimension, above and beyond technology.

A number of works that I freely consulted dealt with various historical aspects of information science.

Among those works are:

- Shera and Cleveland,
- Bourne,
- Herner,
- Salton,
- Cleverdon,
- Swanson,
- Lilley and Trice,
- Farkas-Conn,
- Buckland and Liu, and
- Rayward.

Still, a comprehensive history of information science is a project for a future historian of science. As yet only historical pieces and different perspectives of pieces exist. A history of any field is a history of a few powerful ideas. I suggest that information science has three such powerful ideas, so far. These ideas deal with processing of information in a radically different way than was done previously or elsewhere. The first and the original idea, emerging in 1950s, is *information retrieval*, providing for processing of information based on formal logic. The second, emerging shortly thereafter, is *relevance*, directly orienting and associating the process with human information needs and assessments.

The third, derived from elsewhere some two decades later, is *interaction*, enabling direct exchanges and feedback between systems and people engaged in IR processes. So far, no powerful ideas have emerged about *information*, as the underlying phenomenon, or *"literature"*, as the object of processing.

However, one can argue that the idea of mapping of "literature," that started with exploitation of citation indexes in 1960s, may also qualify as a powerful idea. In a non-historical sense this stage deals with these powerful ideas and with leitmotifs. They form a framework for understanding the past, present, and future of information science.

ORIGIN AND SOCIAL CONTEXT

Information science is a field that emerged in the after-math of the Second World War (WW II), along with a number of new fields, with computer science being but one example. The rapid pace of scientific and technical advances that were accumu-lating since the start of the 20th century, produced by mid-century a scientific and technical revolution. A most visible manifestation of this revolution was the phenomenon of "information explosion," referring to the exponential and unabated growth of scientific and technical publications and information records of all kinds, so masterfully synthesized and illuminated by de Solla Price.

In a remarkable turn of events, the impetus for the development of information science, and even for its very origin and agenda, a respected MIT scientist and, even more importantly, the head of the U.S. scientific effort during WW II.

Bush did two things:

- He succinctly defined a critical and strategic problem that was on the minds of many, and
- Proposed a solution that was a "technological fix", and thus in tune with the spirit of the times.

Both had wide appeal and Bush was listened to because of his stature. He defined the problem in almost poetic terms as "the massive task of making more accessible a bewildering store of knowledge". In other words, Bush addressed the problem of information explosion. The problem is still with us. His solution was to use the emerging computing and other information technology to combat the problem. But he went even further. He proposed a machine named Memex, incorporating a capability for "association of ideas," and duplication of "mental processes artificially." A prescient anticipation of information science and artificial intelligence is evident.

Memex, needless to say, was never built, but to this day is an ideal, a wish list, an agenda, and, some think, a utopia. We are still challenged by the ever-worsening problem of the information explosion, now universal and in a variety of digital formats. We are still trying to fix things techno-logically. We are still aspiring to incorporate Memex's basic ideas in our solutions. A number of scientists and professi-onals in many fields around the globe listened and took up Bush's challenge.

Governments listened as well and provided funding. The reasoning went something like this: Because science and technology are strategically important for society, efforts that help them, information activities in particular, are also important and need support. In the U.S., the *National Science Foundation* (NSF) Act of 1950 established NSF and provided a number of mandates, among them "to foster the interchange of scientific information among scientists in the U.S. and foreign countries" and "to further the full dissemination of information of scientific value consistent with the national interest".

The 1958 National Defence Education Act enlarged the mandate:

"The National Science Foundation shall..undertake programme to develop new or improved methods, including mechanized systems, for making scientific information available".

By those mandates, an NSF division, which after a number of name and direction changes is now called the Division of *Information and Intelligent Systems* (IIS), has supported research in these areas since the 1950s. Importantly, the field-defining studies that NSF supported included, among others, Cranfield IR evaluation studies in the 1950s and 1960s, large chunks of SMART studies from the 1960s to 1990s, and now the Digital Libraries Initiatives.

In the U.S., information science developed and began flourishing on its own in a large part due to government support by a host of agencies, as did many other fields. Historically, the support was a success—it was instrumental in creation of the whole enterprise of information science and even of the information online industry based on IR. But to the credit of information science it kept growing on its own even after government support slackened substantially. This cannot be said of a number of other fields or areas that floundered after government stopped being their main source and resource.

Social Context

It is a truism to state that information was always important for any society in any historical period. But the role of information and its degree of importance differed. With the evolution of the social order to a "post-industrial" society, or "post-capitalist" society or what we now commonly also call "information society," knowledge and information is assuming an increasing central role in every aspect of life. The classic study by Machlup, followed by a number of similar studies, documented the startling structural changes in the economy and society as driven by the growth of information and knowledge production and processing.

Popularly, they were summarized by Drucker:

The change in the meaning of knowledge that began two hundred fifty years ago has transformed society and economy. Formal knowledge is seen as both the key personal and the key economic resource. . . [K]nowledge proves itself in action. What we now mean by knowledge is information effective in action, information focused on results.... The actual products of the pharmaceutical industry is knowledge; pill and prescription ointment are no more than packaging for knowledge.

Addressing the problem of information explosion, information science found a niche within the broader context in the evolution of the information society. In its various manifestations and attempted solutions, the niche is getting broader and bigger. But by no means does information science hold a monopoly in that niche. As the importance of infor-mation is increasing in society, more and more resources and expenditures are channeled into various information-related activities. More and more research funds, projects, and initia-tives are devoted to information in various disguises. It is not surprising then that more and more fields, researchers, professionals, and businesses are turning to information, and even "discovering" information. There is gold in information. Information science has many competitors—it may be even swamped by them.

WHAT IS "INFORMATION" IN INFORMATION SCIENCE

In a scientific sense, the answer to the question is "We don't know." Yes, we can and do provide various lexical definitions of information, and we have an intuitive understanding of its meaning that we apply daily and widely. Thus, we do understand the message-sense in which we deal with information in information science. But that does not provide for a deeper and more formal understanding and explanation. Information is a basic phenomenon. For all basic phenomena—energy or gravity in physics, life in biology, justice in jurisprudence—the same "we-don'tknow" answer applies.

However, the investigation of the basic phenomena is proceeding—that is the basic point of all these fields. It is proceeding by investigating the *manifestations, behaviour,* and *effects* of phenomena under question. While we do not know what information is, or what some of its derivative notions, such as relevance, may be, over the years we have learned a lot about their various manifestations, behaviours, and effects. And we are continuing to learn about them through scientific investigations. "Information" has a variety of connotations in different fields. For instance, from the standpoint of physics and biology, a number of highly ambitious attempts have undertaken to explore information as a basic property of the universe.

In psychology, information is used, at times, as a variable dealing with sensory perception, comprehension, or other psychological processes. These senses of information are very different than the one in information science. In some fields, information science included, the notion of information is broadly associated with messages. For this sense, a number of interpretations exist, which are assumed in different theoretical and pragmatic treatments of information. We can present them as related, but differing manifestations of information in an ordered sequence or a continuum of increasing complexity.

Narrow Sense

Information is considered in terms of *signals or messages for decisions* involving little or no cognitive processing, or such processing that can be expressed in algorithms and probabilities. Information is treated as the property of a message, which can be estimated by some probability. Examples are information in terms of uncertainty in information theory, "perfect infor-mation" in game theory, or information as related to decision-making and market equilibrium in the theory of uncertainty and information in economics of information.

The latter has been surveyed by Hirshleifer and Riley, who provide this illustrative explanation: In the economics of uncertainty, an individual is assumed to act on the basis of current *fixed beliefs*, *e.g.*, deciding whether to carry an umbrella based on one's present estimate of the chance of rain, while in the economics of information a person typically is trying to arrive at *improved beliefs*, *e.g.*, by studying a weather report before deciding to take an umbrella.

Information may be considered as causing a difference between fixed and improved beliefs. The value of information is calculated as the difference between the decision maker's expected utility of the decision made without the information, and the expected utility of the best possible choice in decision made after receiving and analysing the information. The huge, and sometimes insurmountable, problem, of course, is estimating appropriate probabilities. A number of pragmatic applications follow this interpretation, such as computerized trading.

Broader Sense

Information is treated as directly involving *cognitive processing and understanding.* It results from interaction of two cognitive structures, a "mind" and a "text." Information is that which affects or changes the state of a mind. In cases of information services, information is most often conveyed through the medium of a text, document, or record, *e.g.*, what a reader may understands from a text or document.

The interpretation by Tague-Sutcliff fits:

- Information is an intangible that depends on the conceptualization and the understanding of a human being. Records contain words or pictures absolutely, but they contain information relative only to a user... Information is associated with a transaction between text and reader, between a record and user.

Broadest Sense

Information is treated in a context. That is, information involves not only messages that are cognitively processed but also *a context*—situation, task, problem-at-hand, and the like. Using information that has been cognitively processed for a given task is an example. In addition to other senses, it involves motivation or intentionality, and therefore it is connected to the expansive social context or horizon, such as culture, work, or problemat-hand.

In information science, we must consider the third and broadest sense of information, because information is used in a context and in relation to some reasons. The point was implicitly understood from the beginning of information science, particularly as reflected in the practice of information retrieval. This interpretation of "information" in information science is not new. Such a broad interpretation of information that explicitly incorporates cognition and context was, among others, elaborated by Wersig and Neveling and Belkin and Robertson. It is also implicit in the social role of information science.

INFORMATION RETRIEVAL

In the early and mid-1950s, a critical mass of scientists, engineers, librarians, and entrepreneurs started working enthusiastically on the problem and solution defined by Bush. By 1960s this became a large and relatively well-funded effort and organized activity. Often, there were heated arguments and controversies about the "best" solution, technique, or system.

These arguments brought on the tradition of evaluation, a major staple of IR research and development. What is now TREC started with Cranfield evaluations in the late 1950s and early 1960s. Remarkably, the basic evaluation principles developed then are still the underpinning of TREC today. Calvin Mooers, an active and highly visible pioneer of information science, coined the term *information retrieval* in 1951. The term took hold, and today is a part of the English language.

At that time, Mooers not only coined the term, but also defined the problems to be addressed:

> "Information retrieval embraces the intellectual aspects of the description of information and its specification for search, and also whatever systems, techniques or machines that are employed to carry out the operation.

Today, we would add that IR also and particularly involves interaction in all of these, with all the contextual-cognitive, affective, situational—aspects that interaction embraces. An expanded Mooers' conception is still valid. As it advanced, IR produced a number of theoretical, empirical, and pragmatic concepts and constructs. Numerous IR systems were developed and successfully deployed. A great many historical examples can be given to illustrate the remarkable evolution of IR systems and techniques, adapting the ever-evolving information technology, from punch cards in the midcentury to the Internet at its close. Based on IR, an online information industry emerged in the 1970s, and grew through its own version of information explosion, as chronicled by Hahn. IR is one of the most widely spread applications of any information system worldwide. It has a proud history. Surely, information science is more than IR, but many of the problems raised by IR or derived from objects and phenomena involved in IR, are at its core.

Approaches and Paradigm Split

The approach taken by Mooers was to concentrate on the building of systems. This systems emphasis which was formulated early in the 1950s, was the sole approach to IR for some decades. It still predominates in a good part of IR research to this day.

Consequently, most of the IR research and practice concentrated on retrieval systems and processes. However, starting in the late 1970s and gaining steam in the 1980s, a different line of reasoning and research evolved-one that concentrates on the cognitive, interactive, and contextual end of the process. It addressed users, use, situations, context, and interaction with systems, rather than IR systems alone as a primary focus.

The retrieval cluster started splitting into subclusters, as noted by White and McCain, and before by others such as Saracevic and Harter. We now have two distinct communities and approaches to research in the retrieval cluster. They became commonly known as *systems-centred* and *user-centred.* Both address retrieval, but from very different ends and perspectives. The split is not only conceptual, looking very differently at the same process, but also organizational. The systemscentered side is now mostly concentrated in the *Special Interest Group on Information Retrieval* (SIGIR) of the *Association for Computing Machinery* (ACM), while the user-centered cluster congregates around the *American Society for Information Science* (ASIS).

Each has its own communication outlets-journals, proceedings, and conferences. There is less and less overlap of authors and works between the two outlets. We have two camps, two islands, with, unfortunately, relatively little traffic in-between. The systems-centered approach is exemplified by work on algorithms and evaluation based on the traditional IR model, a model that does not consider the users or interaction. The massive research that evaluates a variety of IR algorithms and approaches within TREC is a culmination of this approach.

In contrast, cognitive, situational, and interactive studies and models, involving the use of retrieval systems exemplify the human-centered approach. Following that approach, interactive models, differing significantly from the traditional IR model, started to emerge. Even in TREC, a group of researchers started an interaction track, but so far have a hard time conceptually and methodologically, thus demonstrating the difficulty in merging the traditional and interactive models and approaches. Let me characterize, in a simplified way, the relationship between the two approaches or subclusters addressing different sides of retrieval.

On the one hand, the human-centred side was often highly critical of the systems side for ignoring users and use, and tried valiantly to establish humans as the proper center of IR work. The mantra of human-centred research is that the results have implications for systems design and practice. Unfortunately, in most human-centred research, beyond suggestions, concrete design solutions were not delivered. On the other hand, the systems side, by and large, ignores the human side and user studies, and is even often completely ignorant of them. As to design, the stance is "tell us what to do and as suggested, do it." But nobody is really telling, or if telling, nobody is listening.

As a rule, in systems-oriented projects, people and users are absent. Thus, there are not many interactions between the two camps. Let me provide some examples. A rough analysis of the 1997 SIGIR proceedings found only 3 papers of some 34 that dealt in some way with people and users; in the ACM's Digital Libraries 1997 conference proceedings, of 25 papers only 3 mentioned people and users. If one reads authors such as Dervin and Nilan, and many of their successors, who champion the human centered approach, one gets the impression that there is a real conflict between the two sides and approaches, and that there is an alternative way to the "dreadful" systems approach.

In a way, this stance is a backlash caused by the excesses, failures, and blind spots of systems-centered approaches not only in IR, but also in great many other technological applica-tions. Unfortunately, sometimes the backlash is justified. All of us who work on the humancentered side are not that dismissive of the systems side. But the issue is not whether we should have systems-*or* humancentered approaches. The issue is even less of human*versus* systems-centered. *The issue is how to make human*and *systems-centered approaches work together.* In this sense, a number of works have addressed integrating usercentered and systems-centered approaches in IR, but this has been discussed mostly by researchers from the usercentered side.

Examples are works by:

- Bates,
- Belkin,
- Cool,
- Stein,
- Thiel,
- Fidel
- Efthimidiadis,
- Robertson and
- Beaulieu.

To reiterate, it is not one camp against the other but how can we incorporate the best features of both approaches and make them work jointly. The issue is how to deliver and incorporate the desired design features that will improve systems orientations towards users, integrate them with systems features, and use advantages provided by both, humans and technology. In other words, the issue is *putting the human in the loop* to build better algorithms and to exploit computational advantages. Real progress in information science, and by extension in IR, will come when we achieve this. Lately, the NSF has championed human-centered design involving an interdisciplinary approach to information systems. Hopefully, this will go beyond rhetoric. It is not easy to do. But, that is what research is for—to address difficult, not only easy problems.

Proprietary IR

By the 1980s, the commercial information industry based on IR became successful and profitable. Out of academe, grants, and government, IR became a money-making propo-sition. This, of course, is another and important sign of success. Not surprisingly, a number of former IR researchers, practitioners, and graduates of IR programmes ventured out to become IR entrepreneurs.

Sure enough, throughout information science history there were many entrepreneurs, and they were highly significant in development of the field. But this generation of entrepre-neurs was different. They ventured to develop and market a variety of IR procedures based on algorithms, applicable and scalable to large files, multiple applications, and/or various advanced technologies. It was knowledge industry at its purest. But, as in all commercial knowledge industries, the product was proprietary. While it was not that hard to guess the base of these various proprietary algorithms and how they worked—after all they were derived from publicly available knowledge and experiences, such as those that came from SMART experi-ments—they remain unpublished and "secret."

A new kind of IR evolved, separate from the rest, not communicating as to intellectual advances with the rest. None of these ventures became a high commercial success, as measured by Silicon Valley standards. But the World Wide Web, emerging in the first half of the 1990s, changed all this. The acceleration of the growth of the Web is an information explosion of the like never before seen in history. Not surprisingly then, the Web is a mess. No wonder that everybody is interested in some form of IR as a solution to fix it.

A number of academic-based efforts were initiated to develop mechanisms, search engines, "intelligent" agents, crawlers, and so forth, to help control the Web. Some of these were IR scaled, and adapted to the problem; others were a variety of extensions of IR. Many had few, if any original, developments, besides new packaging or labeling; and a good number were just the usual hype. The wheel was reinvented a number of times. But out of this, and fast, came commercial ventures, such as the pioneering Yahoo!, whose basic objective is to provide search mechanisms for finding something of relevance for users on demand.

And to make a lot of money. These enterprises pride themselves on having proprietary methods by which they are accomplishing the retrieval tasks. The connection to the information science community is tenuous, and almost non-existent. The flow of knowledge, if any, is onesided, from IR research results into proprietary engines. The reverse contribution to public knowledge is zero. A number of evaluations of these search engines have been undertaken simply by comparing some results between them or comparing of their retrieval against some benchmarks.

Some evaluations were done within, others outside of information science. Results were not complimentary. The Web-based proprietary IR is expanding and flourishing outside of the field. It is addressing a vexing problem, the like we have not seen before. But as yet, the success is elusive and questionable.

RELEVANCE

As information science pioneers developed IR processes and systems in the 1950s, they defined as the main objective retrieval of *relevant* information. Effectiveness was expressed in terms of relevance. From then to now, IR is explicitly geared not towards any old kind of information, but towards *relevant information*. Various IR approaches, algorithms, and practices were, and still are, evaluated in relation to relevance. Thus, relevance became a key notion in information science. It is also a complex phenomenon with a long and turbulent history in information science transcending IR, going back to early 1950s. Of course, there was a choice.

Relevance did not have to emerge as the key notion. Uncertainty was one choice suggested by a number of theorists to be the base of IR, and thus to reflect effectiveness. But it did not take. In contrast, uncertainty is the basic notion underlying expert systems. If the pioneers had not embraced relevance, but instead, let's say, uncertainty, as the base for IR, we would have today a very different IR, and probably not that successful. In general, relevance, according to *Webster*, means having significant bearing on matter at hand. As with many other concepts, relevance assumes related but more specific meaning in more specific contexts and applications.

In the context of information science, relevance is the attribute or criterion reflecting the effectiveness of exchange of information between people and IR systems in communi-cation contacts based on valuation by people. With relevance as the criterion, and human judgements of relevance of retrieved objects as the measuring instrument, the measures of precision and recall are widely used in evaluation of IR systems. The strength of these measures is that they involve people—users—as judges of effectiveness of performance. The weakness is the same: it involves judgement by people, with all the perils of subjectivity and variability. Relevance indicates a relation. For relevance, many relations have been investigated.

An consensus has emerged in information science that we can distinguish between several differing relations that account for different manifestations or types of relevance:

- *System or Algorithmic Relevance:* Relation between a query and information objects in the file of a system as retrieved, or as failed to be retrieved, by a given procedure or algorithm. Comparative effectiveness in inferring relevance is the criterion for system relevance.
- *Topical or Subject Relevance:* Relation between the subject or topic expressed in a query and topic or subject covered by retrieved texts,

or, more broadly, by texts in the system file, or even in existence. Aboutness is the criterion by which topicality is inferred.

- *Cognitive Relevance or Pertinence:* Relation between the state of knowledge and cognitive information need of a user and texts retrieved, or in the file of a system, or even in existence. Cognitive correspondence, infor-mativeness, novelty, information quality, and the like are criteria by which cognitive relevance is inferred.
- *Situational Relevance or Utility:* Relation between the situation, task or problem at hand and texts retrieved by a system, or in the file of a system, or even in existence. Usefulness in decision making, appropriateness of information in resolution of a problem, reduction of uncertainty, and the like are criteria by which situational relevance is inferred.
- *Motivational or Affective Relevance:* Relation between the intents, goals, and motivations of a user and texts retrieved by a system, or in the file of a system, or even in existence. Satisfaction, success, accomplish-ment, and the like are the criteria for inferring motivational relevance.

Practically, IR systems assess systems relevance only-that is, they respond to queries-hoping that the objects retrieved may also be of cognitive relevance, and even more so of utility. However, a user may judge an object by any or all types of relevance-for a user they may interact dynamically. Difficulties arise when an object is of system relevance but not of cognitive relevance or utility, or conversely.

If items are of cognitive relevance or utility, but were not reflected in the query, they are not and cannot be retrieved. At the bottom of IR research is a quest to align systems with other types of relevance. People all over have a strong intuitive understanding of relevance, thus, they intuitively understand, without manuals, what IR is all about. This makes IR systems generally understandable and acceptable-a critical attribute in their widespread application.

DISCIPLINARY RELATIONS

Two things introduced interdisciplinarity in information science. First and foremost, the problems addressed cannot be resolved with approaches and constructs from any single discipline-thus, intedisciplinarity is predetermined, as it is in many modern fields. Second, interdisciplinarity in information science was introduced and is being perpetuated to the present by the very differences in backgrounds of people addressing the described problems. Differences in background are many; they make for richness of the field and difficulties in communication and education. Clearly not every discipline in the background of people working on the problem made an equally relevant contri-bution, but the assortment was responsible for sustaining a strong interdisciplinary characteristic of information science. I will concentrate on interdisciplinary relations with two fields: librarianship and computer science. Obviously, other fields, most notably cognitive science and communication, have also interdisciplinary relations, but these are the most significant and developed ones.

Librarianship

Librarianship has a long and proud history devoted to organization, preservation, and use of graphic records and records in other media. This is done through libraries not only as a particular organization or type of information system, but even more so as an indispensable social, cultural, and educational institution whose value has been proven manifold throughout human history, and across all geographic and cultural boundaries.

Researcher defines the library as:

- . . .Contributing to the total communication system in society. . . Though the library is an instrumentality created to maximize the utility of graphic records for the benefits of society, it achieves that goal by working with the individual and through the individual it reaches society.

The common ground between library science and information science, which is a strong one, is in sharing of their social role and in their general concern with effective utilization of graphic and other records, particularly by individuals.

But there are also very significant differences in several critical respects, among them:

- *Selection of Problems Addressed and the Way they were Defined*: A majority of the problems were not and are not addressed in library science;
- *Theoretical Questions Asked and Frameworks Established*: The theories and conceptual frameworks in librarian-ship have no counterpart in information science, and *vice versa*;
- *The Nature and Degree of Experimentation and Empirical Development and the Resulting Practical Knowledge and Competencies Dderived*: There is very little overlap in experimentation and development between the two, and professional requirements differ as well to a significant degree;
- *Tools and Approaches Used:* A most telling example is the very different approach undertaken in relation to utilization of technology in IR and in library automation; and
- *The Nature and Strength of Interdisciplinary Relations Established and the Dependence of Progress on Inter-disciplinary Approaches*: Librarianship is much more selfcontained.

All of these differences warrant a conclusion that librarianship and information science are two different fields in strong interdisciplinary relations, rather than one and the same field, or one being a special case of the other. This is not a matter of turf battles, or of one being better or worse than the other. Such arguments, while common between many fields, matter little to progress of either field. But differences in selection and/or definition of problems addressed, agenda, paradigms, theoretical base, and practical solutions *do* matter. Thus the conclusion that librarianship and information science, while related, are different fields. The differences are most pronounced in the research agenda and directions.

Interestingly, research on OPACs, now that they are incorporating more and more IR features, is bringing the two fields in closer relation. Probably, so will the research in digital libraries, but at this time, it is too early to tell. The conclusion is not without heated controversy.

Among other authors, Vakkari contends on information science and librarianship being one and the same field, with the now commonly used name of "library and information science." Does it matter? Administratively yes, very much so, particularly in universities and professional societies. Otherwise, no. The issue is, and always will be, in the problems addressed and solutions undertaken. I contend that they differ significantly.

Computer Science

The basis of relation between information science and computer science lies in the application of computers and computing in IR, and the associated products, services, and networks. In the last few years, this relation also involves research on the evolving digital libraries, with their strong technological base.

To illustrate the connection, we use a definition by Denning:

> "The discipline of computing is the systematic study of algorithmic processes that describe and transfer information: their theory, analysis, design, efficiency, implementation, and application. The fundamental question underlying all of the computing is: "What can be automated?"

Computer science is about algorithms related to infor-mation interpreted in the first, whereas information science is about the very nature of information and its use by humans, interpreted in the third or broadest sense. Computer science is about symbol manipulation, whereas information science is about content manipulation, where symbol manipulation is the indispensable infrastructure. The two concerns are not in competition, they are complementary—they lead to different basic and applied agendas. Computer science is also many times larger than information science.

A number of computer scientists have been involved in research and development on information and its many spin-offs, to the point of being recognized leaders in information science. Gerard Salton is a prime example. In addition, there are several streams of research and development in computer science that had no connection with the early evolution of information science, but have addressed information problems similar to those in information science. Among others, these include works on expert systems, knowledge bases, hypertext, and human-computer interaction.

More recently, this involves research and development on digital libraries, a "hot", financially heavily supported area by a host of government agencies in the U.S. and many other countries. Bolstered by heavy support, interest in digital library research exploded on the scene in 1990s, attracting the attention of computer scientists from a wide variety of streams, as well as people from many other disciplines. These areas have a significant informational component that is associated with information representation, its intellectual organization, and linkages; meta-information, information seeking, searching, retrieving, and filtering; use, quality, value, and impact of information; evaluation of information systems from user and use perspective; and the like-all traditionally addressed in information science.

Conversely, these streams of computer science research and development provide a different outlook, framework, and approach, and even a different paradigm, not only for information science research and development, but also for its academic and continuing education. Again, as with librarianship, the issue is not about turf. It is about paradigms, theoretical foundations, and pragmatic solutions; and ultimately, it is about their appropriateness to human information problems.

EDUCATION

That education is critical for any field is a truism that hardly needs to be stated. In particular, research lives by education, it cannot be better than the education that researchers receive and then extend and plow back into education. Unfortunately, education in information science has not received the attention that it deserves. This may explain the many difficulties in the field that I have discussed. Educational models that evolved differed to a degree or even substantially from country to country. I am concentrating here on the U.S. models only.

In the United States, two educational models evolved over time. I call them the Shera and Salton models, after those that pioneered them. Both have strengths and weaknesses. Jesse H. Shera was a legendary library school dean from the 1950s until the 1970s at Western Reserve University. Among others, he was instrumental in starting the Center for Documentation and Communication Research in 1955. Shortly thereafter, the library school curriculum started to include courses such as "Machine Literature Searching" and several other more advanced courses and laboratories on the topics of research in the Centre.

The basic approach was to append those courses, mostly as electives, to the existing library school curriculum, without modifications of the curriculum as a whole, and particularly not the required core courses. Information science became one of the specialty areas of library science. The base or core courses that students were taking rested in the traditional library curriculum. Information science education was an appendage to library science. A few attempts to spin off information science as an independent degree and curriculum were not followed widely. But Shera's model was. Library schools in the U.S. and in many other countries imitated Shera's model.

They used the same approach and started incorporating information science courses in their existing curriculum as a specialty. Out of this was borne the current designation "library and information science." Shera's model is still the prevalent approach in schools of library and information science. The strength of the Shera model is that it posits education within a service framework, connects the education to professional practice and to a broader and user-oriented frame of a number of other information services, and relates it to a great diversity of information resources.

The weakness is a lack of a broader theoretical frame-work and a total lack of teaching of any formalism related to systems, such as development and understanding of algori-thms. The majority of researchers in the human-centered side, as I described earlier, came from or are associated with this educa-tional environment. Gerard Salton was first and foremost a scientist, a computer scientist, and the father of modern IR.

As such, he pioneered the incorporation into IR research a whole array of formal and experimental methods from science, as modified for algorithmic and other approaches used so successfully in computer science. His primary orientation was research. For education, he took the time-honoured approach of a close involvement with research. Salton's model was a laboratory and research approach to education.

As Shera's model resulted in information science educa-tion being an appendage to library science education, Salton's model of IR education resulted in it being a specialty of and an appendage to computer science education. Computer science students that were already well-grounded in the discipline, got involved in SMART and other projects directed by Salton, worked and did research in the laboratory, completed their theses in areas related to IR, and participated in the legendary IR seminars.

They also published widely with Salton and with each other, and participated with high visibility in national and international conferences. From Harvard and Cornell, his students went to a number of computer science departments where they replicated Salton's model. Many other computer science departments in the U.S. and abroad took the same approach.

The strength of Salton's model is that it:

> "Starts from a base of a firm grounding in formal mathematical and other methods, and in algorithms, and

- Relates directly to research.

The weakness is in that it:

- Ignores the broader aspects of information science, as well as any other disciplines and approaches dealing with the human aspects that have great relevance to both the outcomes of IR research and the research itself, and
- Does not incorporate professional practice where these systems are realised and used. It loses users.

Consequently, this is a successful, but narrowly concen-trated education in IR as a specialty of computer science, rather then in information science. Not surprisingly, the researchers in the systems-centred approach came out of this tradition. The two educational approaches are completely independent of each other. Neither is connected to the other. Neither reflects fully what is going on in the field. While in each model there is an increase in cognizance of the other, there is no educational integration of the systems-and usercentered approaches.

The evident strengths that are provided by Shera and Salton model are not put together. Their weaknesses are perpetuated. It is high time for communities from each model to try to integrate education for information science. It is an open question whether the human-and systems-centered approaches can fruitfully work together as urged in all those calls for human-centered design until an educational inte-gration occurs.

While library education receives formal attention from the *American Library Association* (ALA), and education for computer science from ACM, no such formal attention is paid by any professional/scientific society to education for information science, or for IR in particular. Neither ASIS nor SIGIR, as primary homes for information science, have been involved to any great extent in educational matters, such as setting of standards or devising model curricula. Clearly, there is a need and an opportunity for more substantive involvement by both organizations in educational issues.

DIFFERENT TYPES OF INFORMATION SERVICE

Information service, in the most general sense, is the process of assisting library users to identify sources of information in response to a particular question, interest, assignment, or problem. Sometimes referred to as reference service, the *Reference and User Services Association* (RUSA) of the American Library Association defines reference transactions as "information consultations in which library staff recommend, interpret, evaluate, and/or use information resources to help others to meet particular information needs". These reference transactions can take place in person or via the telephone, e-mail, or virtual reference technologies.

Librarians are also creating Web sites, answer archives, and links to answers to "frequently asked questions" all designed to anticipate user questions and help people find information independently. Traditional reference desk service continues to be highly valued by library users in many settings, but the newer forms continue to grow in popularity. Consequently, it is all the more important that librarians understand the range of enquiries that can be expected, allowing them to provide a full and ready answer, regardless of the form in which the query arises.

READER'S ADVISORY SERVICE

Reader's advisory service, sometimes considered a type of information service, is the quest to put the right book in the hands of the right reader. Librarians are increasingly expected to provide an answer to the dreaded question, "Can you help me find a good book?" Fortunately, as demand has increased, so too has the ease of providing this service. Although there is no substitute for one's own knowledge or experience, many new technologies serve to make the reader's advisory far easier than it was in the past. Many online databases, for example, have functions that automatically recommend other books for those who like a given title. Others have searchable lists of works by genre, helping readers match their favourite books to others like them.

As always, however, remember that reader's advisory, like other reference work, is predicated on the interaction between librarian and library user. Asking directed questions, listening carefully to the users' responses, and tailoring assistance accordingly is the basis of excellent, truly helpful service. The reader's advisory service is generally associated with public libraries and tends to be employed primarily by those looking for fiction. In academic libraries, it is far less common as users rarely come in searching for a mystery to read. Even so, reader's advisory may be needed to help lay researchers looking to deepen their knowledge of a particular field.

A patron who has read and enjoyed Stephen Ambrose's *Undaunted Courage*, but is troubled by allegations about Ambrose's questionable accuracy and academic honesty, may want to know the titles of books about the Lewis and Clark expedition that are both reputable and engaging. Successful reader's advisory librarians are skilled at asking users questions that enable them to assess users' reading level, language, or educational background. They must know a great deal about various genres of fiction and non-fiction and be intimately familiar with their library's collection. Significantly, it is important that they be able to convey their expertise in a friendly and conversational manner.

ANSWERING REFERENCE QUESTIONS

In light of the immense diversity and range of possible questions, being approached by a patron with a reference need can seem like a daunting prospect. Indeed, much of the difficulty of information services arises from uncertainty about the kind of service or breadth of information called for by a given question. Categorizing reference questions by type is a useful way to make sense of such concerns. Three common types of information service are ready reference questions, research questions, and bibliographic verification. *Ready reference questions* such as "Where was Abraham Lincoln born?" "Who won the 1992 World Series?" "What is the capital of Nicaragua?" or "Where can I find a copy of the United States' Declaration of Independence?" can be readily answered using one or two general reference sources.

The librarian may be tempted to tell the user the answer to simple ready reference questions. Yet here the old saying that "giving a man a fish feeds him for a day while teaching him to fish feeds him for a lifetime" is proven true. No matter how simple they seem initially, ready reference questions provide the possibility of teachable moments. Whenever possible, librarians should lead users through the process of looking up the information rather than simply providing the solution.

Librarians who assist users with ready reference enquiries on a regular basis sometimes choose to create a "ready reference" section of the most commonly used resources either in print or on the library's Web site to answer quick questions. Typically, such sections include a general all-purpose encyclopaedia, dictionaries, almanacs, and handbooks. Care must be taken to keep the sources uptodate and to avoid depending so heavily on this subset of the collection that other sources are overlooked by library users and librarians.

Librarians may find that ready reference questions have diminished due to the ease of answering basic questions through online information portals such as Google. Nevertheless, ready reference remains a cornerstone of information services, and librarians should be primed to provide it at any time. *Research questions* are more complex, may take much longer to answer, and typically require multiple sources of information. These questions often require the user to consider a variety of sources and viewpoints and to subsequently draw conclusions.

Sometimes questions that initially seem like ready reference questions are far more complex as previously hidden facets of the user's enquiry are revealed. Here, the variety of possible sources increases with the complexity of users' questions. Librarians should, for example, guide the user in the use of bibliographic sources, citations, and the back-of-the-book bibliographies. Likewise, users with complex questions may need to be taught how to find or request the full text of articles for which only citations are given in a search of electronic databases, allowing them to move beyond cursory surveys of the literature.

Research questions, especially if the user is unable to fully articulate the nature of his or her query, require librarians to ask questions of their own, trying to get at the nature of the request before setting out to help the patron answer it. The librarian may, for example, have to determine how much information is needed, what level of information is needed, and what other sources have already been consulted. Information services call for mutual engagement, especially with more complex questions.

Reference librarians should never be passive participants, pointing the way to an answer. Instead, they should play the part of dynamic guides, joining users on their journeys to knowledge. Naturally, the extent of such engagement may vary from one circumstance to another. Different types of libraries tend to have their own standards for how long librarians should spend with users on research questions. Many public libraries recommend that users be given five or ten minutes of personal assistance and then asked to return if more help is needed.

A university library may have a similar standard, or depending on the institution, may be able to invite the user to make an appointment for more in-depth research assistance. Some libraries may suggest that users call or e-mail ahead of their visit so the librarian can be prepared to offer the best possible assistance. Other libraries, including special libraries, may only be able to provide a basic level of help during the first visit. Libraries may refer users to other libraries with more specialized materials in the area of the user's research or may offer to call back if additional information is found.

Finally a library user may seek *bibliographic verification* when he or she has already obtained the information needed but must verify the sources. Sometimes this service is a matter of fact checking, whereas on other occasions users may have completed their research but lack full citation information. As users increasingly depend on electronic databases for information, compiling and formatting bibliographic citations becomes easier. Verifying and citing material found on Web pages is more difficult since the information needed for the citation is not always easy to find.

INFORMATION LITERACY

User instruction, which is now usually referred to as *information literacy*, may range from showing an individual how to use the library's online catalogue and basic print reference sources to formal classroom sessions about conducting research in the library. The basic component of information literacy includes demonstrating how, when, and why to use various reference sources in an integrated way that will capture the user's attention at the teachable moment. In today's educational settings, the ease of using electronic resources often results in a failure to teach more traditional research strategies. While finding superficial information has grown easier, in-depth information has become increasingly obscure for many students.

In the library too, approaches to instruction may vary and librarians often question whether to simply answer questions posed by users or to teach users how to employ the available resources. This may be contingent on the mission or purpose of the library. Academic institutions may call on their librarians to help students understand how to engage effectively and independently in the research and information evaluation process. Public librarians, by contrast, may try to teach users about reference sources in a more informal manner as they lead users to the answers they seek.

Thus, while instruction is always an important part of reference work, the degree to which they go about providing it is highly contingent on the circumstances.

In any case, all reference librarians must be skilled at helping users find information and answers quickly and be ready to teach users how to use the reference sources that are available. The best reference librarians develop an intuition for when to be information providers and when to be bibliographic instructors.

In some libraries, only specific, designated librarians are charged with conducting library instruction courses. Nevertheless, an increasing number of librarians are required to participate in their libraries' bibliographic instruction programme, and library school graduates are expected to be capable of teaching basic classes on the use of library resources. As should be clear, even those librarians not charged with providing formal instruction have the opportunity to teach those they serve.

THE BIG PICTURE: STRUCTURE OF INFORMATION SCIENCE

Any field is structured along some distinct, larger areas or subdisciplines of enquiry or practice. Think of a number of areas of medicine, computer science, librarianship, and so forth. Information science is not an exception. It has a distinct, two-partite structure. A number of authors observed that the work in information science falls in two large areas or subdisciplines, each, of course, with further subareas or specialties.

White and McCain conducted a monumental bibliometric study of the domain of information science by providing extensive analysis of co-citation patterns for 120 authors over a period of 23 years. Borrowing from White and McCain, visualize a map of information science as an ellipse with authors inside, distributed or clustered according to their connections. There are two large clusters at each end of the ellipse, with only a few authors spanning both. In other words, there are two major areas or subdisciplines.

I liked their metaphor:

As Things Turn Out, Information Science Looks Rather like Australia: Heavily coastal in its development, with a sparsely settled interior.

In one of the coastal sections, fall authors that worked on analytical study of literatures; their structures; studies of texts as content-bearing objects; communication in various populations, particularly scientific communication; social context of information; information uses; information seeking and behaviour; various theories of information and related topics. As yet, there is no good label for that cluster. Some call it "information analysis." For simplicity, lets call this the *domain cluster,* as did White and McCain, although "basic" may be a good label. In the other coastal section are authors who concentrated on IR theory and retrieval algorithms; practical IR processes and systems; human-computer interaction; user studies; library systems; OPACs; and related topics.

Let's call this cluster the *retrieval cluster,* although "applied" may also be a good label. Basically, most of the areas in the domain cluster are about study of fundamental manifes-tations and behaviour of phenomena and objects that information science is all about. They are centered on the phenomenon of information and its manifestations in literature. The retrieval cluster deals, by and large, with a variety of implementations, on both practical and theoretical levels.

It is about implementation, behaviour, and effects of the interface between literatures and people, including, of course, all kinds of retrieval aspects. Unfortunately, these two main clusters are largely unconnected.

Only a very small number of authors spanned the two clusters. In other words, there are very few integrating works. The last text that undertook an integrative approach encom-passing both clusters. A rare example of such an effort in research is the last work by Tague-Sutcliffe, where she related the notion of informative-ness with evaluation of IR systems.

Several modern texts are specifically aimed at IR but none on information science as a whole. I dare to venture a prediction: fame awaits the researcher who devise a formal theoretical work, bolstered by experimental evidence, that connects the two largely separated clusters, *i.e.*, connecting basic phenomena with their realization in the retrieval world. And a bestseller is awaiting an author that produces an integrative text in information science. Information science will become a full-fledged discipline when the two ends are connected successfully. The two clusters are not equally popu-lated. The retrieval cluster has significantly more authors, not to mention total number of works. As in many other fields, more effort is expanded on the applied side than on the basic side.

In part, this is due to availability of funds for given topics—not surprisingly, research goes after moneyed topics. By and large, over the last decade or so, major granting agencies funded only applied research in information science. For instance, I have been unable to identify a single grant addressing any of the topics in the domain or basic cluster from NSF Division of Information and Intelligent Systems since its preceding Division of Information Science and Technology was reorganized and included in the Directorate for *Computer and Information Science and Engineering* (CISE) in 1985. In de Solla Price's concepts and words, the domain cluster is "little science", while the retrieval cluster is "big science," and the connection between the two has presently no science.

PROBLEMS ADDRESSED

General

Webster routinely defines information science as "the science dealing with the efficient collection, storage, and retrieval of information." It is a general definition of problems addressed by information science. The definition follows pretty much an early and popular one given by Borko as a part of a wide discussion and controversy about the nature of the field in the 1960s. More specifically, information science is a field of professional practice and scientific enquiry addressing the problem of effective communication of knowledge records—"literature"—among humans in the context of social, organizational, and individual need for and use of information. The key orientation here is the problem of need for and use of information, as involving knowledge records.

To provide for that need, information science deals with specifically, oriented information techniques, procedures, and systems. To elaborate, the specific concentration of information science is on human knowledge records as *content-bearing objects*, in all forms, shapes, and media. The primary emphasis is on content of these objects, in terms of their potential for conveying information. "Literature" may be used as a generic term for these knowledge records, but "literature" has many other connotations, thus requiring a careful restriction in its use in information science. Because of these connotations, "literature" will not become popular in information science.

Realizing this, I am using the term here only as a shorthand, as did White and McCain, when they elegantly stated:

> "The proper study of information science is the interface between people and literature . . . modeling the world of publications with a practical goal of being able to deliver their content to enquirers on demand . . . While many scientists seek to understand communication between persons, information scientists seek to understand communication between persons and certain valued surrogates for persons that literature comprises.

In all of this there is a technological imperative, reflected in efforts to take advantage of modern information technology. While information science is not about technology, the problem of providing effective computer applications pervades the field. Following is a word on the extent and borders of infor-mation science.

Focusing information science on the content-bearing properties of literature, and on associated techniques and systems dealing with providing effective access to and use of literature, provides a restriction for information science.

Thus, the field does *not* deal with great many other information systems, such as payroll, inventory, decision support systems, data processing, airline schedules, and a zillion others, nor does it deal with direct communication among and between persons. Information science is about a specific manifestation or type of information that defines its scope and its systems. Information science, as many other fields, also involves a professional component. Starting in 1950s, the profession of information science grew from research and applications in IR, to become a powerful component of the field, and in many ways a leading one in respect to innovation.

As in many other fields, there is an uneasy relation between the scientific or research-oriented component and the professi-onal or practice-oriented one. The profession is responding in its own way to needs of its users and organizations, and chartering its own technological applications, many times independently of research advances, and even in different directions. At present, the connection and feedback between profession and research in information science is not as well established as it is in older fields, such as engineering or medicine. This is a serious inhibitor for progress of both.

More Specific

A number of authors suggested a breakdown of specific areas of information science, beyond the structural analysis offered above. The breakdown among different authors is in significant agreement, although the labels differ somewhat. I will take the breakdown and labels provided by White and McCain. They provided a factor analysis of co-cited authors and extracted 12 factors as specialties.

In descending order of how authors loaded, they labelled the specialties as:

- Experimental *information retrieval* (IR);
- Citation analysis;
- Practical retrieval;
- Bibliometrics;
- General library systems theory;
- Science communication;
- User studies and theory;
- OPACs;
- General imported ideas—other disciplines;
- Indexing theory;
- Citation theory; and
- Communication theory.

While one may quibble with some of the classes and labels, these specialties provide a fairly accurate picture of problem areas in which information scientists worked over the past quarter of a century.

Over time, there were shifts in emphasis and there were movements between specialties. Nothing is permanent. But these are the specialties of information science. New areas are clearly on the horizon. For the 1990s, I would suggest that the major new areas include interaction studies; searching of the Internet; multimedia IR; multilanguage IR; and digital libraries.

These are prime examples of the new significant areas of concentration, not yet evident in the historical record. At the same time, the old area of experimental retrieval is blossoming like never before, courtesy of the *Text Retrieval Conference* (TREC), a government-sponsored mechanism for comparative evaluation of a variety of IR techniques and approaches that involves large test beds. IR was, and still is, the major and most populated area of information science.

INFORMATION TECHNOLOGY AND YOUR LIFE

This stage is about computers, of course. But not just about computers. It is also about the way computers communicate with one another. When computer and communications technologies are combined, the result is *information technology,* or 'infotech.' *Information technology (IT)* is a general term that describes any technology that helps to produce, manipulate, store, communicate, and/or disseminate information. IT merges computing with high-speed communications links carrying data, sound, and video. Examples of information technology include personal computers but also new forms of telephones, televisions, appliances, and various handheld devices.

GOVERNMENT AND ELECTRONIC DEMOCRACY

A Rutgers University study suggests that the internet has great potential for civic betterment because it is fast and cheap for users and facilitates communication among citisens better than do mass media such as radio and TV. And a study by the Pew Internet and American Life Project found that internet users are much more likely to contact government than are Non-users because of the ease of finding information online and of contacting officials through e-mail.

Some cities have adopted Neighbourhood Link, a free, easy-to-use system of Neighbourhood Web sites in which residents can communicate with one another and with local governments. In Denver, for instance, the system serves 405 Neighbourhoods. In Austin, Texas, an entrepreneur formed E-The People, which describes itself as 'America's Interactive Town Hall' and is designed to connect citisens with their government officials, local and national, everywhere in the United States.

In Nevada, citisens visit the state legislature's hearings and floor voting sessions by accessing the legislature's Web site, where they can either listen to internet broadcasts or read the text of legislation. In Seattle, citisens can go to their city's Web site to deal with everything from absentee ballots to youth and family services. Besides cutting expenses for stamps, paper, and employees, e-government helps reduce lines and offers people more convenience in paying taxes and parking tickets, renewing vehicle registration and driver's licenses, viewing birth and marriage certificates, and applying for public sector jobs.

The internet and other information technology have also changed much of the political process, both for good and for ill. On the one hand, the net has enabled political candidates and political interest groups to connect with voters in new ways, to raise money from multiple small donors instead of just rich fat cats, and to organise street protests.

On the other hand, computers have allowed incumbent legislators to design voting districts that make it nearly impossible for them to be dislodged; electronic tools have also made it easier than ever for political parties to skirt or break campaign laws, and computerised voting machines still don't always count votes as they are supposed to. Still, Web sites and bloggers have become important watchdogs on government. The Web site E-Democracy, for instance, can help citisens dig up government conflicts of interest, and Web sites such as Project Vote Smart outline candidates' positions.

JOBS AND CAREERS

Career and Use of Computers

Today almost every job and profession requires computer skills of some sort. Some are ordinary jobs in which computers are used as ordinary tools. Others are specialised jobs in which advanced computer training combined with professional training gives people dramatically new kinds of careers.

Consider:

- In the hotel business, even front-desk clerks need to know how to deal with computerised reservation systems. Some hotels, however, also have a so-called computer concierge, someone with knowledge of computer systems who can help computer-carrying guests with online and other problems.
- In law enforcement, police officers need to know how to use computers while on patrol or at their desks to check out stolen cars, criminal records, outstanding arrest warrants, and the like. However, investigators with specialised computer backgrounds are also required to help solve fraud, computer break-ins, accounting illegalities, and other high-tech crimes.
- In entertainment, computers are used for such ordinary purposes as budgets, payroll, and ticketing. However, there are also new careers in virtual set design, combining training in architecture and 3-D computer modeling, and in creating cinematic special effects.

Clearly, information technology is changing old jobs and inventing new ones. To prosper in this environment, you need to combine a traditional education with training in computers and communications. You also need to be savvy about job searching, resume writing, interviewing, and postings of employment opportunities.

Advice about careers, job hunting, occupational trends, and employment laws is available at Yahoo!, Google, and other Web sites. Some starting annual salaries for recent college graduates are shown; note that jobs involving degrees in computers and information systems occupy four of the seven top-paying starting salaries. Computers can be used both for you to find employers and for employers to find you.

Ways for you to Find Employers

As you might expect, the first to use cyberspace as a job bazaar were companies seeking people with technical backgrounds and technical people seeking employment. However, as the public's interest in commercial services and the internet has exploded, the focus of online job exchanges has broadened. Now, interspersed among ads for programmers on the internet are openings for forest rangers in Idaho, physical therapists in Atlanta, models in Florida, and English teachers in China. Most Web sites are free to job seekers, although many require that you fill out an online registration form.

Ways for Employers to Find you

Posting your résumé online for prospective employers to view is attractive because of its low cost and wide reach. But does it have any disadvantages? Certainly it might if the employer who sees your posting happens to be the one you're already working for. In addition, you have to be aware that you lose control over anything broadcast into cyberspace. You're putting your credentials out there for the whole world to see, and you need to be somewhat concerned about who might gain access to them. If you have a technical background, it's definitely worth posting your résumé with an electronic jobs registry, Since, technology companies in particular find this an efficient way of screening and hiring.

However, posting may also benefit people with less technical backgrounds. Online recruitment is popular with companies because it prescreens applicants for at least basic computer skills. If you've mastered the internet, you're likely to know something about word processing, spreadsheets, and database searching as well, knowledge required in most good jobs these days.

One wrinkle in job seeking is to prepare a résumé with web links and/or clever graphics and multimedia effects and then put it on a Web site to entice employers to chase after you. If you don't know how to do this, there are many companies that—for a fee—can convert your résumé and publish it on their own Web sites.

Some of these services can't dress it up with fancy graphics or multimedia, but Since, complex pages take longer for employers to download anyway, the extra pizzazz is probably not worth the effort. A number of Web sites allow you to post your résumé for free. Another wrinkle is to pay extra to move your résumé higher in the listings so that it will stand out compared with competing résumés. For example, for an extra $20–$150 apiece, Careerbuilder.com will move your listing Towards the top of the search heap, and the company says that employers click on upgraded résumés 200 per cent more often than regular ones.

6

Information Technology-based Library Services

New information technology can potentially support a range of traditional and Non-traditional library services. Most of the library services generated using information technology resemble closely to those generated manually with improvements and modifications to suit the requirements of automated services.

OPAC AND WEBPAC

Remote access to the Library catalogues (OPAC) was possible only through a telnet connection before the Web was launched. The web-based interfaces are now available for most of the integrated library software packages including Libsys. Web sites are increasingly providing links to their webPAC instead of telnet links to their Library OPAC.

Exploiting the provisions of hyperlinking that the web provides, various searchable elements of a bibliographic record in a webPAC are hyperlinks to other records in the database. For example, an author is a hyperlink to all records in the database for that author, a series is an hyperlink to all serial title under that series; a keyword for a record is a link to all records in database having that keyword, etc. In effect, a web PAC adds softwarebased functionality to a conventional OPAC. A user has additional incentives to visit the library web page hosting webPAC.

With web-based resources and services in place, many libraries are phasing out their dumb terminals. The library web sites are increasingly becoming a more logical gateway to the catalogue and other web-based library resources. The acceptability of web-based interfaces to the Library OPAC is much greater because web interfaces are familiar to the users with its graphical and navigational interfaces. The users can click complex subjects instead of typing them or remembering complex commands.

INFORMATION ALERTING SERVICES

As the name implies, information alerting services or Current Awareness Services (CAS) are produced by the libraries for their users to alert them about new developments in a given field of study. Information alerting services are issues periodically by the libraries either for internal distribution amongst staff and employees or externally to other users.

The alerting service may be issued as a newsletter reporting new developments, programmes, forthcoming seminars and conferences, events, training programmes, etc. It may also consist of recent additions of books and other documents in the library for a specified time period. Most library integrated system facilitate generation of such a service organised according to subject category for a given time period.

Alerting service may also consist of an indexing service issued by a library or a commercial publisher or a society that regularly indexes the contents of periodicals and some other publications systematically in a specified subject field. Such indexing services are issued at a regular interval. Abstracting services are essentially indexing services wherein an abstract of articles are included in addition to its bibliographic details. Index India and Reader's Guide to Periodical Literature are examples of indexing services. Biological Abstracts, Chemical Abstracts and Index Medicus are example of abstracting services. Most indexing and abstracting services are now available as web-based databases with sophisticated search interface.

Selective dissemination of information (SDI) is a personal form of Current Awareness Service (CAS). It refers to the mechanism of selectively directing new items of information from primary or secondary sources to individuals based on their current interests in a particular subject. SDI is delivered based on a user interest profile which is matched with updates on databases for finding the items of interest for a given user. Push technology or personalisation are more recent terms that are used in place of SDI.

DIGITAL REFERENCE SERVICE

Reference service and imparting instructional training to the library users are key areas of activities for any library. The technology now allows reference librarians to reach out to the users using the network instead of waiting at the reference desk for users to come by. Besides, imparting instructions on mechanisms of using a library, a reference librarian is also involved in delivering reference service that require deep intellectual understanding of subject.

Although automated libraries are not yet sufficiently advanced to offer interactive reference services, electronically-mediated reference services are increasingly available through libraries and information centres. Digital reference service, also called 'Ask-An-Expert' or 'Ask-A-Librarian' services are Internet-based question and answer service that connect users with individuals who possess specialised subject knowledge and skill in conducting precision searches.

As opposed to static web pages, digital reference services use the Internet to place people in contact with people who can answer specific question and instruct users on developing certain skills. The people who serve as digital reference experts (also called volunteers or mentors) are most of the time information specialists, affiliated to various libraries.

LIBRARY CHAT ROOMS

Several libraries have started experimenting with offering real time digital reference service, using chat software, live interactive communication activities, call counter management software, web contact software, bulletin board services, interactive customer assistance system or related technologies. Many libraries are experimenting with Internet chat technology as an innovative method to extend and enhance traditional and remote reference service.

While digital reference service is asynchronous method of information delivery, the Internet chat providing the benefit of synchronous communication between a user and a reference librarian (or mentor). Interactive reference services facilitate a user to talk to a real, live reference librarian at any time of day or night from anywhere in the world. Unlike with e-mail reference, the librarian can perform a reference interview of a sort by seeking clarifications from the user.

The librarian can conduct Internet searches and push Web sites onto the patron's browser, and can receive immediate feedback from the patron as to whether his or her question has been answered to his satisfaction. Most libraries currently involved in real-time reference service are part of a collaborative network so that they can share staffing and work around the clock to truly provide reference service any time. Library of Congress Collaborative Digital Reference Service is one of such services.

Several institutions including Cornell University, Internet Public Library, Michigan State University and North Carolina University are offering Internet chat-based services using software like LivePerson, AOL Instant Messenger, Conference Room and Netscape Chat. The librarians have observed that their relatively new chat-based service logged significantly more questions in a relatively short time than their well-established e-mail digital reference service. LiveRef(sm) maintains an online registry of real-time digital reference services.

ELECTRONIC DOCUMENT DELIVERY SERVICES

The term 'electronic document delivery systems' implies delivery of electronic version of a document that might involve reproduction of an electronic copy of a document if it is not available in electronic format. The libraries had been using fax machines for immediate delivery of photocopies of articles via telephone lines.

The first use of electronic document delivery was based on scanning technology. With maturity of scanning equipment and technology, document supply services started scanning the documents as bitmap page images. Applications are built in such a way so as to automatically produce a hard copy together with a header page containing the address of the applicant which can again be send by snail mail or facsimile. A software package known as 'Ariel' is used in several libraries in developed countries for delivery of scanned articles via Internet.

The Ariel software is loaded on an Internet-enabled computer, can receive and send electronic information to other libraries which have installed Ariel. Availability of most of the peer reviewed research journals in electronic format, inexpensive technology to scan articles and improved electronic delivery mechanisms are some of the enabling factors that have contributed to well-established electronic document delivery system now available commercially. More recently most of the secondary services that were available on CD ROM or through online search services are now available on the Internet where the bibliographic references are linked to their full-text on the publisher's site.

The technology has now been perfected and there are several electronic document delivery services that allow a user to download an article in full-text from their site or deliver them electronically as attachment to e-mails. Most electronic publishers and aggregators like OCLC, OVID,etc., are offering full-text of articles through their web sites. Different vendors have various payment options; some charge each time the journal is used, whereas others provide open access for a set annual fee. A user who wishes to have the item delivered can enter a credit card number and specify a delivery method (postal, UPS, fax, e mail, etc.,) and indicate whether it is a rush item (with a rush order fee attached.) The ADONIS (Article Delivery Over Network information Systems) can be considered as a landmark development in electronic document delivery system. The project was launched by a consortium of five major publishers - Academic Press, Blackwell's Scientific Publications (merged with Wiley InterScience), Elsevier Science Publications, and Springer Verlag.

The project uses combination of laser scanning, printing and digital optical storage technology for storage and retrieval of complete pages of over 650 scientific, technical and medical journal articles. The issues of journals are available on CD ROM with weekly updates for distribution to each centre in various countries licensed to use the system for document delivery.

LIBRARY WEB SITES

Libraries are using web technology to create home pages as starting points or as gateways for searching information about the library. A home page reflects characteristics of an academic institution.

It provides an opportunity to the library to propagate its services and facilities to the academic community worldwide. The home pages of libraries are increasingly used as an integrated interface designed to deliver detailed information about a library as well as to provide access to all computer-based services offered by a library.

Several library web sites facilitate virtual guide to the physical facilities including collections, services and infrastructure available in the library through their web sites. Most library web sites provide library layouts and floor plans to guide users to physical location of facilities and services along with link to relevant information. Besides offering information, the library web sites of academic institutions invariably hosts subject gateways or subject portals that contains links to web resources for subjects of interest to the institution. Most of the IT-based library services mentioned in this article are offered through the web sites of libraries. The library web sites can have features like have Frequently Asked Questions (FAQ) along with their answers, library calendar listing events or show information for forthcoming events, Web forms for inviting feedback. Moreover, libraries may also use bulletin boards, threaded discussion forum and listservs to help promote and evolve web-based library services.

WEB-BASED USER EDUCATION

The www provides a dynamic environment for distributing information over a large network and web-based instructions is a suitable tool to do so. Web-based guides and teaching tools can be easily updated, accessed, and printed on demand. They may include colour graphics and screenshots. The web-based user education provides a high degree of interactivity and flexibility to the users offering them the benefit of self-pace, graduated to teach from basic to highly advanced levels and designed in a wide range of formats that accommodate diverse learning styles.

The proliferation of digital resources will generate greater demands on reference and instructional services. With availability of digital resources that can be used anywhere at any time, requirement for instructional and reference services would also grow. Failure to develop both the technological aspects and required service components would lead to under utilisation of digital resources. The library web sites can use web-based user education for imparting training to users in the following areas:

- Basic library skills along with glossary of library terms;
- Using Library OPAC/ webPAC, locating books, magazines and other library materials;
- Instructions for searching CD ROM and web-based databases and other electronic resources; and
- Instructions on subject searching training, using Boolean operators and searching Internet resources through search engines.

The web technology provides for incorporating both synchronous and asynchronous interactivity in the web-based user education.

LIBRARY SERVICES

The libraries have transformed drastically from store-houses for books and journals to the powerhouses of knowledge and information since the middle of the 20th century. The information and communication technology is responsible for this revolution. The very existences of libraries are dependable on users' satisfaction. Users are getting satisfied when the library is able to rise to his or her expectation or meet the actual needs. A quality service is said to be one, which satisfy the users' expectation resulting a good experience.

Throughout the history, libraries were mainly concerned with collection development and processing. The library profe-ssionals gave less concern to quality in product and services, never checked whether the users were satisfied or not. Gradually the social and economic changes have prompted the libraries to develop services. The staff has a vital role in the satisfaction of users. The library being a service organization, its prime objective is to provide the right documents, infor-mation and services to its users. Only the users' satisfaction survey will facilitate the assessment of their satisfaction with products and services offered. There are various methods, tools and techniques to measure, control and improve the quality of library services. Quality measurement and evaluation assumes great importance in modern libraries, as it brings immense benefits to the library as well as user community. Different methods such as collection of data for measuring the performance and quality of libraries; The SERVQUAL method, a multiple item scale to measure service quality; The LibQUAL, a tool developed on SERVQUAL for measuring the quality of library products and services.

WHAT IS QUALITY

The word 'quality' has several definitions. The conven-tional definition is " One that wears well, is well constructed will last for long time" and the strategic definition is "meeting customers' requirements."

- According to Juuran 'The quality is fitness for purpose'.
- According to Robinson, "Quality is meeting the requirements of customer-now and in the future."
- According to Sarkar "Quality of a product or service is the ability of the product or service to meet the customers' requirements.

QUALITY CONCEPT IN LIBRARY SERVICES

The library is an organization to offer reference and information services to its users. Library service is the combination of the services-process and its delivery. In a library, the service offered from acquisition section, technical section, maintenance section etc. are the processes carried out there and thereafter delivered to the users. The quality should start from the acquisition section, which should be carried uniformly to circulation section. A user who had an unpleasant experience from the library will tell it to many people, but a good experience will be told to very few. Therefore it is very necessary for librarian to understand the users, what they want, how they want, and when they want the documents and information.

HOW TO IMPROVE THE QUALITY IN LIBRARY SERVICES

In this information age it is very easy to make a quality based library if the parent body or concerned authority assist financially as well as collectively. It is very necessary for the librarian and its parent body to look forward for the present and future generation to cope up with international phenomena. A user must be educated with proper technology to use the library effectively.

He or she should have knowledge of what facilities and services are available in the library and information centre and how to access those efficiently and effectively. To improve the service quality the user satisfaction survey is a tool that provides both quantitative and qualitative data. It is an important part of libraries for process and performance measurement.

Main steps to measure users' satisfaction are:

- Conducting sample survey.
- Data collection.
- Process and analysis of data.
- Interpret and present the data.
- Finding out result.

With the help of the result the librarian can take new steps for development of library. The regular survey will enable the library to understand the changes in users satisfaction and to plan the services accordingly.

The Users' Satisfaction is based on Many Factors Like

- A source of up-to-date information, knowledge, accessing facilities and assistance.
- The library should organize its facilities visible to the users; otherwise they may not have it and get dissatisfied.
- *Accessibility:* The library resources and services should be easily accessible. Books should be arranged in shelves in proper classified order, so that the users can locate books quickly. In case of electronic library the electronic database like OPAC will help the users to find out the books in stacks.
- *Tangibles:* The tangibles of libraries, namely the building, furniture and other physical facilities, collection, staff, machines etc. should be sufficient and appropriate and useful for the users.
- *Courtesy/Friendliness:* The library staff should be very courteous and friendly with the users.
- *Physical Appearance/Atmosphere/Cleanliness/Comfort:* The appearance of library, its facilities, collection, staff and services should be attractive and pleasant. A Welcoming atmosphere should be must. Furniture, floor, racks, documents etc. should be neat and clean.

- *Process-Reliability/Communications:* The processing part of the library should be dependable and efficient that suffices the expectations of the users. The way of communication, assistance and guidance also greatly affect the satisfaction of the users.
- *Some Useful Criteria to Measure Users' Experience in a Library are:*
  - Speed of services delivery (Access time, location, processing, etc.);
  - Value added services such as Xerox service, CAS, SDI etc.; and
  - Technology used.

It is observed that if something goes wrong that can be very easily learned from the users, so the users' complaints can be taken as good measure of user satisfaction.

Steps for Staff to Meet the Users' Needs

- Being responsible for the total service quality to the users both the Technical staff and frontline staff in the library should serve the users.
- Services must be provided to the users in a most effective way.
- Providing maximum benefits to the users form collection and facilities.
- Stay close to users: Library can not understand users' needs, tastes, interests etc. without listening to them, and services without users' interest will be a mere wastage.
- Users must be treated well, informed well and acknowledged well about the services to the users.

IMPACT OF RANGANATHAN'S FIVE LAWS IN QUALITY SERVICE

The five laws of Ranganathan help in quality improvement of service as those are concentrated to the users very seriously. The laws directly advocate towards libraries' collection development, speedy processing, maintenance and quick retrieval of information by users.

The First Law

"Books are for Use" is a direction for measuring the quality of a library; quality in terms of contents, accessibility and availability as and when needed.

The Second Law

"Every reader his/her books" implies needs of users. In order to meet this law the library has to index all micro and macro documents so that every reader can find out his or her requirements.

The Third Law

"Every Book/Information its reader" implies the importance of book/information selection in a library. The law advocates scientific document selection, subject based organization, advanced and in depth indexing, efficient and effective searching and locating tools, Staff assistance, open access, extension services, publicity programmes etc.

The Fourth Law

"Save the time of Reader" indicates the importance of fast and efficient services to the users with the advanced technologies, method, techniques and tools. Open access, digital services, classified arrangement of documents in shelves, location and directing guides, excellent searching tools, and techniques *i.e.* Online public Access Catalogue (OPAC) in an automated library, Xerox facility, Online Information services, qualified and experienced staff will ensure fast service to the users.

The Fifth Law

"The Library is a growing organism" implies collection development, changing of all components of a library.

Everyday the world of documents and information is changing tremendously. Now the information is recorded not in papers alone, to many media, the latest being the electronic and digital form. So in today's world the library may called as information and knowledge house of world as a whole if it is supported by advanced information and communication technologies.

MEASURING QUALITIES OF LIBRARY SERVICES

The important measuring tools and techniques are:

- TQM (Total Quality Management).
- SERVQUAL.
- LibQUAL.

The TQM is one of the techniques used for the improvement and maintenance of quality or performance of the library. It is to provide the right information to the right users at the right place and time and also at the right cost.

The most important components of TQM in a library are:

- Benchmarking.
- Performance Measuring and Monitoring.
- Qualification and experience of staff.

Benchmarking is a process of comparing the operations, products and services of a library with a library doing quality processes and offering quality products and services to the users. Performance measurement is necessary to identify the problems, if any and find out new ways for improving the products or services. It requires both qualitative and quan-titative data.

The major performance indicators of the library functions are:

- *Acquisition:* Efficiency, effectiveness, cost productivity.
- *Classification:* Accuracy, Time factor, cost.
- *Cataloguing:* Efficiency, Time effectiveness.

- *Technical Processing:* Efficiency, effectiveness, cost productivity.
- *Collection Management:* Efficiency, ease, accessibility, effectiveness.

Quality of service depends on quality and experience of staff. The TQM supports user education, sufficient and convenient technical infrastructures. SERVQUAL is the most popular assessment tool of service quality. It is designed by the marketing research team of Berry, Parasuraman, and Zeithaml. SERVQUAL evolve a set of five dimensions to assess the service quality-

- *Tangibles:* Appearance of physical facilities, equip-ments, personnel, and communication materials.
- *Reliability:* Ability to perform the promised service dependably and accurately; giving correct infor-mation asked.
- *Responsiveness:* Willingness to help users and provide prompt service making new information available.
- *Assurance and Empathy:* Knowledge and courtesy of employees and their ability to convey confidence to users. It involves politeness, friendliness, skill to provide information.
- *Access:* It means there are adequate staff and equipments as well as hours of operation. Location of library is central and convenient.
- *Communications:* It involves understanding the users' needs precisely, provision of user education, teaching library skills to users, the use of language understandable to different categories of users.
- *Security:* It involves physical safety within the library, and keeping library dealings secured.

LibQUAL + is a library service quality measurement tool based on the SERVQUAL models of assessing service quality. It is standard survey instrument used in many libraries.It is a tool measuring users' perception of service quality and identifies gaps between desired, perceived and minimum expectation of services. LibQUAL +TM 2002 is the latest version to listening the users

USERS' EXPECTATIONS: QUALITY OF SERVICES

- Modern building and furniture are required for a good library.
- A good library provides excellent facilities and services.
- Required books and journals in adequate number will be available with attractively displayed in a good library.
- In a good library, the staff will assist the users for locating a document.
- Accurate information and proper records will always be available in a good library.
- The staff of a good library will have sufficient knowledge to answer user's questions.
- Easy accessing and convenient working hour should have in a good library.

USERS' PERCEPTION: QUALITY OF SERVICES

- My library has modern building and furniture.
- My library provides me excellent facilities and services.
- Necessary books and journals in adequate number are available displayed attractively in my library.
- My library assists the users for locating the documents needed.
- Accurate information and proper records are always kept in my library.
- The staff of my library has proper knowledge to answer my question.
- My library is easily accessible with convenient working hours.

FACILITIES IN A QUALITY BASED LIBRARY

Physical Facilities:

- Good library is easily accessible.
- Good layout for a good library.
- Sufficient Space, lighting and ventilation.
- Clean, tidy and hygienic.
- Cozy and comfortable furniture.

Library Collection:

- Good collection of textbooks, journals, reference books, online journals, ebooks, etc. is needed in a good library.
- Good library displays new arrival of books in separate shelves.
- Good library offers open access to the collection.

Library Staff:

- Staff in a good library should be experienced with knowledge of modern technology.
- Staff should help the users to locate the documents needed and do their works in time.
- Sufficient staff to run the library.

Technical Processing:

- Good library acquire new documents in time.
- Shelf arrangement and rectification is a never ending process in a good library.
- Good library has proper catalogue or database for collection (OPAC etc.).
- Good library has prompt processing, charging and discharging system.

SERVICES IN CENTRAL LIBRARY, IIT GUWAHATI

The Central Library, one of the important central facilities of the Institute, currently has about 85,000 volumes, including textbooks, reference books, conference proceedings, back volumes, standards, and non-book material such as CD-ROMs, audio tapes, video tapes, slides. The Library also subscribes to about 484 current periodicals. All operations of the Library are automated with the help of an integrated library software package (LIBSYS). The database for the entire collection has been created and available through On-Line Public Access Catalogue (OPAC) to the users via campus network. Now this facility is also available through Institute's Intranet as a Web enabled OPAC.

The Library is a member of INDEST consortium (Indian National Digital Library in Science and Technology Consor-tium), under the aegis of the MHRD, provides online access to few important science and engineering abstracting database services, such as COMPENDEX and INSPEC, MathSciNet, SciFinder Scholar, Web of Science etc and several full-text journals and Indian Standards. The Central Library Intranet Page provides the IP based online accesses to these resources. Opening hours is from Morning 8 a.m. to 11 p.m. Average number of users in library is 200 per day.

IT'S ROLE IN MANAGING ORGANISATIONAL CHANGE

IT and Environment - Goals-Structure

Researcher defined environment as those factors which not only are outside the system's control but which determine in part how the system performs.

Uncertainty is the difference between the amount of information required to perform the task and the amount of information already possessed by the organisation:

- *Proposition* 1: Turbulent environment drives organisations to use IT for monitoring the preferences of the environment. System theorists have recognised the importance of 'feedback' for the survival of the system and for maintaining a 'steady state' or 'homeostasis'. Organisations are purposive systems that learn of the impending threats by scanning. Scanning is the process by which the organisation acquires information for decision making. The modes of scanning are primarily determined by the external environmental stimuli and are determined by the magnitude and by the direction of the discrepancy between the goal and its realisation. While surveillance is useful for information-gathering process, search is oriented towards finding a satisfactory solution to a specific problem. Complex systems require complex controllers. IT will provide the 'complex controller" to the increasingly complex organisation. The information systems of an organisation need to evolve to remain consistent with the changing organisational structure. Referring to the obscurity of causal laws of turbulence, Aldrich argued that scanning could provide the firm with the desired 'competitive edge.'
- *Proposition* 2: Turbulent environment drives organisations to use IT for translating the information on environmental preferences into goals. Continuously changing environment requires organisations to

continuously reassess their goals. Effective structuring requires a consistency among the design parameters and contingency factors have demonstrated that organisations' goals can be generated by external forces, such as other groups seeking to use the organisation to further their own ends.

- *Proposition* 3: Turbulent environment drives organisations to use IT to align their structure with environmental preferences. The very efforts of the organisation to maintain a constant external environment produce changes in organisational structure. Scott argued that organisational structure and goals are driven by the preferences in the environment. The structure is determined by the information-processing capacity requirements of the organisation which in turn are governed by the IT being used. Aldrich, Perrow, Walker and Woodward have attributed structural differences to the organisation's technology. Mintzberg had suggested that the organisation's environment and technology are the independent variables that determine the structural variables of the organisation. Fowles, in his narrative on the history of organisational communications technologies contends that the phenomenal expansion of organisations can be largely attributed to advances in the technologies of organisational communication. Yates argued that in absence of technological communication organisations could have evolved differently. Preliminary econometric analyses of the overall U.S., economy for the period 1975-1985 further confirms that the increased use of IT is correlated with decreases in firm size and vertical integration.

IT and Organic Structure

- *Proposition* 4: Turbulent environment drives organisations to make more use of IT for increasing their 'organic' characteristics. 'Organic' firms are better equipped to sustain themselves in turbulent environment. A dynamic environment will drive the structure to an organic state despite other forces; the more complex the environment, the more decentralised the structure. Introduction of IT at the 'operating core' level transforms a bureaucratic administrative structure into an organic one. Effectively, automation of routine tasks eliminates the source of many of the social conflicts throughout the organisation. Law of requisite variety implies that the rate of change of organisational systems must correspond to the rate of change of environmental systems, *i.e.*, organisations with complex environmental interactions would develop complex structures like adhocracies or networks. Adhocracy is suitable for a dynamic and complex environment, when the firm has sophisticated technical systems and the focus is upon consistently offering differentiated products for retaining the customers. Future organisations would be 'networks' characterised by adhocracies with flexible systems of projects and teams brought together quickly to accomplish specific tasks. Some existing organisations have already 'farmed out' their operations by establishing them as separate organisations or contracting them out to other organisations.

- *Proposition 4a:* Turbulent environment drives organisations to use IT for empowering workers at all levels. Growing availability of telecommunications has offered technologies like distributed systems and client-server architecture that facilitate the process of empowerment of the lower levels. In the 'informated' organisation, workers would be 'empowered' by virtue of access to necessary information to perform higher-level tasks. Ramstrom has argued that tactical decisions relating to 'soft' information would be delegated to the 'grass-roots' where there is easy access to relevant information concerning the immediate environment, at the same time providing these levels with the information generated within the system by means of 'cheap' internal information systems.
- *Proposition 4b:* Turbulent environment drives organisations to use IT for increasing the spans of control. Information technologies, by facilitating the standardisation of coordination would facilitate larger spans of control or work units which would be characterised by extensive lateral communication and self- contained authority structures.
- *Proposition 4c:* Turbulent environment drives organisations to use IT for increasing lateral communications. Selective use of lateral decision processes for situations involving task uncertainty increase the information processing capacity of the organisation. Bringing the points of decision down to the points of action reduces the information overload on the managers. Since specification of 'procedures' in complex situations creates inefficiencies, organisations in turbulent environments would use more IT resource for delegating the decision-making to workers. Increased use of groupware for lateral coordination will spell the demise of middle management.

IT and Differentiation - Integration

- *Proposition* 5: Turbulent environment drives organisations to reduce their 'dimensions' by focusing on core competencies by leveraging their use of IT.
- *Proposition 5a:* Turbulent environment drives organisations to use IT to reduce differentiation and integration to focus on increased specialisation. Organisations structure themselves to minimize coordination costs and group together similar activities to achieve the benefits of process

specialisation. Environmental uncertainty or 'task predictability' is the basic independent variable influencing the design of the organisation. Faced with increased uncertainty, organisations can reduce the need for information processing by decreasing the 'diversity of outputs'. Reduced differentiation and integration of activities would decrease the coordination effort involved thus reducing the information processing requirements. Reduced coordination costs with IT would result in the substitution of IT for human coordination. Greater specialisation would be achieved by focusing on few core competencies.

IT's Role in Managing Organisational Interdependencies

- *Proposition* 6: Turbulent environment drives organisations to actively seek Inter-organisational relations to leverage their core competencies. Cooperation, especially in the international context, will be necessary to gain a competitive advantage in the future. To survive in an increasingly competitive environment, firms would form alliances that would bring together their core competencies to create the 'best of all" products.
- *Proposition 6a:* Turbulent environment drives organisations to reduce environmental complexity and uncertainty by seeking interdependencies with other organisations in the environment.
- *Proposition 6b:* Turbulent environment drives organisations to use more IT - effort to establish coordinating mechanisms with other firms.

To survive in the fast-changing environment the 'adaptive organisation" would be more like a shifting 'constellation' that has 'linkages' with independent and semi- autonomous organisations. Use of inter organisational linkages such as EDI would enable new forms of organisations and reduce the coordination costs of increasingly market-driven organisations. Increasingly, electronic linkages are becoming the necessary condition of doing businesses with larger firms. Using an analogy to the study of community chests conducted by Litwak and Hylton, we observe that in the increasingly global competition, the firms are competing for the common customers' 'fund' and the increase in one firm's revenue would come at the expense of other firm's loss. Coordination, being a function of interdependency, should grow in periods of increased competition for 'funds.'

The IT Paradox

- *Proposition* 7: Increasingly turbulent environment would feed the need for further advancements in IT which would further increase turbulence.

Business needs are incessantly driving the demands for increased capabilities of IT. In turn, increasingly advanced IT is being utilised in more and more sophisticated ways by the businesses to outdo competition. IT, which is being deployed as a solution to the increased complexity and uncertainty of the environment, has paradoxically contributed to the situation by 'compressing time and distance.' In absence of the present day advances in IT, would we be talking of globalisation or time based competition? Perhaps, not.

The pace of complexity is increasing fast. Hopefully, the advances in technology would be able to keep up with the environmental changes. Turbulence refers not to chaos in the environment, but to an increasing causal interconnection that renders environments obscure to local observers. Thus how can IT help organisations in responding to the challenges of an increasingly complex and uncertain environment? How can IT help the organisations achieve the 'flexible' organisation structure? We provide academic libraries as a living educational example that has been impacted by the strong trend of convergence of the technological advancements.

ROLE OF INFORMATION IN CONTEMPORARY ECONOMY

In the information economy, many private sector firms and government agencies have become consolidated around a framework of telecommunication networks and related information technologies. However, integrating communications and information technologies into their organisations have affected organisational processes, including production, distribution, and administration of products and services.

Researchers have noted that organisational processes in both the public and private sectors have become characterised by applications, such as electronic data exchange, distributed databases, computer-based communication, and client server computing.

Other researchers have indicated that geographic concepts, such as space and location, are significant factors in the distribution of data as it flows between individuals and organisations across communication networks, therefore, the use of geographic information systems in the facilitating and analysis of data has also increased greatly. The development and integration of geospatial information in a variety of administrative, production, and service functions within organisations in both the public and private sectors can have an effect on the role that libraries play in the information economy. The geospatial information that is used by individuals and organisations in the information economy is often produced by a mix of private developers and government agencies.

The data used by geographers and geographic information systems analysts in their operations is diverse and distributed across a wide network of server locations, over a complex series of information nodes. Libraries can provide a unique entry point to this multitude of sources. Economic activities during the past few decades have increasingly been characterised by different functional uses of information. The establishment and growth of diverse information industries, such as statistical bureaus, marketing associations, trade journals, and consulting agencies, have integrated information in their operations.

The development builds on early studies of how information not only impacted, but helped define, different economic processes. During the decades following World War II, individuals in the banking and accounting sectors began defining information as having value and affecting production. Statements, such as the 'Statement of Basic Accounting Theory,' asserted that accounting systems could be conceptualised as an 'application of general theories of information to the problem of efficient economic operations'. The National Science Foundation began to fund research about the economics of information.

Other organisations, such as the Organisation for Economic Co-operation and Development (OECD) and the United Nations Economic, Scientific, and Cultural Organisation (UNESCO), were also debating policy issues about the economics of information. However, to develop an information policy, one must first understand that policy is '... the generic name of any formulation, simple or complex, vague or exact, general or special, discretionary or detailed, of guidance for action in the face of circumstances which, lying necessarily in the future, can be approached only by conjecture and imagination'. The first bibliography of information economics was published in 1971.

By the mid 1970s, developments in the literature illustrated how the general theories of information were being investigated by economists and other researchers in the sciences and social sciences. Clearly, "... the existence of learning processes and likely variation in policy criteria in a business organisation imply that the decision-making unit is undergoing continual change".

Further, "those responsible for shaping information policy must determine the appropriate mix of information inputs to achieve social objectives, while at the same time they must have regard for equity considerations". By 1976, the American Economic Association officially recognised information as an economic topic and incorporated it into core ideas. By the 1980s, research into this area was generating much debate among researchers about what comprised information economics. Among the ideas being debated was the emergent issue of how to incorporate information into modes of production and thereby study its effects in different sectors of the economy.

Early economists described three factors of production that included land, Labour, and capital. The competing theories on defining just how these three factors relate, especially capital, in a system is contentious and open to debate. Economists differ on how to define capital. It can be described concretely as something of value as in money or more abstractly as an association with Labour and consumption.

In examining the value of transformative functions of an economic activity, the definition of capital can be more broadly interpreted, in some cases to include information. For example, the definition of human capital is the "sum total of skills embodied within an individual: education, intelligence, charisma, creativity, work experience, entrepreneurial Vigour, ... it is what you would be left with if someone stripped away all of your assets-your job, your money, your possessions". A number of articles and other publications that were produced in the 1990s discussed different forms of intangible capital including information, cultural capital, linguistic capital, and social capital.

Social capital would involve "networks of communication and communication-based institutions and their rules, norms of social practice, and relationships of trust". Networks themselves would be considered as facilitating a sum of knowledge that would have value as a factor in production. Another perspective on integrating information into economic theory was in examining how change in the economy is affected by information.

Braman suggests that "the production of knowledge and its transformation into technologies and other applied mechanisms such as competition can alter the order of different sectors of the economy and thus its equilibrium". Since, the "defining trend of the modern economy is the shift to the intangible. The economic landscape is ...moulded by intangible streams of data, images and symbols.

The source of economic value and wealth is ... the creation and manipulation of dematerialised content ...Non-linear and Non-deterministic, the intangible economy raises a whole series of measurement issues. More fundamentally, it changes the role, the function, and the perception of economic measurement data. Because information is its key resource and output, the intangible economy is highly data-sensitive and intrinsically self reflective".

However, as Goldfinger suggests, the effects of the applications of information and technology are only apparent over a period of time when it is possible to perform analysis with systematic data. Recent studies have focused on defining the role of technology in causing economic growth. Some researchers consider economic change as being influenced by aspects of the innovation process, aspects that are characterised as being 'information intense' or more developed technologically than what had currently existed. There has been much speculation on the correlation between technological development and economic growth and the social consequences of economic activities. In Marshallian neo-classical economics, externalities refer to by-products of activities that affect the well-being of people, where those impacts are not reflected in market prices; the costs (or benefits) associated with externalities do not enter standard cost accounting schemes.

The backbone of the information economy is in the linkages that combine to form a network. If the network is a combination of technology and human activities that processes information as they traverse the network, then the uneven flow of information across the network can cause externalities to manifest themselves. These externalities can be caused by incomplete information that can result in the fluctuating prices of a commodity.

The effect of content of information on the economy is up to debate. Are the contextual aspects of information processed in the economy irrelevant or do the contextual aspects of information in the economy have distinct sociopolitical value? For those who argue the latter, the contextual aspects of information do shape the perception and understanding of economic processes themselves. The cultural variability of information creates difficulties in determining the locational aspects of data.

Data may be associated with a physical carrier, but it is not bound by the location of that carrier. This aspect of information has created challenges to economists who have attempted to illustrate Braman's concept that would "distinguish between the costs of information at different stages of an information production chain". Further, the value of the information chain hinges upon relevance that "is a subjective question of mapping an utterance on the conceptual map of a given user seeking information for a particular purpose defined by that individual" and the "utility of a piece of information will depend on a combined valuation of its credibility and relevance". Most of the economic models that attempt to illustrate an information production chain have the elements of information creating, processing, flows, and use incorporated into their structure.

A number of organisations have created models that have the elements of information acquisition, production, assembly, storage, monitoring, interpretation, and exchange. United States federal documents describe an information cycle that includes information creation, collection, processing, and distribution as do international organisations. Creators, or individuals who are involved in the innovation of new concepts and new industries, are highly valued.

However, the idea of an information sector is not new. In 1962, over 50 industries were identified that comprised an information sector. Other economists preferred to identify information sector industries by using existing industry classifications, as identified by Standard Industrial Classification (SIC) codes. However, critics of the approach questioned the validity of defining information on so specific a criteria, fearing that existing industrial classifications "ignore a major part of the processes of investment in information in the economy" and that "most significant information activities do not produce goods in tangible form and thus not included in the SIC system". The debate over how to classify industries in the information sector illustrates the variability of trying to define information for econometric purposes.

The debate is further magnified when trying to define the economic aspects of information in an international sense. Cultural context is a factor in defining what comprises the information sector, with definitions varying between countries and methods that describe material and information related production. Even though legal negotiations about the nature of information and production between countries, such as with the General Agreements on Tariffs and Trade (GATT), have attempted to arrive at some definitional parameters for information, the process of trying to understand how information works in an international trade environment is problematic due to the great variability production across different countries. For example, the North American Industry Classification System (NAICS) was adopted in 1997, replacing the old Standard Industrial Classification (SIC) system. Developed jointly by the U.S., Canada, and Mexico to provide new comparability in statistics about business activity across North America, the NAICS also better distinguishes between manufacturing and information sectors. Although imperfect, the NAICS is an essential tool to determine service and product providers in the information sector, to remain current on industry analyses, statistics, and leading companies. The international economic environment is indeed a complex one, and in defining how information operates within economic systems, one can examine the redefining of economic components such as the agent, the firm, and the market.

As discussed in classical economic theory, agents tend to act in ways that put themselves in a better position than previously held. Braman questions the decision-making processes of economic agents as they improve their position according to economic theory. Processes including 'rationality, perfect information, and individualistic independence' are subject to myriad influences and the amount of information available. Further, there are limits to the amount of information that an individual agent can have access to or even process in order to maximise his position.

Research in the fields of psychology, that is, cognitive miserliness has indicated that there are cognitive and neurological limitations that affect how information is perceived and understood. Technology limitations can also affect the capture, recording, and transmission of information, thereby, affecting its cognition by an agent or organisation. The cultural context of information, as well, can have an affect on how information is understood. The social organisation of society can have an significant impact on the flow of information creating barriers that can slow or impede the finding of information by individual agents. The concept of social organisation and community is also important in understanding how information is processed in regards to economic function. In classical economic theory, economic agents act purposively.

Since, they have an end in mind and find means to attain those ends, the actions of individual agents bear a causal relationship to overall market outcomes. Further, an economic agent uses information in order to "obtain satisfaction or benefits gained from consuming a particular good or service according to a hierarchical ranking of preferences". The social context of how information can be pursued and utilised also affects the actions of an individual economic agent.

An individual may use information and acquire goods and services beyond what is necessary for the maximising of their position and thus, may not make the best use of information in a classical economic sense. Cultural processes can affect preferences for a particular commodity adding or detracting from its value. The decision-making process is interconnected among various individuals in society, which can affect the utility factor in economic activities.

Societies and communities can be conceptualised as components of a larger structure or market in which economic activities are performed. The larger structure can operate as an "informational mechanism" with different types of information arrayed spatially across it. How economic agents operate within markets is subject to much debate as economists advocate different operational models about the functioning of markets.

One model centers on the prices of commodities and services that are distributed across a market. Economic agents enter the market with a certain knowledge level and assumptions about prices that influence their interaction with the market. The search for further price information for an eventual outcome process frames their activities in the market. Social aspects and cultural ties that are part of the market structure affect how information interacts with markets. The distribution of information across markets has an impact on the economic decision process of the firm as well as the individual. If a market is a social arrangement that allows buyers and sellers to discover information and carry out a voluntary exchange of goods or services, the firm is an alternative system of allocation to the market that exists to organise production in a Non-price environment. Although there is a distinction between a market and a firm, most economists admit that the two shade into each other.

A business model describes the elements and relationships that express the business logic of a firm. Just as NAICS classes businesses into sectors, firms are often classed into 'internally consistent sets of firms," referred to as strategic groups or configurations, allowing typologies and taxonomies to explore the determinants of performance. Early studies of information flow within existing business entities usually focused on individual managers. In a market environment in which reliable information was at a premium, business managers made decisions based on an individualised perspective that made use of personal social networks as well as market information.

The growth of larger business enterprises with extensive production and distribution linkages increased the need for accurate market information, which led to the eventual progression Towards extensive record keeping overseen by professional managers. The availability of accurate market information and information on other firms in related enterprises began to affect business decisions.

An increased efficiency in record management usually decreases what some economists have labeled transaction costs, or the searching for information needed for a particular type of economic activity. Early studies in the nature of transaction costs within business processes determined that firms usually invested in those transaction costs that were more expensive, while leaving the more inexpensive transaction costs to the marketplace. The application of advanced telecommunication technology by firms has encouraged commercial enterprises to distribute their transaction costs on an even wider basis for more efficiency. Contemporary studies in the nature of firms and different economic sectors have expanded the focus of study beyond the single firm to a hierarchy of firms or even larger social constructs, such as networks.

Research into the role of information and economic theory bridges the mathematical boundaries of idealised econometric models to account for information sector variability and the irrationality of human Behaviour. Research in the social dynamics of industries that comprise the information sector should take a wider, holistic approach. Studies on the information sector should integrate concepts and analytical methods from other disciplines.

One such discipline is political science, which has often focused on the effect of uneven flows of information and of the impact of imperfect information on decisions. In expanding their descriptive scope of the components of the information sector, economists expanded their idea of the firm and the market by including variables with wider spatial structures. Such structures include telecommunication networks and social communication networks.

It is with the physical network of the telecommunications sector that some researchers, especially in the field of geography, have sought to combine spatial concepts of space, place, and landscape to provide a rigorous and quantifiable platform in which to measure the complex socioeconomic phenomena that comprises the information sector.

EMERGENCE OF INFORMATION AND KNOWLEDGE SOCIETIES

Some 10,000 year ago the early ancestor of mankind, subsisted by hunting and gathering, started to building agrarian societies. The old agrarian societies began their transitions to industrial societies in mid-18th centuries. Expansion of intellectual activities in industrial societies, such as industrial production, international trade and transactions, and technological advancement, stimulated mass distribution of education and creation of libraries. Industrial societies continued their enormous material development throughout the 20th century.

The information society has passed through four transformational stages of development, the most radical stage starting at the tail end of the 20th century. This stage has brought a never-ending revolution, particularly with the introduction of information and communication technologies. During this period, there have been unprecedented developments, profoundly affecting the social structure–the decline of manufacturing sector as compared to the prospering information-rich service sector is one example of such developments.

The concept of knowledge societies is often used to denote a development in or second generation of information society.

Whereas the information society aims to make information available and provide the necessary technology, the knowledge society aims to generate knowledge, create culture of sharing and develop applications that operate mainly via the Internet. The goal of knowledge society is to fill social needs, create wealth and enhance the quality of life in a sustainable manner. India is moving fast towards becoming an information society as the Government of India is paying due attention to the use of information technology (IT).

The Prime Minister of India constituted a National Task Force on IT and Software Development in May 1998 with the purpose of formulating a long-term National IT Policy to convert India into an IT software superpower. These steps are helping India to shift from an 'economy of goods' to a 'knowledge economy' or 'knowledge driven economy'. The beginning of the knowledge society has been made through creation of parks and corridors, and the Prime Minister has given a mission of converting India into a 'knowledge society' by the year 2008. Today, India is one of the largest exporters of knowledge workers.

ROLE OF LIBRARIES

In the modern society, where the use of electronic services and Web-based information sources constantly increases, libraries are managed in a more democratic way, have more flexible communication system and work organisation, and their service development is based on the quality and user-orientation of services. In the modern knowledge society libraries have a new role and there are various types of library models.

These are as follows:

- Traditional library as a memory institution
- Library as a learning and research centre
- Library as a cultural and communication centre
- Electronic library
- Digital library
- Virtual library as library without walls

Libraries had been performed many important roles in the past agrarian and industrial societies. But those roles were limited in scope. In the 21st century, libraries have to perform pivotal roles in disseminating and sharing the culture of knowledge. In this age of knowledge libraries should be repositories of all of the knowledge and information accumulated by human kind.

They will have to store all kinds and forms of material and information and disseminate beyond the geographical boundaries. Today's advanced information technology is enabling libraries to accomplish this immense task. Exchange of knowledge has always been the most important objectives of libraries. Various systems have been developed to share and exchange the records of human knowledge. Universal Bibliographic Control and Universal Availability of Publications are two major Programmes of IFLA (International Federation of Library Associations and Institutions) to exchange knowledge world over. OCLC is the world leading library network in USA for sharing intellectual knowledge among academic community in all over the world. But libraries in the 21st century should fulfill more dynamic role. They should exchange knowledge and information with users inside and outside their country, thus going beyond their traditional reference and lending services. This would possible when libraries agreed to expand their roles beyond the geographical boundaries by using sate of art technologies.

The modern libraries certainly can not be passive repository for books and other printed materials. The opposite requirements of storing increasing collection in various forms and of maintaining easy access to most part of it can only be balanced by deploying information and communication technologies. Libraries should upgrade their services by digitising their resources for online use.

These services should be accessible to anyone, regardless of time or location, through digital communication devices. Libraries can play significant role in providing a good education and knowledge of high quality. Individuals around the world, no matter how poor they may be, can access whatever knowledge and information they need by visiting libraries via the internet, such as the library of congress.

PROBLEMS AND OPPORTUNITIES FACING LIBRARIES IN INDIA

Library and information services are fundamental to the goals of creating, disseminating, optimally utilising and preserving knowledge. They are instrumental in transforming an unequal society into an egalitarian, progressive knowledge-based society. It is well known that in India most of the libraries function in the government sector.

These are in academic and research institutions and under the public library system, which is again under the state and central governments. At present, education being a state subject and coming under the purview of different apex agencies, there is no common direction or coordination among them. It is imperative that all libraries (public, academic, research and special) change gear and develop at an accelerated pace. Developments in information communication technology (ICT) have enabled libraries to provide access to all, and also bridge the gap between the local, the national and the global. Yet the Library and Information Services (LIS) sector in India has not kept pace with the paradigmatic changes taking place in society.

There are a few libraries which are using state of art technologies to disseminate knowledge to their respective user community. There is lack of cooperation among the libraries of different organisations and which cause the lack of union catalogues at national level.

The national library failed even to do this immense task. One of the major problems faced by LIS sector in India is lack of bibliographic control at national level which causes duplication in research. A considerable number of libraries had not been developed bibliographic databases of their documents for putting them on network. To summarise, the major constraints faced by the libraries which militate against effective dissemination and use of information are:

- A considerable percentage of the population is illiterate or functionally literate making libraries of minimal use to them.
- Poor resource allocation for infrastructure improvement and collection development for public libraries.
- Lack of sufficient sanctioned posts, forcing most services to be operated by voluntary Non-professional staff, which damages information organisation and services.
- Lack of national policies promoting ICT as a tool for development of library systems and services.
- Lack of adequate trained manpower in the use of IT.
- Lack of funds for acquiring necessary hardware and software facilities.
- Resistance on the part of library staff to change from their traditional practices to the use of IT.

Despite the problems, Library and Information Services (LIS) sector in India has got remarkable achievements. Efforts had been made to set up networks at local, regional and national level to deploy information and communication technologies and to build electronic information sources. Besides INFLIBNET at the national level to support university and college libraries, a number of other national networks and various library networks have also been developed including NICNET (National Informatics Centers Network), ERNET (Education and Research Network), CALIBNET (Calcutta Library Network), DELNET (Developing Library Network), etc.

A number of educational institutions are members of such networks. These networks, especially INFLIBNET and DELNET, are engaged in compiling union catalogs, creating various databases of experts, providing training to library staff, ILL, online facilities, reference service, assistance in retrospective conversion, etc. To overcome the problem of financial crunch and the rising costs of journals, librarians have formed consortia to subscribe all the required journals and databases. Some special libraries and research organisations have established consortia known as FORSA (Forum for Resource Sharing in Astronomy) to share electronic access to journal literature.

NISCAIR (National Institutes of Science Communication and Information Resources), one of CSIR labs, has formed a consortium for CSIR labs for accessing e-journals and databases. In order to solve the problem of universities and college libraries, UGC launched a major initiative called UGC-INFONET that provides high speed Internet connections so as to have electronic access to professional literature including research journals, abstracts, review publications, and databases from all areas in science and technology, as well as in social sciences and humanities.

The Ministry of Human Resource Development (MHRD) has set up the "Indian National Digital Library in Science and Technology (INDEST) Consortium" for the subscription to electronic resources for 38 academic institutions, including the Indian Institute of Sciences, Indian Institute of Technology, Regional Engineering Colleges, Indian Institute of Managements, and about 60 centrally-funded/aided government institutions through the consortium. For the improvement of quality of library and information services through the systematic acquisition, organisation and dissemination of knowledge, various library associations have been set up at national and state level.

They annually organised conferences, seminars and training Programmes to trained and update library professionals with latest development in LIS. Recently libraries and research organisations realise the importance of digital libraries and they started the work of digitisation of important documents. NISCAIR and the Department of Indian Systems of Medicine and Homoeopathy (ISMandH) have entered into an agreement for establishing a Traditional Knowledge Digital Library (TKDL) on Ayurveda. TKDL will be available in English, German, French, Spanish and Japanese Since, these languages account for more than 98 per cent of the international patent applications.

TKDL in the first phase targets Ayurveda. But as a whole it would encompass, in addition to Ayurveda, Siddha, Unani, Yoga, Naturopathy and Folklore medicine. The Indian Institute of Science (IISc), Carnegie Mellon University (CMU), the International Institute of Information Technology, Hyderabad (IIITH) and many other academic, religious and government organisations, totaling about 21 'Content Creation Centers', have become partners in the Digital Library of India (DLI) initiative for the digitisation and preservation of Indian heritage present in the form of books, manuscripts, art and music.

Each centre brings its own unique collection of literature into the digital library. DLI has a vision to build a universal digital library of world knowledge. One million books have already been available through this project. India perhaps has one of the oldest and largest collections of Manuscripts in the world. These manuscripts are in different languages and scripts; written on different materials such as birch bark, palm leaf, cloth, paper,etc. They are in the custody of libraries, museums, monasteries, mutts and individuals.

A significant proportion is not preserved scientifically. Experts estimate that almost all palm leaf manuscripts may perish due to wear and tear over next 50 to 100 years. In this regard the National Mission for Manuscripts has taken a step to save the most valuable, intellectual property of our cultural inheritance. The missions has started a pilot project for digitising the manuscripts in five states across India covering five caches of manuscripts and for the same four digitising agencies have been selected.

Importance of open access archives, institutional repositories and open access journals has been realised by the library and information professionals in India. This movement has been accelerated by the availability of open source software namely DSpace, EPrints, Greenstone, etc., Indian Institute of Science, Bangalore, INFLIBNET Centre, Ahmedabad and Documentation Research and Training Centre (DRTC), Bangalore are the leading institutions who made this movement a great success. Among the top 25 publishing countries, India ranks 12th for the overall number of journals, but drops to 18th for journals with online content. At present there are more than 150 open access journals in India.

The open access journals in India are mainly initiated by six journal publishers, namely, Indian Academy of Sciences, Indian National Science Academy, Indian Medlars Centre of National Informatics Centre, Medknow Publications, indianjournals. com and Kamla-Raj Enterprises. The Indian Institute of Science was the first in the country to set up and interoperable institutional archive ePrints@IIScr. The archive now has more than 7000 records, with over 90 per cent having full text. Presently there are 25 institutional archives in India which are registered in the Registry of Open Access Repositories (ROAR). An open access statement is likely to be ready by this year. The CSIR also has a plan to setup a national digital repository of research literature. NISCAIR has already started to work on the project known as National Science Digital Library. National knowledge Commission is also formulating similar open access policies and guidelines for the higher education and R and D sectors to improve access to research literature and disseminate research literature to the global communities. The National Knowledge Commission has submitted its report to the government on how to redefine the information services sector. The report of Knowledge Commission on library sector suggests that "Every state should establish a registry and archives of knowledge based digital resources which should be made accessible to all".

INFORMATION TECHNOLOGY (IT) PRODUCTS

MOST IMPORTANT PRODUCTS OF THE '90S

The 1990s was a decade of rapid technological advances. Client-server architecture evolved into a viable alternative to mainframe computing. Enterprise applications such as groupware, inventory control, supply chain, and systems management emerged as platforms for the evolution of business systems. The PC became a Ubiquitous and increasingly powerful desktop tool. And the Internet was embraced as a communication medium, consumer platform, and business conduit. Here are 10 of the most important and influential products introduced in this decade.

1. *Sun Microsystems' Java:* The brave little embedded operating system started out as a platform for write-once-run-anywhere computing and ended up as the Web's favourite tool.
2. *Nets Cape Navigator:* There's probably no greater development in the history of IT than the emergence of the Internet and World Wide Web. By the time Marc Andreessen and Jim Clark launched their graphical Web browser, Navigator 1.0, in 1994, there were more than 1 million Internet hosts. While Mosaic was the first widely distributed browser, Navigator set the standard in terms of look and functionality. And in the process, it shook Microsoft to its core—no small feat.
3. *Lotus Notes:* Lotus Development Corp. licensed Notes, the product most commonly associated with the term groupware, from Iris Associates in 1989. By the time IBM bought Lotus in 1995 for $3.5 billion—primarily to acquire the groupware technology—Notes had an installed base of almost 2 million seats. Lotus made a successful effort to integrate Notes with the Internet when it introduced Domino in 1996.
4. *Microsoft Office:* Microsoft didn't come up with the idea to bundle a spreadsheet, word processor, and graphics package into a productivity suite, but it made the most of the concept-and created a business computing standard. Microsoft has continued to enhance the bundle, including links to the Internet.
5. *Oracle's Relational Database:* The original work on relational database technology was done by Edgar Codd when he was at IBM in the early 1970s. However, Oracle took the relational model and established it as a database standard, through both rapid technological advance and aggressive marketing. In the 1990s, Oracle continued to enhance the basic architecture to incorporate symmetric multiprocessing and object extensions.
6. *Sun Microsystems' Enterprise 10000 Server:* Sun made believers out of many of those who had been skeptical about the scalability of symmetric multiprocessing servers when it shipped the 64-node E-I0000 in May 1997.
7. *SAP Rl3:* The third version of SAP's suite of enterprise applications, introduced in 1992, integrated and automated back-office systems and convinced many companies to re-engineer their business processes to accommodate the software.
8. *Computer Associates' Unicenter:* Introduced in 1993, CA's systems management software unified a disparate set of products and processes, and provided a comprehensive view of IT systems. CA continued to strengthen the product with the introduction of the graphical, object-oriented TNG version in 1997 and the three dimensional TND version in 1998.

9. *Intel's X86 Architecture:* Intel led the PC industry on a price/performance curve that mirrored Moore's Law-and then some. When Intel launched the 66-MHz Pentium processor in 1993, it set the stage for a quantum leap in desktop processing, making possible powerful personal productivity applications and eventually online commerce.
10. *Microsoft Windows:* In the spring of 1990, Microsoft CEO Bill Gates introduced the latest iteration of the company's graphical front end, Windows 3.1 and it was an instant hit with the public. Since then, billions of copies of the operating system have been sold, and, along with its siblings, Windows NT and Windows CE, Windows has proved to be one of the highest-impact products in IT.

WELCOME TO THE INFORMATION SUPERDORM

Malone regard that "we are now at the threshold of a new era, driven this time not by the technologies of production and transportation, but by the technologies of information, communication and coordination." An extraordinary array of information technologies is providing not only powerful new tools for dealing with these changes, but also a promising framework for creating entirely new opportunities. Advances in computers, software, telecommunications, networking, and electronic media are vastly increasing the quantity, quality, and accessibility of all forms of information.

Internet

Internet as a "bunch of communications protocols that enables millions of computers to talk with each other. It is already replacing overnight mail and faxes as a way to communicate quickly and over long distances.

Begun as a research project of the US Defence Department in the 1970s, it has become the:

- Technological trend in academic libraries of the '90s with dial up databases such as CompuServe, small corporate and university databases that are interconnected via the Internet.
- Thousands of companies have started to promote and sell products over the Net and at the same time, businesses are discovering that they can streamline operations and increased productivity by connecting their in-house networks to the Internet.

Almost overnight, the net grows from an academic resource into an ocean of capitalist dream.

World Wide Web

Subscribing to the Internet opens the door to many different types of information and communication possibilities. The World Wide Web, a *subset* of the

Internet and one of the Internet's most popular and employs simpler computer applications, such as Windows, and more transparent commands then the internet.

By using browser software and fast modems, a subscriber can easily:

- View individuals' and organisations' home pages.
- Graphical tables of contents to more-detailed files contained within.
- Best of all, a user need not be a computer pro or a rocket scientist to surf the Net.

With the attributes such as multimedia, hyper linked, dispersed, dynamic, versatile and multi platform, the reason for Web popularity is the ability it affords to send and receive graphics, photographs, movies, and sound along with text. Several factors have contributed to this rapid growth, "most notably, technological advances in software, hardware, and communications that have made connections more economical".

Electronic Mail (E-Mail)

A way for computer users to exchange messages in completely different offices, locations, organisations, cities, countries, even continents using the e-mail programme available through the *Internet Service Provider* (ISP) to create, read, and manage the e-mail messages. Educationally, e-mail has continue to grow more important. It has also become easier to exchange not only textual messages but a variety of files, including graphics, software programmes, spreadsheets, and databases. Ingram believe that e-mail will become part of a total distance-education system that might include elements of videoconferencing, interactive multimedia, and other learning tools.

Lotus Notes

A complete 'environment' or 'platform' for several computer applications and can be used:

- to send electronic mail,
- As an electronic calendaring system,
- As a scheduling system.
- As a bulletin board.
- As a publishing system for the web,
- As an automated workflow system and
- As a group ware system.

Intranets

James view Intranet as a network that lets people within an organisation share the kind of information one's can experience—and create—with Netscape Communicator Professional such as:

- Pages full of text, graphics, sound, and video;
- Fill-out form;

- e-mail with pictures;
- Specialised newsgroup and interactive conferences;
- Directories full of files one's can download; and
- A broad range of custom-tailored resources for research, education, or business.

Thus by using a standardised methods, or protocols for moving information from one computer to another, an entire office, or even a corporation with many physically remote sites, can communicate without worrying about specific hardware or software.

Multimedia

Multimedia tools enable us to express ideas that are more difficult to describe with words than they are to demonstrate in some way. For those who are aural or tactile learners, for example, multimedia provides a fresh new means of comprehending something.

Videoconferencing

Ingram claim that videoconferencing is increasingly used for individual and group meetings as well as to deliver education and training at a distance. Brown University Computing and Information Services view videoconferencing as an interactive audio/visual meeting channel to sites worldwide via high speed telephone lines. Thus, videoconferencing combines the benefits of face-to-face interaction with the power of telecommunications.

As claimed by Littman, the videoconferencing rationales are as follows:

- Enhance the quality and intensity of communications.
- Engender a sense of responsibility and involvement among individuals who could not otherwise meet with each other.
- Lead to the articulation of policy, goals, and objectives through consensual decision making.
- Enable academic librarians to hold interactive sessions regardless of location on such topics as Internet access and use, intellectual freedom and copyright.
- High school students can be introduced to resources in an academic library, thus saving field trip and liability insurance costs.

Virtual Reality

Virtual reality has captured most organisations. It benefits an organisation, by gathering information on customers/users, competitors, and potential markets.

Cavanaugh describes the creation of 'virtual offices' that has enable:

- Communications between employees and vendors.
- Advertise products and services globally.
- Deliver new products or packages of services.

CD-ROMs

Rogers view that the advent of CD-ROMs in libraries was the introduction to the world of high-tech ware for many librarians. CD-ROMs are found in every library today and are loaded on most business networks but are often simply presented to end users, from car mechanics to astronauts. This technology is revolutionising the way students and professionals can assemble and access information.

Being fixed systems:

- The *content* on CD-ROMs is finite, although the amount of information on a disc is still impressive.
- The *functionality* of CD-ROMs and the number of tricks they can perform is finite.

Amendments to the software, indexing, and content are done at the will of the developer and information provider. A number of business databases available on CD-ROMs has increased steadily over the past few years. At the same time, most major public libraries, colleges, and *university libraries* have made available at no cost numerous CD-ROM databases for user and customer use.

CD-ROMs Into the Future

Beiser stresses that the emergence of a high-density CD (HiCD) technology opens exciting new possibilities for all sectors of our society—not the least of which are *libraries.* CD-ROMs was a distribution and publishing medium, and not a competitor to hard disk drives. Meanwhile, HiCD can deliver text, graphics and multimedia content as well or better than a high-speed link. It is the stuff of memory cells, the repository of incredible amounts of otherwise evanescent data, a resource without which libraries will be unable to perform their designated role in an information intensive universe.

Online Databases

It offers full texts of journal and magazine articles. Tenopir claimed that academic librarians are actively looking for alternatives to print journal collections:

- As serials budgets stagnate,
- Print journals take up as much space.
- Patrons want to locate and access everything from a single workstation.

Some examples of online databases are EBSCO Elite Periodical Database, FirstSearch Online Databases, INFOTRAC Periodical and Newspaper Databases, etc.

Electronic Journals

Researcher claimed that electronic journals are mushrooming online, on the Web and in CD-ROM format. This phenomenon is due to the rapid advancement of information technologies including the Internet and digitising techniques. The quantity of e-journals is growing larger although no exact number is available.

In recent years, many more journals have been earmarked for digitising, a necessary process for turning a paper journal into an electronic one. In addition, a considerable number of journals are now published only electronically, which significantly enlarges the size of the e-journal pool. Among all the users of e-journals, academic libraries especially, are the major subscribers of e-journals.

INFORMATION SERVICES USING CLOUD COMPUTING

While forecasting the next must-have library information service can be difficult, it is likely that the service will be available in the cloud. Library IT vendors more frequently offer hosting options along software and are developing new systems that leverage cloud architecture to share data and make adoption and management easier for libraries. In addition, open source projects such as DuraCloud and Omeka are using cloud computing to facilitate adoption and generate income. This means that libraries have new choices to make when selecting information services but also means that they must evaluate IT platforms as well as information services. This stage explores some of the criteria that libraries can use to make these decisions and examines the long term implications of the cloud-computing trend.

FACTORS THAT INFLUENCE IT ADOPTION

The choice to adopt a particular IT service depends on a number of organisational, technical, and community factors. Differences in funding sources, IT staff expertise, information service needs and policy and legal issues means that there is no one right solution for libraries exploring whether or not to adopt cloud-based IT services. Before we consider the longer-term implications of cloud computing adoption we will consider each of these factors.

COST

Ongoing service cost and requirements of funding sources can be a major barrier to cloud adoption. Many IT organisations are focused on a capital or one-time investment model for technology assets. On the other hand, libraries have a background with subscription-based financial models and may feel more comfortable with lower capital but higher ongoing costs than their IT department counterparts. A way to understand the differences in cost is to complete a high-level return on investment (ROI) analysis comparing the differences between cloud and local IT services. Reese provides an overview of how to compare ROI on cloud and local IT services including start-up vs ongoing costs, staffing/ support costs and direct service vs required infrastructure costs. He suggests comparing cloud and local approaches based on your organisation's capital depreciation schedule to better understand the long term costs. While this enables an apples-to-apples comparison it also masks some of the advantages that cloud platforms offers in service flexibility and scalability.

EXPERTISE

Having a strong understanding of local IT staff expertise and capacity is particularly important when selecting an IT infrastructure. Capacity can be defined as the ability of an IT department to provide technology and staffing resources to ensure quality service. In contrast, expertise can be defined as the technical ability of staff to support a service. While these two factors are often directly correlated (*e.g.* an increase in expertise results in an increase in capacity) this is not necessarily the case. In my own research many libraries cited expertise as either a motivating factor (*e.g.* lack of local organisational IT capacity motivated the library to seek external support) or an inhibiting factor (*e.g.* lack of internal IT expertise limited which cloud solutions were explored).

Expertise and capacity in your organisation can be difficult to quantify but tools such as a time-allocation analysis or skill survey may be useful. If your IT staff's skills typically do not include server or datacentre management skills, then infrastructure as a service (IaaS) based cloud solutions are not likely to be successful. If, in contrast, your IT staff has considerable expertise in software development and tweaking, then platform as a service (PaaS) will provide them tools that may expand their service support capacity.

Defining capacity and current workload can be difficult, but at the least should include understanding your staff's recurring tasks and ongoing workload. Scholars explore capacity planning from a staffing perspective in depth in their chapter on Organisational Structures and discuss tasks including service deployment, ongoing management, end-user support and service decommissioning.

SERVICE QUALITY

Service quality is often where libraries begin their exploration of a new application. Service improvements may include new discovery features, better mobile accessibility, or wider research resources. In deciding whether or not an IT service will be of higher quality in a local or cloud-based platform depends in part on how the data being provided in the service can be managed locally over time.

For example some information services depend on rapidly changing data that can only be managed via an outsourced subscription (*e.g.* OpenURL resolvers and journal subscription services).

Because many library services feature large data repositories there are a number of services including journal databases, resource linking applications and 24/7 research support services that are often only available as a cloud-based or at least externally supported service.

In these cases, the ability of the vendor to update the database is an important consideration that may sway libraries towards a SaaS versus a locally implemented approach. Other systems, such as digital library applications, integrated library systems, research support and web site services, however, may be influenced more by other factors including expected uptime and reliability, speed and interoperability. Understanding these issues and how they relate to capacity and skill issues can help libraries understand the essential elements of what will make a service successful.

POLICY AND LEGAL FACTORS

Organisational policy and legal factors should be one of the first areas to explore when considering cloud-based services. Understanding the implications of privacy and accessibility laws on information services and having an appreciation of organisational policy can save time by eliminating solutions that are a poor fit. In addition to speaking with organisation experts about service regulations it is important to evaluate Service Level Agreements (SLAs) of cloud providers to ensure that their services are in compliance. When exploring SaaS providers it is also important to understand which cloud platforms these providers are using to provide their services.

While it is important to be aware of these issues, it is equally important to not get bogged down in them when exploring potential IT solutions. Low risk or low sensitivity services may be entirely appropriate for cloud platforms that do not provide bulletproof SLA agreements while services that have private data or management requirements are best in locally managed environments.

WHERE SHOULD LIBRARIES FOCUS THEIR IT RESOURCES

With an understanding of these four factors (cost, expertise/capacity, service quality and policy/legal) libraries can make better informed decions about their IT environments. Libraries operate in a complex information environment comprised of multiple information systems and guided by professional ethics including an interest in ensuring free, open and ethical use of information. Cloud computing provides both an opportunity and a challenge for libraries seeking to hold onto these principles as they adopt new information systems. It is increasingly common to find software vendors and open source software developers that offer systems on hosted platforms. DuraCloud, Equinox and Omeka are just a few examples of open source software offered by non-profit and commercial hosting organisations that also engage in software development. Many commercial developers offer some form of hosted or cloud-based service as well.

This approach has been successful in growing the market for co-operative library services in the US. For example, the Georgia Pines Library system that led the creation of Evergreen not only succeeded in migrating its branch libraries to a new single-ILS platform, it also led the way for other states seeking the opportunities for data sharing and economies of scale. This is good news for open source projects seeking to find long term viability. A recent Ithaka research report discussed the difficulties associated with finding ongoing support for open source projects including new projects, shifting priorities and lagging community involvement. By leveraging cloud-computing hosting, some open source projects are both expanding their community of adopters and benefiting from a revenue stream to enable ongoing development.

My research on cloud computing adoption in libraries showed that it was more common for libraries who had turned to cloud computing to have turned to a SaaS as opposed to PaaS or IaaS platforms. SaaS solutions also pose a long-term challenge for libraries by eliminating local capacity and expertise and ultimately impacting the ability to migrate to new systems. In contrast, PaaS and IaaS solutions provide libraries with tools that level the playing field by preserving local expertise and expanding capacity. Unfortunately, it can be rather difficult, if not impossible, to implement many current commercial and open source systems in a PaaS or IaaS environment.

Many open source and commercial products operate on very specific IT stacks. Although PaaS providers, including Heroku, Cloud Foundry and Google Apps Engine are expanding support for different programming languages and database platforms, library applications have not been developed using these frameworks or deployment techniques. This means that the redundancy, replication and backup features that come with PaaS platforms is out of reach of libraries who either must rely on a vendor-provided SaaS approach or turn to local or IaaS solutions.

Further complicating the situation is the difficulty inherent in migrating to new platforms for libraries using SaaS or IaaS solutions. While PaaS providers may not always support easy migration, by focusing on building applications using industry standard frameworks, vendors and open source communities could make migration more realistic. Unfortunately, few if any commercial or open source library systems operate in these environments. This limits the range of IT solutions available to libraries and can push libraries towards either largely localised or outsourced options.

While cloud computing offers new opportunities for large and small libraries, it also raises the stakes on information service selection. Libraries are increasingly moving towards network-based data and more complex information services. At the same time they are grappling with constrained resources and a new range of IT platforms. In selecting an information system and IT platform, it is important that libraries choose solutions that improve service while also ensuring that their choices are good for the long-term.

EDINBURGH LIBRARIES AND SOLUS

Rather than roll over and accept this, the City of Edinburgh has chosen to harness the very technology cited as a threat and engage with new audiences in new ways. The primary aim has always been to attract physical users to their facilities, however if this is not possible then the next best thing is to engage digitally with their audience. If you think about citizens in a new way, as mobile, digitally accessible, yet unique and focused on receiving the service that they want whenever they want it, technology gives them and you the opportunity to build a new relationship. Once in place, it also enables you to market your services free of charge, increasingly important in these austere times.

Liz McGettigan, Library and Information Services Manager at the City of Edinburgh Council, realised the requirement to engage with developments in web 2.0 services, or risk being left behind in an increasingly digital world. She saw the opportunities for promotion that social media enabled and created a team of people within the library to pull all electronic resources into one location. Finally, she employed the best technology available to engage with Edinburgh's citizens, in facilities, on the web, socially and on the go.

- *Your Library*: the Web Portal – This unique portal unites all digital resources including catalogues, databases and other web sites.
- *Tales of One City*: This is an integrated approach to social media, engaging citizens and local communities with Edinburgh's blog, Facebook site, Twitter feed, Flickr and YouTube sites. It's push and pull communication that connects with their audience.
- *SOLUS*: This gives Edinburgh the power to schedule content from their web-based Content Management System to digital signage, web and desktop video players, a library app and to social media channels.

SOLUS, a member of the Capita Partner Programme, provides Edinburgh with a unique digital communications capability and helps maximise efficiency in a market where cost saving and best value is critical. Jim Thompson, Edinburgh's Development and Quality Manager, stated, "The premise behind SOLUS is the ability to create once and schedule many. SOLUS allows us to use one system to upload a promotional video file to our digital signage network, make it available to view across our desktops, embed it into our web portal and intranet, schedule it to our mobile app and distribute it automatically to all our social media channels."

SOLUS has also fully integrated with the Capita LMS to provide functionality for "Your Library App" and this has enabled additional benefits. Most recently added and most popular stock can now be automatically promoted across other platforms managed by SOLUS, such as digital signage and social media. Neil Wishart, Director of SOLUS, was recently at Downing Street, discussing the potential of "Your Library App" with Nick Jones, Director of Digital Communications for No. 10 and The Cabinet Office. Following the meeting Neil commented:

> "One of the key requirements for government at all levels is to engage more efficiently and effectively with citizens. The digital citizen is

real and their dependency on technology is increasing. Rather than being a threat, it provides libraries with the biggest opportunity in a generation to engage with new users in increasing numbers. At the same time, it will let them do this more efficiently and effectively. For the citizen, libraries can offer easy and immediate access to services that can save them money. If people are cutting back due to their personal budgets being squeezed, libraries can take advantage."

To take advantage, access must be 24/7, slick and with instant gratification. V2 of Edinburgh's Library App will allow users to scan a barcode in a shop and automatically search the library catalogue. This is already reality - the recently launched Haringey Library App, which is powered by SOLUS, allows users to scan, search and reserve within seconds. If they don't know how to get to the reserved item, the app will take them there and if an Ebook is available, users can get that instant gratification!

Of course, the proof is in the pudding and Liz McGettigan has solid evidence to prove this innovative use of technology is working. In the last year digital visits have increased by 135,000, PC usage is up by 145,000 sessions, attendance at events has increased, up 32 per cent, and significantly, the decline in physical visits has been reversed with an extra 30,000 people attending libraries. Wishart stated, "It's a classic case of inbound marketing, where effective online positioning has a direct impact on offline behaviour. It's fantastic for Liz to be able to report back to her stakeholders that she has improved access to services and achieved a direct return on investment, both in relation to time and money."

What's next? Creating an app, using social media and installing a digital signage network are all great foundations, but maximum uptake can only be ensured through effective ongoing promotion. The next step in the partnership between Edinburgh Libraries and SOLUS is to develop a range of collaterals to shout about libraries. Liz commented, "There is no point in having the world's best kept secret, we want as many physical and digital users as we can possibly attract. We are actively working on materials with SOLUS to promote our App and these will be resources that can be shared with other libraries across the UK. There is no point replicating spend - if we can all make further efficiency savings and at the same time develop really exciting material, it benefits the whole library community."

Libraries now lead the way in Edinburgh, with other departments continually looking to implement their successful strategy.

7

Library Information System and Information Technology

INTRODUCTION

In library information system, information technology has had a clear and persuasive impact in almost every area of the library. The most significant development in information technology over the last few years or so is digital technology. Digital technology is revolutionizing the traditional concepts of preservation and access in library and archive communities. The applications of digital system and computing system in the libraries have been a subject of interest to present day professional librarians.

More recently the libraries have sought to implement increasingly complex solution that involved distributed networking and access to remote information resources. During the eighties, the whole focus of the librarians shifted towards library automation but in the nineties it has shifted towards digitization. The phrase library automation has been generally accepted within the profession to encompass early automation activities, yet it does not do justice to the current state of affaires as libraries have move well beyond the automation of internal procedures. In Manipur, however, applications of technologies in libraries are lagging far behind.

There are two university libraries, 74 affiliated colleges, nine public libraries, one state central library at Imphal and others at different districts of Manipur and many high and higher secondary schools libraries. But most of the libraries function in the traditional way with conventional printed shelf collection except some libraries like Manipur University library, Central Agricultural Library, RIMS Library, DOEACC Library etc. These libraries have initiated automation. Manipur University Library started automation since 1989 in the areas such as cataloguing, serial control, information retrieval and circulation recently.

This library provides internet facility, OPAC and has become one of the important nodes in the academic libraries system. As far as college libraries are concerned collections of information resources which support the faculty and students are not up to the mark because of lack planned systematic approach to the development of resources. Many of college libraries built up their collection of printed materials as activities and services are yet to be automated. Only one college library *i.e.* Modern College library has started Data entry using CDS/ISIS.

Books are still the only important channel for dissemi-nation of information. The librarian and other supporting professional staff are not well qualified and trained with the new modern technology. As far as infrastructures are concern a large majority of libraries have not yet automated their activities as they are handicapped to switch over to computeri-zation and modernization because of lack of infrastructural facilities like computer hardware, software, and human-ware. And most of the libraries are not provided internet facility.

Regarding school and higher secondary school libraries, majority of school libraries are not able to provide even the facilities of a traditional library. From the discussion it is evident that the libraries in Manipur, except some, automation of the operations and services progressing very slowly. Automation as well as conversion of digital library will not be possible within five year though plan for automation exist. In Manipur it is not an easy task to develop digital library system as automation in the library is totally absent. Keeping in views of the reasons, authority should take initiative for promoting library automation by implementing new IT in the libraries of Manipur so that users from different communities can get the universe of knowledge available in the digital format.

PROBLEMS OF DIGITAL LIBRARIES SYSTEMS

Problems faced while entering into a digital libraries systems in Manipur can be summarized as:

- Libraries exist only in the traditional form and there is no electronic library/digital resource;
- Most of the libraries function with inadequate number professional staff required for smooth functioning and there is a general unwillingness to develop digital library system;
- Even if the librarian and some professionals are qualified they certainly lag behind because of lack of awareness about value of information, cooperation and coordination in the resource building and sharing of information and poor communication skill;
- Total absence of hardware, software and trained human power is another reason;
- A highly irregular and unpredictable power supply; and
- Libraries lack standardization of methods due to unwillingness to adapt to new requirements;
- Presently large majority of library have no computer and no internet facility and other infrastructural facilities required to exploit the

opportunities provided by electronic media. Therefore, the best use of electronic publication on-line and network access are not possible;

- Lack of financial support due to the acute financial problem the state is facing.

In fact, the main problems faced seem to be lack of financial resources and lack of computer education without which automation in the libraries are not possible.

PROSPECT OF INFORMATION REVOLUTION

The dawn of information revolution is considered to be one of the marvelous achievements of the 20th century. The rapid growth and development of IT has resulted in the development of digital library, tools and skill relating to encoding information objects in digital format. The application of digital technologies within the library comes along with the development of computer technology. Keeping the points in view it is necessary to consider some perspective of digital library. Digital library not only creates and develops modern libraries but also transforms many existing libraries.

Digital Library introduced the concept of hypertext, facilitates networking in order to communicate and exchange digital information from source location to destination. It also facilitates preservation, storage, and communication of diverse multimedia objects but also provides intensive access from multiple locations and enrich teaching and learning environment which is not possible with the traditional library. Due to information explosion and existence of information society, everybody is aware of the newly developed technologies. This new developments are reflected in LIS education and in those libraries with existing infrastructure, services and network. In fact, there is a complete change in activities, role of library, librarians and other professionals (staff).

Most of the librarians in Manipur have now entered in the technological era of communication dominated by film and electronic media. The libraries are expected to be an automated information system having pervasive impact in almost every areas of library-be it the online catalogue, online database, online searching, document delivery, inter library loan, circulation etc. Clearly, the impact of automated system in libraries has been pervasive and significant.

INFORMATION EXPLOSION AND THE DIRECT RELATION OF INFORMATION TO DEVELOPMENTS

The present information explosion and the direct relation of information to developments in all walks of life emphasizes the need to give greater priority to the planning of systems which give library and information services to the people. Such systems can only be planned at national levels, if the total information resources of the nation is to be pooled together in a federal country like India, and shared between the cons-tituent states to make it available to all the users who require it in an equally and unbiased way at optimal cost.

Such library and information systems are to be founded upon sound legislation, if they are to attain their objectives the Society's information need has become so imperative that, many of the national and international library organizations has started to stress the urgent need for national library systems working together and sharing their services and materials at international level to provide better services to the people. Better can be defined here in quantitative and qualitative terms. Such national level and international level networking and resource sharing between library systems make possible service at lower cost, convenience of access, access to more materials and more rapid availability of materials.

PREAMBLE OF STATE ACTS

The preamble of a Library Act should summarise and state the aims and objectives of that Library Act. Even though the preamble of KPLA went on to explain the existing situations and the intentions with which the Act was initiated in an elaborate and vague form, it has given what is to be in preamble just before the preamble in precise and clear words as a long title ofthe Act. This summary or long title of the Act which we have to consider as preamble contains the basic concept of modern public library service which the actual preamble failed to state and the KPLA in its totality failed to support.

Like the Model Act, this summary provides for the establishment and maintenance of a system of public libraries and for the comprehensive development and organisation of all kinds of library and information services required for the people. The long title that follows the title of the Act in KPLA states, it is: An Act to consolidate and unify the library laws in the State and to provide for the reorganisation of the entire library system in the State of Kerala with a view to the develop-ment and maintenance of a comprehensive rural and urban library service and for matters connected therewith or incidental thereto.

Ranganathan has laid clear emphasis on legislation for public library service and for the organisation of a comprehensive library system. But all other Acts except KPLA provides for establishment and maintenance of public libraries only. They all cling to the obsolete concept of treating public libraries as independent units in their collection and services. So in this statement of the purpose of the Act, KPLA has accepted the most modern concept of Public Library legislation and the statement is a distinct improvement over those in all other existing State Acts.

THE MODEL ACT OF S.R. RANGANATHAN

To attain these objectives Dr. S.R. Ranganathan had framed the first model public libraries Act in 1930 which he placed for discussion at the Educational

Conference at Banaras. Before framing the Act, this internationally reputed library scientist had travelled through most countries of the world where library legislation existed and had evaluated them and in many countries his ideas helped them to improve the systems.

In his Library Development Plan which he submitted in 1947 to Government of India he had included a union library bill and a revised state library bill also which envisaged the national public library and information system according to the most modern principles. Another model library Act was drafted in 1963 by a committee under the chairmanship of D.M. Sen on behalf of the Ministry of Education, Government of India. In 1966 the Library Legislation Sub Committee of the Planning Commission also prepared a model bill. The library Acts that came into existence in Madras, Hyderabad, Andhra, Karnataka and Maharastra totally or partially accept the ideas of Rang ana than as reflected in his Model Acts and bills. These States became the laboratories where the ideas evolved by Ranganathan were experimented and observed.

In the light of these observations and suggestions contained in the other model bills and Acts, Ranganathan has improved his model Act by rectifying the clauses found to be defective in working and by adding new provisions that seemed essential. This model libraries Act was published in 1972. This is the latest and most advanced Model Act. Ten States out of the 25 States and 7 union territories have enacted library legislation. They are Madras 1948, Andhra 1960, Karnataka 1965, Maharastra 1967, West Bengal 1979, Manipur 1985, Kerala 1989 and Haryana 1989.

Others are Goa and Mizoram. But none of them are considered perfect or efficient. So in this comparative analysis of the essential aspects of State Public Library Acts, the Model Public Library Act, 1972 of Dr. S.R. Ranganathan is taken as the measuring rod or ideal situation with which the State Act is compared. Whenever some notable additional provisions or improvements are found in other existing Acts the same is discussed at the concerned contexts. The Kerala Act to which stress is given in this study and Ranganathan's Model Act of 1972 will be referred herein after as KPLA and Model Act respectively.

PURPOSE AND ADVISING OF STATE LIBRARY COMMITTEE

The Model Act provides for a *State Library Committee* (SLC) for the purpose of advising the SLA on all matters arising under the Act. All existing State Acts and Model Bills enacted or drafted in India provide for appointment of such a Committee or Council. KPLA names it as Kerala State Library Council. All Acts of the states except Kerala's have prescribed its membership on somewhat similar lines. All Acts provides that this body will be headed by Minister for Education. Despite differences in nomenclature and composition the function of this committee or council envisaged everywhere is basically the same *i.e.,* to advise the SLA or State Government in all matters arising out of the Act.

Kerala State Library Council (KSLC)

A careful analysis of the Kerala State Library Council (KSLC) in comparison with the SLC as provided in the Model Act or other State Acts will reveal that it is not a councilor committee of advisory nature as SLCs are. KSLC is an SLC and at the same time an SLA by itself. Naming it as a council is a difference in terminology only. Instead of appointing a Minister as SLA as in Mysore it appoints a body as SLA. But the Act fails to name it as SLA. The duties, powers and functions assigned to KSLC is inclusive of all those assigned to SLA and SLC in Model Act.

Sub-section 1 of the Section 3 of KPLA dealing with the constitution and composition of KSLC states9; KSLC shall be a body corporate having perpetual succession and a common seal with power, to acquire hold and dispose of property, both movable and immovable and to enter into contracts and shall by its name sue and be sued. This is an adaptation of the class related to Karnataka State Library Authority of Karnataka Act. No other Act including Model Act has so clearly defined the nature of this body and assigned so much powers as this like the Acts of Kerala and Karnataka. The powers and functions assigned to KSLC includes both the advisory functions of the committees and councils provided by Model Act and other Acts and the duties assigned to SLA by Model Act and Karnataka Act.

Sub-sections of section 8 of KPLA provides that the KSLC may:

- Advise the government of all matters connected with the administration of that Act and . . . the overall library policy of the State.
- Co-ordinate the working of the District Library Councils and Taluk Library Unions and...supervise and direct all matters relating to library service in the state.
- Establish one or more State Libraries . . . at such place or places in the State as may be considered necessary.
- Appoint and control such officers and servants as may be necessary for the efficient performance of its duties and functions under this Act and the rules made there under.
- Give to the District Library Councils and Taluk Library unions directions in the performance of their functions under this Act and . . . they shall not in-the discharge of their functions under this Act depart from directions given by the KSLC.

While we consider these classes and compare them with the parellel sections of the Model Act or other Acts it becomes clear that the classes which assigns the duties, powers and functions of KSLC is a distinct improvement from all others. KPLA has identified most of the functions and duties expected from such a body and very clearly assigned them to it without giving space for doubt and vagueness.

Composition of KSLC

If KSLC is to become able to fulfil such duties and functions expected from it, the composition of the body should be done accordingly. Membership of such a body should include persons who have contributed to the growth of knowledge, who has evolved or developed methods and techniques for collecting, organising and disseminating information and who have wide experience in related fields of activity. It is not the method of representation but the quality of representation that will make possible the efficient functioning of the system.

The sections which prescribe the membership of SLA in Karnataka Act and SLC in Model Act and other State Acts prescribe their membership on somewhat similar lines. Prof. P.B. Mangla in his study of library legislation opines that it should be a body having representatives from various institutions, organisations, government etc. interested in and connected with the growth and development of library and information services in the State.

The Model Act, the opinion of experts and recommen-dations of committees set for studying library legislation agrees that such a body should include among its members; the Minister for Libraries if there is one, otherwise Minister for Education, then Minister in charge of Local-Self-Government, Director of Libraries, State Librarian, sufficient number of representatives from State Legislative Assembly by election from among themselves, Secretary to Government for Education, representatives elected from Local Library Authorities by rotation to limit size of the body, representatives of associations of library profession and experts with specialization in library and information services and represen-tatives of Universities of the State.

It would be essential that the Minister in charge of Libraries should act as *ex-officio* chairman and the Director of Public Libraries or State Librarian should act as ex-officio secretary of the committee.

The rationale behind such a composition of this body is that it is a body which is to advise the government and discuss continuously on a most important responsibility of the government, that is organisation and dissemination of information required by the society. But disregarding all these principles KPLA provides for constituting a body of members who were not suitable to undertake this work.

The section 3 sub-section (2) related to the composition of the KSLC in KPLA provides: The KSLC shall consist of one member each from Taluks, elected by the general body of the District Library councils, and five members of whom one shall be a librarian, another a person belonging to the scheduled caste or scheduled tribe and another a woman nominated by the government. Library and information service is an intellectual service. It goes without saying that this body as provided in KPLA will not be able to fulfil satisfactorily the purpose for which it is intended.

In these days of information explosion and flooding of vast and varied types of books and other printed materials that originates every minute without wide familiarity of all spheres of knowledge and expertise in handling their information in most effective way at minimum cost the body which heads such a system will be having a mere formal and useless existence. As we have seen in section 8 of KPLA the most important function of KSLC is to advise the government on all matters connected with the administration of this Act and overall library policy ofthe State.

It is not clear how this committee will be competent to render such expert technical advise when it has only persons as members, who has come through election without expertise or knowledge about information work and without even any educational qualifications. Library and information service to the people if provided efficiently will be the continuously active service of government and will require expert advise everyday on many matters.

The KSLC's inability to provide such expert advise will make government's efforts futile and to overcome this, govern-ment will be forced to create a continuous chain of Advisory Committees which is also not very practicable. While no hard and fast rule can be laid down about the size of this body it is generally felt that it should not have more than twenty members. The KSLC may remain a supreme body in name only for real powers of the council have been passed over to a smaller body which is the executive committee. But it also becomes an unwieldy body with membership of 25 persons.

Thus KSLC has acquired all the defects existing in SLAs and SLCs into one body. This Executive Committee is a new addition in our library Acts. But the findings of Ashok Mehta Committee and various committees appointed by many State Governments to study Panchayat Raj Institutions advise us against such an elected body like KSLC for organising important service as library and information service to the people. Instead of adopting the constitution and composition of SLA and SLC provided by the Model Act or followed by the other State Acts KPLA gave legal sanction to the organi-zational set up of an association that was already existing there, that is Kerala Granthasala Sangham.

The constitution and composition of KSLC and its Executive Committee is the same followed by Sangham for its general body and Bharanasamithi. In all other provisions KPLA follows the same pattern of Sangham with some minor alterations. For more than half a century Sangham was pressurizing the Government to give legal sanction to Sangham to be the SLA and to accept its system as it is,as State's Library System.

But experts have continuously pointed out during this period the futility of such a system for library and information service. But Sangham objected government's all other attempts to enact a modern library system legislation and at last come out successful in legalizing its own system. But this in fact totally prevents the State from having an advanced library legislation and developing its library and information services in conformity with the requirements of the time.

CONCEPT OF THE STATE LIBRARY AUTHORITY

The concept of the *State Library Authority* (SLA) underwent an evolution from State Library Committee to Minister of Education or Libraries; everywhere in the world. The Model Act recommends that for the purpose of promoting and organising a library system in the State the Ministry for Education of the State shall be the SLA.

It shall be the duty of the SLA to provide; for an adequate library and information service in the State and, for the progressive development of the institutions devoted to the purpose and to secure the effective execution by *Local Library Authorities* (LLA) of the national policy for providing adequate library service to the people in every locality. In the existing' State Acts only Karnataka Public Library Act, 1965 provides and clearly names SLA.

The Act provides for the constitution and composition of the SLA.6 SLA shall be a body corporate having perpetual succession and a common seal with power, to acquire, hold and dispose of property and to contract and may by the same time sue and be sued. It consists of twenty members from the fields concerned with information creation, organisation and services, with Minister for Education who shall ex officio be the President and State Librarian who shall ex officio be the Secretary of SLA. But it is desirable to make only one person, instead of a corporate body to be the supreme authority for providing this very important service, for that gives a unified command from administrative points of view.

And this person should not be any person less than the Minister for Education, because he is directly responsible to the legislature and his term of office being limited to a period of five years he is ultimately responsible to the people. Hewit who made a study of the library legislation in India; it will be observed that two kinds of supreme authority are favoured in existing legislation and in the drafts of the model bills framed in India. One is a body of persons *i.e.,*

State Library Councilor Committee and second is a Minister of State. He suggests the second as the better of the two, mainly because a Minister is responsible to his legislature, and through it, to the electors and many be called to account therein. A body of persons even though a Minister may be President or Chairman thereof is not so easily questioned.

In any case; so important an activity as the provision for public library and information service to the people fully justifies direct representation in State Legislature. So all the studies on library legislations and the evaluation of existing legislations throughout the world and especially in third world counties, like that of Gardners's study comes to the conclusion that providing up of a body or a person as SLA and clearly naming and defining its powers and functions is certainly essential for the successful working of library Acts. But KPLA is very vague in this aspect and it fails to name a person or body as SLA.

DEPARTMENT OF PUBLIC LIBRARIES AND OFFICIALS

It is generally emphasized that in order to develop a system of public libraries in a State or country on proper lines, it is essential that a separate department of public libraries be created at par with the department of education and that the former should not be a part of the later or any other' department. The Acts of Andhra, Maharashtra, West Bengal and Karnataka prescribe for the creation of separate department of Public Libraries.

Director of Public Libraries

Most of the recommendations related to public library system legislation emphasizes that the department of Public Libraries should be headed by a Director of Public Libraries (DPL), whose rank must be equivalent to that of Director of Education. He must be a person with qualification and experience in Library and Information Science. Emphasis on his being a professional is laid because it is he to whom the whole public library system in the State would look for guidance and inspiration and his professional outlook would normally greatly help the development of the system on desired lines.

The first public library Act in this country; the Madras Public Library Act, 1948 provided for the appointment of DPL. Andhra, Maharastra and West Bengal also prescribes for the creation of DPL. In Madras and Andhra the Director of Public Instruction is made the ex-officio Director of Public Libraries also.

The disadvantages of such an administrative set-up are quite obvious. The Department of Public Libraries becomes an additional burden to the Director of Public Instruction. This new department will be looked upon as an uninvited guest. A. R. Hewit has rightly pointed out that many of the duties of Director of Public Libraries would require technical knowledge and skill in librarianship. So professional experts only can undertake this responsibility efficiently.

State Library

All the Acts except KPLA which is not providing for these offices, combines the responsibilities of developing and managing the State Central Library Superintending and directing all matters related to the State library system in a single person called State Librarian or DPL.

The Model Act also recommends this pattern. But the Sinha Committee report suggested the creation of two separate posts for this purpose when it said "The DPL may have the overall responsibility to organize develop and supervise the public library system as the Head of the Department of Public Libraries.

The State Librarian should have the responsibility to manage supervise and develop State Central Library and should be the Chief Technical Advisor of the DPL, with no responsibility for the administration of the service in the State. This responsibility should be entirely that of DPL. But in KPLA there is no provision for appointing a Director of Libraries or State Librarian. While the class by class discussion of the Bill was going on in Assembly Mr. V.M. Sudheeran; member presented an amendment to add a new clause in the Act providing for appointment of a Director of Libraries. But was not considered.

Administration

For the administration of public libraries all the State Acts have created a department or directorate of public libraries. It is put under the charge of Director of Libraries or State Librarian who is to be the *ex-officio* Secretary of SLA. The functions of these posts as prescribed by all Acts including the Model Act are: to supervise and direct all matters relating to public libraries, to direct and control the working of LLAs, submit reports to Government and deal with schemes and plans relating to libraries. Many of the highly technical and specialized works of State Central Library also is to be supervised by them.

So it is clear that these posts which are carrying heavy responsibility concerning various matters-financial, advisory, administrative, technical, supervisory and so on-under the Act would require technical knowledge and skill in library and information service. So the Secretary or High Officer of this body should be a whole time officer having the prescribed qualifications to practice the library profession. Disregarding all the facts KPLA assigns all these duties and powers to a Secretary elected by members of the Executive Committee ofKSLC.

Section 3 sub-section (5) of KPLA provides that the elected members of the Executive Committee shall elect a President, Vice-President, Secretary and Joint Secretary from among themselves to be the President, Vice-President, Secretary and Joint Secretary respectively of the State Library Council and of the Executive Committee. Their term of office will be for three years.

KPLA assigns to the Secretary of KSLC the duties and powers which other State Acts assign to State Librarian or Director of Libraries. Section 9 Sub-section (1) States: the Secretary of the State Library Council shall be Chief Executive Authority of KSLC.

The nature of the office of Secretary of KSLC requires professional knowledge and experience as well as continuity of office for the successful operation of the Act, so it is inevitable that this provision will prevent KPLA from fulfilling the objectives for which a modern library legislation should exist. This serious defect of the Act has been pointed out by many members during the discussion of the bill.

Dr. M.Kuttappan has brought to the notice of the Assembly that such an important system like that for library and information service requires qualified government officials as their secretaries at State, District and Taluk levels. The period of an elected non-official member may be over by three years and if he misappropriates government fund allotted for library development it will not be possible for the government to take action on him. Sri Ishac Kurikkal suggested an amend-ment to the Bill to provide that the Secretary of the SLC shall be appointed by the Government on the advice of the Kerala Public Service Commission.

Another member Sri Kodiyeri Balakrishnan opined that the Secretary of KSLC should be appointed by Government and the Act should specify the qualifications and method of appointment for this post. Sri Ramesh Chennitthala presented an amendment to add the following sub-clause in KPLA namely: The Secretary shall be a person not below the rank of a Joint Secretary to Government appointed by Government from among persons qualified and competent to hold such post. But all these suggestions were rejected and principles were disregarded to maintain a democratic system for constituting the SLA.

Library Co-operation

To make the best possible use of the document resources not only in the public library system but also in other types of libraries in the State such as universities, special libraries etc, a system of inter library co-operation needs to be developed in the state as a whole. It would also be useful and economical if centralization of different aspects such as acquisition programme, technical processing etc. of documents should be introduced at State level or at different levels of the system. The KPLA gives no such provision for co-operation or centralized processing and the institution which is to give leadership in such activities that is SCL is absent in KPLA.

State Central Library

The existing State legislations and the Model Act provide for a State Central Library (SCL) as an integral part of the Public Library Service. The SCL is normally the copy right collection. It should collect as far as its resources allow, expensive work and literature published abroad, material for which the local public library would have little need and could not afford. All the countries of the world possessing adequate library systems, have national library systems and all have national central library as distinct from the other libraries in the system, but is accessible to all through any library of the system.

The same role of National Central Library to the National system is done by SCL to the State system. Usually the library legislations designate the biggest collection available in the State as SCL and makes its resources and services available to the system. Even though various Acts and Model Act give different names to SCL like State Service Library, etc. in a public library system only one such library will be maintained and its resources will be shared by all participating units. Maintaining more than one SCL is unnecessary duplication of work and waste of resources.

Most of the State Acts and Model bills drafted, designate the biggest public library existing in the State as SCL and adopts it to the system and shares its resources among participating units. But instead of designating Trivandrum Public Library, the oldest and biggest collection in the State as SCL, the KPLA deems it to be one of the many State libraries it will establish.

The Act provides for no SCL in its system. Instead it provides that KSLC shall establish one or more state libraries at such place or places in the State as may be considered necessary. The relation of State libraries with other state libraries and different level service units and the purpose of more than one such institution is not defined in the Act.

State Library Service

State Library Service brings the manpower of the State in one pool and thus avoids the waste of time and money involved in filling up posts that would otherwise involve, if every Local Library Authority were to appoint the staff independently. A State Library Service further avoids the influence of members of the Local Library Authority in day-to-day management of libraries. Mysore Act has created a special state library service and it ensures proper administration and economy through State Library Service. But KPLA gives to KSLC and Local Library Authorities that is DLC and TLU the powers to appoint and control required officers and servants.

INFORMATION STORAGE, ORGANISATION, AND RETRIEVAL

The purpose of this chapter is to focus briefly on basic concepts of the field of 'storage and retrieval' that seem particularly relevant to pro-cognitive systems. Some of the ideas of this field have already been mentioned in our example in which documents were retrieved with the aid of descriptors and a thesaurus. We have also illustrated applications of passage-retrieval and question-answering techniques - techniques that penetrate the covers of documents and deal with sentences and paragraphs or -with 'ideas' and 'facts.' Let us now examine those and related techniques a bit more systematically.

The basic unit of knowledge appropriate to our purposes may well be akin to the 'idea' of popular and sometime philosophical usage, but we shall not try to exploit that possibility because 'idea' is discouragingly nebulous. Alternatively, the basic unit may be closely related to the mathematical concept of 'function,' or to the logical concept of 'relation' that figured centrally in our earlier discussion of relevance networks. Again alternatively, the logical systems of predicate calculus, particularly the so-called higher-order predicate calculi, offer formalisms for the expression of complex attributes and attributions. Some of these systems not only provide implement able procedures for deduction but also have the advantage of being well developed and thoroughly tested. Finally, there is the apparatus of linguistics, with several syntactic categories and myriad rules of grammar. Despite the ready availability of the foregoing concepts, most of the work that has been done in the field of information storage, organisation, and retrieval has been based on the simplest of ideas about sets. The next most popular schema, if we count implicit as well as explicit application, has been geometric space. We may organise our examinations of this area, therefore, by considering storage, organisation, and retrieval systems based on the following models:

- Sets and subsets,
- Space analogues,
- Functions and relations,
- Predicate calculus, and
- Other formal languages.

SYSTEMS BASED ON SETS AND SUBSETS

In most systems based on the ideas of sets and subsets, the fundamental concepts are set, partition, item, name, term, prescription, storer, organiser, and retriever, and the logical connectives. Although details of the concepts and the names used in referring to the concepts vary considerably from system to system, the same fundamental ideas appear repeatedly. The items are the things to be stored and retrieved: documents, facts, and so forth. There is a set of items. Each item mayor may not have a name. Terms are associated with items by being written, usually by storers, on the items themselves or on tags or cards associated with the items. Prescriptions are made up mainly of terms and are usually written by retrievers. For each system, there is a rule that determines whether the terms associated with.a given document sufficiently match those of a given prescription. The rule and the mechanism for implementing it are devised by organisers. The object of retrieval, in systems based on sets and subsets, is to partition the set of items in such a way as to separate the items a retriever desires from those he does not desire. In order to establish a perspective, let us examine briefly, and somewhat abstractly, some familiar retrieval schemes.

PARTITIONING BY NAMING

The very simplest retrieval method achieves the partition by naming the elements of the desired subset. That method is not applicable to such items as sentences and facts that do not have names. Moreover, when the retriever does not know the names of the items he desires, the method does not work even with those items that do have names, such as books and journal articles. Nevertheless, the method and the location-coded cards often used in implementing it are simple and widely used.

HIERARCHICAL INDEXING

If the items have no names, or if the names of desired items are unknown to the retriever, it is necessary to fall back on the use of descriptive terms to specify the desired items. In most term-based systems, either it is assumed that the retriever knows the terms, or glossaries or thesauri listing the legal terms of the system are provided. In a hierarchical system, first the over-all set of items is partitioned by organisers into mutually exclusive and exhaustive first-echelon subsets or categories, and a unique term is assigned to each. Then each first-echelon subset is partitioned into mutually exclusive and exhaustive second-echelon subsets or categories, and a unique term is assigned to each of them.

This process of subdivision is continued until there are as many echelons as can be handled conveniently or until there are only a few items in each subset of the lowest echelon. The retriever in this system merely composes a prescription consisting of one term for each echelon. He makes his way down the branching, root like structure of the hierarchy, selecting first the first-echelon subset corresponding to the first-echelon term of his prescription, then the second-echelon subset corresponding to the second-echelon term of his prescription, and so forth. When he gets to the bottom, or to a level at which there are not too many items, he examines the items of the subset he has isolated. In practice, the main trouble with this scheme is a trouble inherent in all serial-decision methods: one mistake anywhere in the series, and the game is lost! Perhaps a more basic difficulty is that knowledge does not seem to be naturally susceptible to hierarchical analysis. For these reasons, storage and retrieval systems that set out to be hierarchical often turn into lat- ticelike systems through non-exclusive categorisation and cross referencing.

COORDINATE INDEXING

The difficulties just men]tioned can be avoided by giving up the notion of precedence that orders the hierarchy. Without precedence, all the subsets and all the terms are coordinate. In coordinate indexing systems, the organisers partition the set of items in various premeditated ways and assign a term, not to each subset, but to each partition. The term itself identifies one of the two subsets separated by the partition - usually the smaller one. The retriever then draws up a prescription consisting of terms joined by logical connectives. Often the logical 'and' is the only connective employed. In some systems, use is made also of 'or' and 'not.' The mechanism that fulfills the prescription has to find and deliver the subset of items corresponding to the logical expression. Given, for example, the prescription:

the mechanism would retrieve the items characterised by *A* and those characterised by both *Band* C, and, in addition, those characterised by D but not by *E*. Many commercial and government systems are based on coordinate indexing: *e.g.*, most edge-notched-card systems, the PeekA- Boo Card system, and the descriptor system of the Defence Documentation Center.

INVERSE FILING

The 'natural' or 'first-thought' way to set up a coordinate- indexing system with cards is to assign a card to each item and then to record the terms applicable to the item on the card. Second thought, however, may lead to the opposite procedure: assign a card to each term, and record on each card the names or codes of all the items to which the term applies. A file organised the second way is an 'inverse' file. Its main advantage is that, since ordinarily there are more items than terms, it requires fewer cards. In the Peek-A-Boo system, each card is divided into many small areas, one for each actual or anticipated item, and an item is associated with a term by punching out the item's area, thus leaving a hole, in the card for the term. When the desired term cards are piled, one on top of another, to form a deck, and are held up to the light, one sees light through the entire deck at the location for each item to which all the terms apply. This is, of course, merely one of several convenient implementations of the logical 'and.' It illustrates the natural congruence that exists between punched cards and Boolean algebra.

HYBRID SYSTEMS

Because knowledge has a more complex structure than coordinate indexing can mirror, and still is less perfectly hierarchical than systems based on root like branching and exclusive categories must postulate, there have been several efforts to develop hybrid systems that would combine the advantages and avoid the disadvantages of hierarchical and coordinate indexing.

One such approach is to employ only a very few echelons of hierarchy and to use coordinate indexing within each echelon. Another is to build a quasi-syntactic structure upon the coordinate index base by assigning role indicators to the terms. One may distinguish between R_1, wax made by bees, and R_2, bees made of wax, for example, by establishing an *ad hoc* two-echelon hierarchy:

- Product,
- Source or constituent.

In that case we have:

Alternatively, one can define the role indicators: P = product, S = source, C = constituent. In that case we have:

It seems unlikely, however, that such circumventions will lead to highly sophisticated or truly elegant storage and retrieval systems. The fundamental trouble seems to be that elementary set notation and Boolean algebra are inadequate to express compactly the subtle distinctions and intricate relations involved in a sophisticated representation and organisation of the body of knowledge. In saying that, however, one should be sure to acknowledge that storage and retrieval systems based on sets and subsets have a particularly strong congruence with present-day information-processing technology and that, despite their limitations in sophisticated applications, they seem to be capable of achieving a high level of effectiveness in document retrieval and even in the retrieval of relevant passages within documents.

That is to say, their shortcomings seem likely not to manifest themselves strongly until an effort is made to deduce or infer consequences from the stored representation of knowledge.

SPACE ANALOGUES

The basic notion of topological space analogy is that one item is the 'neighbour' of another item to which it is closely related. Metric space analogy involves the notion of distance in addition to the notion of neighbourhood: two items may be close together or far apart, and the distance between them may be analysed into *n* components corresponding to the *n* dimensions of the space. Metric space analogy is to some extent implicit in the many information-retrieval studies that have used product- moment correlation, multifactor analysis, and related 'linear' methods. However, those studies have not emphasised the space concept, and they have led to little or no consensus even about the dimensionality, much less about the identities of the dimensions, of any such thing as 'information space' or 'semantic space' or 'the space of knowledge.' Doubtless the most literal application of the space concept has been Osgood's 'semantic differential,' based on factor analysis of many human scaling judgements relating linguistic 'objects' to named attributive scales. Osgood and his colleagues have shown, for example, that the same half-dozen basic factors appear in almost all human judgements, and that the fundamental affective dimensions are almost the same the world over - in 16 different ethno linguistic contexts. One can see a possibility of relating Osgood's kind of semantic space to the space in which Swanson has determined correlations among the occurrences of descriptive terms and to the space in which Giuliano has determined correlations of the contexts in which descriptive terms occur.

However, that possibility has not been developed. There has been much use of methods that assume linearity of the basic variables, but not much explicit discussion of geometric space as a milieu for the representation of knowledge or intellectual processes. Much of our knowledge deals with the physical world, however, and must be indexed to the physical dimensions of space and time. Place names are in a sense merely spatial coordinates, and linguistic tense has its roots in physical time. It seems difficult, therefore, to conceive of a representation of knowledge within which a geometric framework does not playa major role. How can the attractiveness of the space analogy be reconciled with the obvious merits of logical and linguistic schemata that involve neither geometry nor continuous variables? The most promising approach, it seems to us, is to accept the notion that, for many years at least, we shall not achieve a complete integration of knowledge, that we shall have to content ourselves with diverse partial models of the universe.

It may not be elegant to base some of the models in geometry, some in logic, and others in natural language, but that may be the most practicable solution.

FUNCTIONS AND RELATIONS

Williams, Barnes, and Kuipers have described an approach to document retrieval based on analysis of natural-language expressions in terms of arguments and functions. In our study, a similar approach was developed in terms of relations.

Functions and relations appear to cover very nearly the same ground. If z is a function F of x and y, which we may write $z = F(x, y)$, the n there is a relation R among x, y, and z, and we may write it $R(x, y, z)$. A relation may have any number of arguments. If it has one argument, it is merely an attribute or property. It seems reasonable to say that a single relation, say, $R_{10}(a, b, c, d..., t)$, might subsume all the interactions described in a long sentence.

The following discussion involves a long example based on a sentence of medium length. The example leads to the statement of a problem and an expression of belief, but not to a solution or a method. Earlier in this report there appears the sentence: 'They will comprise the echelons of the memory hierarchy we have mentioned.' If a pro-cognitive system were to try to make sense of that sentence, it would first have to determine the referents of the pronouns. Let us suppose that it is able to figure out that 'they' refers to computer memories that embody various compromises between small-and-fast and large-and- slow, and that 'we' refers to the participants in the study, or perhaps to the author together with the readers.

The sentence then amounts to the assertion that a complex relation exists among several entities:

- Computer
- The memories
- Time
- The echelons
- Memory
- The hierarchy
- The participants
- Comprising
- Mentioning

To take up the matter a small part at a time, in an intuitively guided sequence, we may note first that there is a component relation that is nothing more than a simple qualification of a part of something by associating with it the thing of which it is a part. Thus we have 'the computer memories,' a relation between *(a)* and *(b)* that we may represent as $R_{ll}(a, b)$.

In 'the memory hierarchy,' we have another qualification, but of a slightly different kind. The hierarchy is not part of the memory. Instead, the memory is part of the hierarchy, or at any rate memory is the stuff with which the hierarchical structure is filled. We may write *R121 (j, e),* using the common initial subscript to signify the similarity, the distinct second subscript to signify the difference, and the third subscript as a hedge against future complications. Next let us look at 'the echelons' and 'the hierarchy.' The echelons are abstract parts of the hierarchy. That relation we may call $R_{122}(f, d)$, indicating that it is similar to, and also that it is different from, $R_{121}(f, e)$.

We put the verbs at the end of the list because verbs seem so much like operators and so different from substantives. Nevertheless, let us represent the relation between 'time' and 'comprising' as $R_3(c, h)$, and the relation between 'time' and 'mentioning' as $R_4(c, \mathrm{i})$. We come now to larger parts of the over-all relation of the sentence. Let us consider 'the authors have mentioned,' and then let us consider 'the memory hierarchy the authors have mentioned.' The smaller segment is $R_5[g, R_4(c, i)]$. The larger, which must include some equivalent to the notion that the memory hierarchy is in the main clause whereas the rest is in a dependent clause, is $R_6\{R_{121}(f, e), R_5[g, R4(C, i)]\}$. The complex just constructed must mesh with 'the echelons of the memory hierarchy.' The two ideas have to fit together in such a way as to indicate that we are planning to move the train of thought forward with the echelons, but that we want to acknowledge that they are parts of a hierarchy, that the nature of the stuff of which the hierarchy is made is memory, and so forth. We may call the abstract meshing relation, together with its nuances, $R_7(X, y)$, and we may make it specific to the sentence in question by substituting the arguments:

$R_7(R_{122}(f, d), R_6\{R_{121}(f, e), R_5[g, R_4(C, \mathrm{OJ}\})$.

Finally, to wind up the example with one big step, we may express the relation among 'the computer memories,' 'comprising' (in the future), and all the rest that we have dealt with as: ₹$[R_{11}(a, b), R_3(c, h), R_7(R_{122}(f, d), R_6\{R_{121}(f, e), R_5[g, R_4(C, \mathrm{OJ}\})\mathrm{J}$. That formula reflects to some extent the order in which the parts were combined. Since certain other sequences of partial combination would have been equally defensible, it is clear that there are alternative formulas that are equivalent to the one developed. Now, although the foregoing discussion is ridiculous in several ways, it is instructive in one way and challenging in another. It is ridiculous in that the relational expressions generated are complex and inscrutable, whereas the sentence itself was fairly simple and fairly clear.

Unfortunately, it is probably ridiculous also in that we were able to set forth neither a taxonomy of relations nor an algorithm for simplifying the relational expressions. Nevertheless, the relational notation impresses us as much closer to an organisable, processible cognitive structure than is the sentence made of words. Note how much detail there turns out to be in a 12-word sentence. The relational notation makes the detail explicit and manipulable. It challenges us to develop taxonomies and simplification procedures. Chomsky's concept of transformational grammars offers a promising approach to both tasks. If Chomsky's methods were fully developed, one could transform any grammatical sentence into canonical form. Some of the information of the original sentence would then reside in a designation of the transformation that was applied, and some would reside in the canonical expression that resulted. On the average, of course, the canonical expression would be simpler and more straightforward than the original.

Even with some of the structural linguistic information factored out, much would remain in the canonical sentence. Some of that information would reside in the syntactic structure; more of it would reside on the non-syntactic facets of the relations among the elements. Indeed there appear to be at least some thousands of significantly different relations among things. It is not entirely clear that the number is finite, even if we make an engineering interpretation of 'significantly different.'

However, it seems somewhere between conceivable and likely that the myriad and diverse observed relations are compounded of a few dozen - perhaps a hundred - atomic relations, and that the great variety arises when the atoms are combined in ways reminiscent of organic chemistry. If it should turn out to be so, then relational analysis will almost surely be a powerful technique for use in the representation and organisation of knowledge. Our initial thoughts along the line of relational analysis were concerned with relational nets, an example of which.

The circles represent entities, relations, and properties. Entities, relations, and properties may participate in relations and have properties. The ultimate property is being a property. The 'input terminals' of relations are marked by black spots. Ordered terminals are identified by numbers. Interpretations of the diagram, such as 'John and Jim are brothers, and John is taller than Jim' and 'Jack has red hair,' are explained in the text. We hypothesise that, in a fully developed relevance net of this kind, the alphabetic labels can be erased without loss of any basic knowledge of the situation represented - *i.e.*, without loss of any information other than that rooted in arbitrary selection of unessential symbols.

Consider the circles labeled 'John' and 'Jim.' That they represent individuals is indicated by their connection by arrows to 'individual.' Individualism - being an individual- is a property, as is shown by the connection from 'individual' to 'property.' Being a property is also a 'property,' as is shown by the recursive arrow. John and Jim are both male, and they are siblings, therefore brothers. 'Sibling' is an 11-argument relation, and being an n-argument relation is a property. Every path ends at 'property. ' There are two 'sibling' circles, for one set of siblings uses up a circle, and Jack and Jill are siblings too. As is shown by the arrows from the two 'siblings' to 'same,' being a sibling is the same as being a sibling. 'Same' is an unordered, 11-argument relation, and 'unorderedness' and 'n-argumentness' are properties. 'Jack' and his 'hair' participate in a whole-part relation and also in a possessor-possessed relation. Both relations have two ordered arguments. The hair is red. Red is a colour. Red and colour are both properties.

Thus Jack has red hair. It is all extremely simple at each step, but there seems to be room for many steps. As the number of relations and properties grows, the lower-level labels that are not wholly arbitrary can be figured out more and more readily from the higher level labels. In a complete relational net, all the unarbitrary information resides in the structure; the labels are entirely superfluous. Relational nets are consequently very attractive as schemata for computer processing. During the last few months of the library study, Marill developed the idea of relational nets in the direction of a predicate calculus.

Marill and Raphael are now simulating net structures on a computer and developing programmes that will organise and simplify nets.

PREDICATE CALCULUS

Much of the research during the second year of the study was devoted to question-answering systems. The system constructed by Black, to be described briefly in Part II, was based on the representation of information in the form of statements in first-order predicate calculus. With the information in that form, and with the aid of computer programmes designed to process it, the computer could deduce from its information base answers to various questions stated in the formalism. We believe this to be a significant development. It demonstrates the advantage of employing a formalism that approaches the sophistication and complexity necessary to represent efficiently the subtleties and intricacies of thought and knowledge. Two other researches are using predicate calculi in ways somewhat similar to Black's. Bohnert, of the Thomas J. Watson Research Center of I.B.M., is using the first-order predicate calculus.

McCarthy, is using a second-order predicate calculus that degenerates to first order when time is held constant. Two severe practical problems are encountered along the path taken by predicate calculus. First, there is as yet no way to translate automatically from statements in natural language to statements in predicate calculus; the translation must be made by people, few people can do it, and the process is time consuming. Second, a small amount of natural language turns into a large amount of predicate calculus. The first problem is, of course, a basic research problem as well as a practical one. The second problem places its demand upon the information technology.

HIGHER-ORDER LANGUAGES

At this stage it seems to be a very good hypothesis that languages of high order are required for compact representation of knowledge, and it seems to be a fairly good hypothesis that such languages are required for efficient processing of knowledge. Even highly complex things *can* be said in very simple languages. For instance, if there were an element in a set for every possible statement, one could make any statement merely by pointing to its element. However, in low-order languages the representation of a complex molecule of knowledge is disproportionately voluminous. Our perception of this matter, though still somewhat nebulous, has led us to a rather firm conviction: that the economic and practical advantages of linguistic sophistication are great, and that the intellectual advantage is even greater. The conviction just set forth is coupled with a second conviction that is less firmly set but is nevertheless a working conviction: in a language to be used in pro-cognitive systems, formality is an extremely valuable asset. Both the lack of formality and the failure to adhere strictly to the rules can cause great difficulties in all kinds -of machine processing of information. The problem is not the inconvenience caused by grammatical errors or ambiguities of vocabulary, but rather the high price that civilization pays for the capability that lets man navigate through his sea of syntactic sorrow and semantic confusion. It is almost obvious that man's inability to organise the corpus of his knowledge tightly is due to his having to squander such a wealth of intellectual resource each time he reads a paragraph.

For all these reasons we strongly favour the idea of developing high-order formal languages and applying them with machine assistance in organising the body of knowledge. Natural English is a high-order language, of course, and, when correctly written or spoken, it may even adhere to a definite form - though surely no one knows quite what the form is. If we try to say what is wrong with English, perhaps we can sharpen the concept towards which we are pointing. The main shortcoming of English, and presumably of any natural language, is its ambiguity. Natural languages are so often used as adjuncts to non-linguistic processes that natural languages do not have sufficient chance to practice independence and to develop self-sufficiency. Moreover, when they are exercised in isolation from non-linguistic processes—in reasoning out solutions to difficult problems, for instance—there is very little opportunity to track down sources of error or confusion.

Thus ambiguity persists because it creates no serious difficulty in situations in which the difficulty could be detected and corrected, and ambiguity is rarely detected in situations in which it creates great difficulty. It is no wonder, therefore, that 'in' and 'of' stand for twenty different relations each, and that 'When locked enter through 3D-l 00' does not tell you what to do when you are locked, nor does it tell you to go through room 3D-l 00 when the door of 3D-IOO is locked. In short, the trouble with English as a carrier of knowledge is the horrendous amount of calculating on a very large base of data that is expended just to decide which of several locally plausible interpretations of a simple statement is correct or was intended. If the greater part of man's capability is wasted in that kind of processing, he does not have enough left to achieve more significant goals.

This conclusion is obvious when the processing of English text is attempted by a present-day computer. It is less obvious but probably just as true for people. The higher-order language that we propose as an effective carrier for knowledge is a kind of unambiguous English. As long as changes of context are signaled explicitly within the language, no serious problem is introduced by dependence on context. The proposed language would recognise most or all of the operations, modulations, and qualifications that are available in English.

However, it would quantise the continuous variables and associate one term or structure unambiguously with each degree. Finally, the system in which the proposed language is to be implemented would enforce consistent use of names for substantives; it would monitor 'collisions' among terms, ask authors for clarifications, and disallow new or conflicting uses of established symbols. All this advocacy of unambiguous, high-order language may encounter the disdainful accusation, 'You're just asking for ruly English!' However, the situation is more favourable now for a ruly version of English than it ever has been, and it will be fully ripe before the new language is likely to be developed.

The situation will be ripe, not because people will be ready to adopt a new dialect, but because computers with large data bases will need the new dialect as an information-input language. The envisioned sequence is: from the natural language of the journal article through a machine aided editorial translation into unambiguous English, and then through a purely machine transformation into the language(s) of the computer or of the data base itself. At any rate, this is a plausible approach that deserves investigation, though the areas discussed earlier, particularly relational nets and higher-order predicate calculi, will surely provide con1petitive approaches.

THE IMPACT OF TECHNOLOGY ON EXISTING GENERATIONAL DIFFERENCES

This online collaborative environment has enabled people to access information, as well as interact with each other to share knowledge, like never before. It is no coincidence that in the face of this online landscape, the physical library is getting smaller. There is much debate in the library profession right now as to how the future will shape up, but there is little doubt that many libraries, public and special, are currently facing budgetary cuts and a reduction in the physical space available to them.

Teams of librarians are being replaced by the rise of solo operations, with little career development or ability to recruit more staff. In addition, services may be increasingly outsourced or long-established information centres closed. Quite simply, where people can go online to fulfil many of their information needs, there is little perceived need to visit a library or use the services of a librarian. There is also a generational shift, reinforced by technology advances, which may also be threatening the survival of the library. Quite simply, many still perceive the library to be a physical space, filled with books and policed by a bespectacled librarian, probably from an older generation, and trained in advanced forms of library cataloguing and indexing.

While they are valuable skills, the younger generation may little relish the thought of following in their footsteps – after all, they have grown up into a world that appears completely different, and that is dominated by instantly accessible online information. In the business world, for example, the proliferation of technology has had a completely transformative effect, enabling vast global expansion because the tools allow for different offices in all locations to streamline operations and communicate. Most people now use technology applications on a day-to-day basis, if only to function effectively in the workplace.

For younger generations, though, this technology drive has been even more revolutionary. From childhood, younger people have been using technology to help with everything, from doing their homework to socialising. And as those younger people have grown up and entered the workplace, so have the days of reading books or even just sitting in a classroom seemed increasingly numbered. E-learning, for instance, is becoming more popular, with many businesses employing sophisticated techniques for delivering employees with 'just-in-time' training at their desks.

Younger employees will also be far more adaptable to these technology tools, having most likely graduated from colleges that also employ tools, such as webinars, to deliver vital training. For this younger generation, the whole concept of the 'library', including the people who staff them, may appear somewhat old-fashioned and irrelevant. Meanwhile, the older generation may not be well-equipped to adapt to this new environment or to educate younger people on the continuing and, indeed, evolving value of library services. While certainly not ignorant of technology advances, the older generation is less likely to view technology as such an integral part of daily life.

Al Podboy has worked as director of library services at law firm Baker Hostetler for 30 years; he knows the firm's culture and its lawyers inside out, and he's also familiar with these changing times. "My generation and a lot of my peers have been working in their firms for a long time. I've seen a couple of generations come through the firm and I've seen the differences between them," he comments. He has also been a witness to intergenerational conflict – he refers to one example where a familiar criticism targeted at the younger generation is that they just don't read. "I get a bit annoyed by this to be honest. We live in a much faster environment than when I started. Younger people do read, just not necessarily books," he says. Such differences highlight a real problem: a potentially growing generation gap that could be particularly harmful for the survival of library services, where the older generation is less likely to keep up with new applications and younger people are less likely to be open to, or understand the worth of library services. And if that means fewer people even enter the library profession, the impending crisis could soon be worse than feared.

For Podboy, such generational differences need to be addressed proactively: "We have to introduce older people to technology and convince them that the younger people are not necessarily doing things wrong," he explains. "We need to ensure that people of my age understand what those technologies are and try to encourage them to adapt to them.

At the same time, though, we need to be able to teach younger people the older forms – the value of a book or of an older mentor, for example, where they can benefit from somebody's direct experience of a particular work or task." But bringing together different generations, so that they can appreciate the merits of different methods of working, may be particularly difficult in this modern landscape. Where Podboy, like many of his peers, stayed with the one firm for his whole career, the younger generations are far more likely to change jobs and even careers several times. According to a 2006 survey by *The American Lawyer*, for example, many associates in US law firms see jumping ship as a 'fundamental career milestone'.

Nearly two-thirds of third and fourth-year associates responding to the survey said they didn't expect to be, or didn't know if they'd be, at the same firm in five years as a partner or senior associate. Quite simply, attitudes to the workplace and lifestyle expectations between generations are often vastly different. Generations X and Y want flexibility, challenges, career-advancement opportunities, learning and development opportunities, and fast appreciation and recognition.

And much of their experience of this will be in a fast-paced, technologicallyenabled, online environment. In contrast, older generations are far more used to working in one company, and having one career for a lifetime, learning via traditional routes, and probably using, but not relying, on technology to function effectively. Not only do their attitudes differ widely, but it is less likely today that they'll even be in the same company for long enough to really benefit from the teachings of each other.

THE DANGER FOR LIBRARIANS

For the library profession, these changes may well prove to be fundamental stumbling blocks in the years ahead. According to America's Career Resource Network (ACRN), the number of people aged 55 and over will increase sharply by 2050, but their labour force participation will increase only slightly.

This means that the labour force overall will shrink. In addition, ACRN expects that by 2014, the workforce will have openings for nine million more degree-holders than will be available. There will be three million surplus openings for two-year degreeholders, four million for four-year degreeholders, and two million for advanced degree-holders.

And such a shortage of skilled/professional workers is not just a US phenomenon – the retiring baby-boomer generation is also likely to cause problems for employers in the UK, and beyond. And for librarians, the difficulties may be even more pronounced.

US government statistics show that there were 5,490 librarians working in business industries (manufacturing, finance, insurance, trade, publishing and transportation) in 2002. It predicts that there will be 6,632 librarian jobs by 2012 – a significant rise of 1,142 or 21 per cent. In keeping with overall workforce statistics, not only does the library profession face the aforementioned shortage of graduates entering the informationservices field, but a larger number of those currently working as librarians will be older and close to retirement age.

They need to find a way now of attracting younger people by demonstrating how the library profession can meet the needs of a younger generation with very different personal and career perspectives. If the profession fails to do this now, there may be significant problems in delivering any kind of library services in the future, once the baby-boomers have retired. In June 2006, Mary Ellen Bates, principal of Bates Information Service Research Association, spoke at the Special Libraries Association (SLA) annual conference on the future of library services.

As part of her presentation, she remarked on how library services were experiencing a period of older librarians, with the question arising of how they would be replaced – or how the library profession could go about attracting younger people. In addition, she touched upon the increasingly technology-savvy graduates who have a Masters in Library Science (MLS) – but might be put off the idea of entering a library environment perhaps because of perceptions of it being outdated or old-fashioned, the remit of an older generation more used to books and classrooms, rather than social software and online collaboration. Indeed, SLA surveys of members suggest that an increasing number of information graduates that might traditionally have entered the library environment, are actually choosing jobs outside the library or information resources centre.

In 2003, the SLA 'Annual Salary Survey' revealed that as many as 18 per cent of Canadian and US SLA members were not working in the library or information resource centre. This compares to 13 per cent in 1999. Other areas of work attracting information professionals today include publishing, the database, directory and software industry, as well as the computer systems design industry.

The trend also shows a growing number of information professionals not only working outside the library, but also taking on different responsibilities compared to the traditionally accepted library remit:

- Analysis is the primary responsibility of 8.1 per cent of SLA members who do not claim to work in libraries. This compares to just 0.7 per cent of those who work in libraries;
- Of those not working in libraries, 3.4 per cent said that information product/ database development was their primary responsibility, compared to 1.0 per cent of those who work in libraries;
- While 2.5 per cent of those claiming to work in libraries have primary responsibility for knowledge management (KM), a higher percentage (3.8 per cent) of those not working in libraries primarily manage KM; and
- Records management is the primary responsibility of 4.1 per cent of those not working in libraries, compared to just 0.7 per cent of those working in libraries.

This means that traditional libraries may not just find themselves struggling to recruit fresh graduates to the field, but they may also find themselves competing for talent against other functions, including records management and KM.

THE GOOD NEWS

There is little doubt that the library profession is presently facing something of a perception problem. As Mary Ellen Bates said at the 2006 SLA annual conference, there is much work to be done to market librarians and library services as something 'sexy', attractive and new. The rather stale and outdated image of a glasses-wearing, book-laden librarian will just not hold up against the fast-paced expectations of the younger business generation. To some, indeed, there now appears to be a very real prospect that libraries as we understand them will soon cease to have a purpose at all; that they will before long be consigned to the history books – which in themselves will disappear down some dark, disused library corridor. But there are also signs that the librarian may be emerging from these difficult times to become something altogether new. Ramon Barquin, president of consulting firm Barquin International, recently argued that librarians are perhaps key to making sense of a world that has certainly moved on technologically, but actually struggles more than ever to manage the sheer amount of information circulating in this online dimension. Librarianship has, and will continue to evolve, beyond books to helping to connect people with what they need to know, in whatever format they need to receive the information.

8

Use of Computer-based System in the Libraries and Information Units

We are living to-day in a world of change and the changes we see all around us due to availability of information quicker than before, faster communication through E-mail, voice mail and video conferencing and the great influence of the Internet and web pages. The use of computer-based system in the libraries and information units is now commonplace all over the world. Computers are used to assist in a variety of functions such as maintaining and providing access to the catalogue of items in the collection, managing the issuing and returning of items from the collection, the acquisition of new items for the collection, controlling the serial publications and allowing the retrieval of information from the databases relating to bibliographic data financial or numeric data or the full text of documents.

DIGITAL INITIATIVES AT J.N.N. COLLEGE OF ENGINEERING LIBRARY

It is experienced that Bar-coding has revolutioned the library activities globally. A Laser Barcode printer was purchased and Bar-coding software was also installed. The Bar-coding labels for each book were generated.

BAR-CODING OF BOOKS

Printing barcode labels and pasting in three places of each book, *viz.*, Title page, Secrete page and due date slip were entrusted with a contractor. This generating of Bar-coding labels and pasting the labels for all 53,500 volumes were completed within five months. Retrieving of information through barcode labels using barcode scanner was tested. The computer displayed the Accession Number and the relevant bibliographic information was retrieved from the book database. The bibliographic information includes Accession Number, Author, Title, Call Number, Publisher and Keywords.

BAR-CODED IDENTITY CARDS

The work of bar-coding of identity cards for all users J.N.N. College of

Engineering. College was entrusted to the Frontier Information Technology, Secundarbad. The identity card contains the attributes: Class, Dept, Eligibility, Valid up to, Blood group, Residential address, residence phone number. A stamp size photo of each member was scanned and printed on each card. Both Librarian and Principal are signed on this ID card. The identity cards looked good rather than the old traditional plastic card. Each user used to carry this card and produce the same in the issue counter along with the books and get it issued. Now user feels happy in handling this bar-coded identity card. They also feel proud in producing the same card wherever he visits either inside the college or outside the campus.

NETWORKING AND MANPOWER TRAINING

J. N. N. College of Engineering, Library is a member of the DELNET. The users of the library access the resources listed in this network through the net connectivity. The library staff had their sufficient training at Frontier Information Technology, Secundarbad on various divisions of the library such as Acquisition, Cataloguing, Circulation and Periodicals control. They received special training with regard to preparation of Bar-coded identity card. Various processes include:

- Scanning of the User's Photo.
- Printing the photo in the special art paper using the colour printer.
- Composing various fields, *viz.*, name class, branch, valid up to, eligibility, blood group, residential address, residence phone.
- Laminating the above paper using laminating machine.
- Books issue through scanner.
- Books return through scanner.

Our Library staffs were sent to nearest libraries to have practical exposure towards developing of barcoded identity cards. J.N.N. College of Engineering Library staff underwent hands on training nearest libraries studied the system form all perspectives. The hands on training assisted the Library staff to develop the barcode identity cards. For this purpose the following equipments have been identified.

- Digital camera.
- Colour printer.
- Scanner.
- Laminating Machine.

J. N. N. College of Engineering Library staff has also studied various operations in DRTC Library, Bangalore.

DIGITAL ASSETS

- Floppies: Certain Books are accompanying floppies; such floppies are assigned the concerned Book Accession Numbers. These floppies are arranged serially and kept in the floppy boxes. J.N.N. College of

Engineering Library has 200 floppies. Users lend and read these floppies in OPAC systems.

- CDs: Some new books contain CDs also. Such CDs are assigned the Concerned accession Number and kept in CD container. There are about 1,400 CDs available in Library. Users refer these CDs through OPAC system.
- Software used in J.N.N. College of Engineering: There was one software, which was developed by one programmer of computer science Dept. It had some limitations. Now, 'LIBRIS SOFTWARE' has been purchased and installed. This software put into use.
- LAN: Local Area Network was established by connecting all 6 systems in Library with a Main Server. Each system was connected Ethernet and Win proxy Card through Co-Axial cables.
- UPS: An UPS was purchased and connected with all 6 terminals in the Library.
- Computers: There are 7 computers available in the Library. PC's Configuration: -
  - Pentium III/650 MHZ and above, 512 KB internal and external
  - Cache memory 815 E-Intel
  - Chipset motherboard 128 MB SD RAM.
  - Minimum 17.1 GB/HDD IDE Drive.
  - 1.44 MB FDD, 32 Bit Graphic Card 52*CD Drive, 17 inch Colour
  - Monitor with electronic turner and energy saving windows
  - Keyboard, Logitech Mouse, ATX Cabinet with preloaded and O.S.Windows 95/98.
- Printers: There are one Dot Matrix and one Laser Printer available in the Library.
- Bar-Code Printer: One Bar-Code Printer is also printing in barcode labels in Laser Printer was purchased along with 2,500 Book Barcode sheets and 5000 ID Barcode Label Sticker Sheets.
- Book Database: A book database was created with 53,500 records. Bibliographic information about each Access No. Title, Author, Call Number, Keywords, Publisher, Price, etc.
- Periodical Database: A periodical database was created entering all current journal's bibliographic information. The data entry for receipt of periodicals is being entered into computer. Reminders for non-receipt of periodicals is taken as print out and sent to the periodical suppliers.

ADVANTAGES

Computerization of Library operations saves much time of the Library Staff and users. Students and Staff members feel happy to handle Bar-coded Membership Card. Bar-coding facilities stock verification of books and journals.

DRAWBACKS

Since we implement computerization, our library staff does dual job entering all operations manually and through computer. Staff finds this as a job. In the beginning it may be do their, jobs through computer only. During power failure time, staff face problems to operate computer. These problems can be solved using UPS. An UPS* was purchased and connected to all systems in the library. This UPS solves power problem up to some extent.

HOW TO IMPLEMENT IN FUTURE

Our library staff will prepare bar-coded identity cards for fresh students in future using the barcode equipments. Similarly barcode labels will be generated and pasted in three places of each new book purchased in future. Stock verification will be done online using the barcode scanner in future.

PURCHASING CD CABINET

To preserve CDs it is proposed to purchase a CD Cabinet. All CDs will be serially arranged and kept in proper order. Whenever a user requires particular CD, Library Staff can provide the same for reference purpose.

ROLE OF OPEN SOURCE IN HIGHER EDUCATION

WHAT IS OPEN SOURCE

Traditionally, a programme is defined as a set of instructions which tells a computer what to do. For example, the Windows operating system by Microsoft is a programme, or a set of instructions, which tells the user's computer how to send information to the disk drive, how to take information from the user, and how to communicate with pieces of hardware such as the modem or the network card. However, these programmes are compiled, which means that they are translated into the binary code which the computer understands. The lines of instructions, which are translated into the binary code, are called the source code of the programme. If a user or a programmer has access to the source code behind the programme, then the user is able to alter the programme, changing the way that it works.

For most proprietary, or closed source, programmes, the source code is not available for users or programmers to alter. This means that if a user encounters a bug in the closed source programme, they will not be able to fix it themselves, but must rely on the software vendor to fix the error. As many frustrated users know, this can often take a very long time. Open source software, by contrast, is software for which the source code is freely available. The web server Apache, for example, is a programme which runs as many as two-thirds of the web servers on the Internet. Apache is open source, which means that anyone can access the source code for Apache and make changes in how the programme works.

OPEN SOURCE PLAIN AND SIMPLE

Open source software (OSS) refers to software programmes that are distributed with the source codehence open source. The open source license allows users the freedom to run the programme for any purpose, to study and modify the programme, and to freely redistribute copies of the original or modified programme.

Open source is a way of building software

Open source software is often constructed using the same time-tested methodologies and practices used to construct proprietary software. However there are a number of interesting differences that result from the difference in rights conferred by the license:

- The software evolves more rapidly and organically. Many individuals and teams working in parallel produce advances beyond the capacity of a single team. The improvements are managed into releases by a core team much like the proprietary alternative.
- Users' needs are rapidly met as the OSS model harnesses their collective expertise and contribution. Improvements to the software are often contributed by users who have fixed a problem or added new features.
- New versions are released very often and rely on the community of users and developers to test it, resulting in superior quality software tested on more platforms, and in more environments than most commercial software.
- The development "team" is often largely volunteers, distributed, many in numbers, and diverse. Often, paid members of the development team will manage the project and organize the work of the volunteers.
- Security is enhanced because the code is exposed to the world. In proprietary packages, shortcuts and poor programming are more easily overlooked because only a select few see the code. Like peer reviewed papers, open source code is subject to much greater scrutiny and thus produces a higher calibre result.

Open Source is a Way of doing Business

Open source is often thought of as free software. In fact, one of the benefits is that anyone can use, modify, and redistribute the software without a license fee. While the code is free, the benefits have much more to do with the freedoms than the cost. On the surface it may appear that free software is in opposition to the 'business' of software and, while the open source model challenges the traditional models, open source represents great opportunity for customers and businesses alike. Without the restrictions of a proprietary software license, any institution or company with the skills can use the software to solve their own needs or offer products and services of value to others. Businesses based on open source software typically add value by:

- Offering services such as implementation, training, and support;
- Packaging and integrating open source software to make its installation and use easier for a wider market;
- Creating complementary, add-on, or enhanced software for sale. Open source affords institutions, as consumers of software, unparalleled control over the use of software to meet business demands and control over where they deploy their budget dollars. Taking into consideration its core competencies and available resources, an institution may use its own people and resources, hire external resources, or partner to share costs. The principles of open source software-freedom to run the programme for any purpose, to study and modify the programme, and to freely redistribute copies and modifications-are simple, yet have powerful and far reaching implications.

COMPARISON TO PROPRIETARY SOFTWARE

One of the great misconceptions about open source is that it is an alternative to commercial software. Rather, open source software is an alternative to proprietary software, but often acquired through or supported by a company-in other words commercial. Fundamentally, the difference between open source and proprietary software has to do with control. Where the open source license imparts freedoms to use, modify, and redistribute the software, the proprietary license restricts use, modification, distribution, and more. Vendors of proprietary software restrict access to and use of the source code because the source is knowledge-and knowledge is power.The open source license corrects the balance of power between producers and consumers of software. Access to the source code is about freedom and choice. After all, most of us aren't software engineers-we can't start adding features and fixing bugs just because we have access. Yet access to the source code is important to all of us because access is control. Open source clearly offers advantages for the consumer, but it also represents a significant competitive advantage to companies that adopt compatible strategies. IBM, HP, Sun Microsystems, Apple Computer, Red Hat, Novell, and many other companies attribute significant revenue from strategies built on commercialization of open source software. Mainstream press coverage of open source has been accelerating all over the world, but the press coverage in higher education has been nothing short of explosive in recent months. Vendors of proprietary software have been carefully crafting their powerful and influential messages about open source. Some attempt to categorize open source as something applicable to research and experimentation. Others cast open source as comparable to open standards. Still others warn about considering open source software for mission critical applications. Each of these messages uses generalizations that distort the truth. Let's examine some of the important attributes and how open source and proprietary approaches compare:

ATTRIBUTE OPEN SOURCE PROPRIETARY

License Licensed to provide freedom to use for any purpose, modify, and redistribute.Licensed to restrict use to "acceptable uses", protect against modification and redistribution.Control Balanced. Consumers and providers of commercial offerings have equal access. Vendor is in control. Often large up-front investments in the software, training, and other implementation costs create a lock-in situation that strips the consumer of control. Innovation Rapid and diverse. Leverages a very large community of users and developers working in parallel. Limited to vendor investments. Typically caters to the features sought by the largest audience. Low levels of innovation. Longevity/ Risk of abandonmentSoftware will always be available as long as it serves a useful purpose. The larger the adoption the safer the investment. No single point of failure. Dependent on the success of the vendor. Single point of failure.Security and reliability As the great tradition of peer review produces high quality academic and scientific works, open source projects produce software that is generally more secure and reliable. Like peer reviewed papers, open source software is subject to greater scrutiny and leverages a larger collective intelligence than proprietary software. *Total cost of ownership* (TCO) Acquisition cost Low or no initial license cost. License costs on the rise in education. Implementation and support costs OS community support and competition for commercial support keeps costs low.

Choice allows consumer to bear costs internally which may further decrease cost. Costs determined by and coupled to vendor. Lack of choice. Alternative service organizations often lead to higher costs. Costs of scale No additional license cost with additional users, servers, etc. License costs generally rise with increased use. Platform support Broader platform and server support increases leveraged investments in existing institutional infrastructure. Platform support limited to what the vendor offers. May not fit well with institutional infrastructure. As we can see from the comparison, open source promises some impressive advantages over proprietary software. While open source has a rich history in education, a recent convergence of powerful drivers and enablers are precipitating a strong movement towards open source in higher education.

ROLE OF OPEN SOURCE IN HIGHER EDUCATION

Open source is changing the nature of the software business in many settings, but the movement is particularly impressive in education. While open source has nearly a 20 year history of success producing leading software, it has mostly been in the infrastructure domain-the protocol implementations, servers, development frameworks, and utilities that enable the e-mail programmes, browsers, and other applications we all depend on. Open source has not been a significant model for producing application software-until recently. In the past few years colleges and universities have begun to produce enterprise open source applications like course management systems and electronic portfolios that compete directly with their proprietary counterparts. These e-learning applications are leading a movement in higher education from proprietary software towards open source. A snapshot of the current proprietary software environment in education reveals some compelling drivers.

- Tight budgets have focused attention on software acquisition costs, and total cost of ownership
- Growing resentment of vendor power, particularly in the wake of price increases and licensing changes that many institutions felt powerless to reject.
- Lack of innovation. Learning technology has not lived up to its potential to improve learning. and some enablers of a more effective model:
- Collaboration technology has made large-scale collaborative work across institutional, geographic, and cultural boundaries more effective.
- Software design patterns, development technologies, and standards have evolved in a way that facilitates modular, interoperable software components.
- Proven business models and education focused companies that embrace open source.
- Strong cultural appeal of open source in academia

We observe many of these drivers and enablers beyond the context of higher education. Perhaps the cultural appeal in academia represents the 'tipping point' for a powerful movement unique to colleges and universities. At the heart of the cultural fit between academia and open source are common philosophy and values. Creating and sharing knowledge for public good is a key part of the mission of colleges and universities, and a core part of the philosophy driving open source software. Colleges and universities are also home to some of the best software engineers in the world. Yet most institutions don't have a plentiful supply of available talent to meet evolving needs-individually. The open source model provides colleges and universities a way to leverage cultural values of collaboration and sharing to gather resources and work together for the common good. Unlike contexts outside of education, working together doesn't blur institutional brand or threaten a school's income. As a result, higher education not only boasts some of the best software engineers, but also has a plentiful supply of willing talent- a critical success factor for open source. A common challenge to developing software is understanding the needs of the users and turning that understanding into a suitable software design. While there are many different approaches and software methodologies, the open source model clearly has an advantage since the individuals most involved in teaching and learning are deeply involved in the development of the software for teaching and learning.

Another critical success factor for open source is the emergence of education-focused companies that embrace open source as the preferred model for business. Although colleges and universities are well suited to develop world class enterprise software, supporting that software for other institutions isn't an activity that helps fulfill their mission. A new ecology has emerged where commercial organizations, colleges, and universities play complimentary and collaborative roles. The Andrew W. Mellon foundation, the William and Flora Hewlett Foundation, and others have recognized the need and the potential and have made considerable financial resources available to seed open source projects and help create the new ecology. While there are literally thousands of active open source projects all over the world addressing most application domains, there are a number of notable projects particularly interesting for institutions of higher education.

MAN-COMPUTER INTERACTION IN PRO-COGNITIVE SYSTEMS

The concept of the pro-cognitive system has been approached and developed from several different points of view. Common to these points of view has been the fundamental purpose, to improve the usefulness and to promote the use of the body of knowledge. Also common to the several points of view has been the central methodological theme, that the purpose can best be achieved through intimate interaction among men, computers, and the body of knowledge. Though we shall use the convenient phrase, 'man-computer interaction,' it should be kept in mind that it is an abbreviation and that the body of knowledge is a coordinate partner of the men and the computers.

In order to come to grips with problems of the projected interaction, it seems necessary to break it down into parts, even though there appears to be no set of components into which the interaction process can be subdivided that do not themselves interact strongly. The traditional approach, which allocates some functions to men and others to machines, is particularly unsatisfactory because, in order for the major functions involved in working with the body of knowledge to be fulfilled efficiently, synergic action is required in which men and machines participate together. Most of the efforts made during the last decade to figure out 'what men should do' and 'what machines should do' have missed this point widely. They have supposed that the fabric of man-computer interaction is a patchwork quilt made of red and blue patches, and that the red patches correspond to functions that can only for human capabilities, the blue patches to functions that can only for machine capabilities. In our analysis, however, the fabric of man-computer interaction is an almost uniformly purple quilt, albeit made of red and blue threads. Woven together, they constitute a useful whole. But when one tries to divide it into human functions and machine functions, he winds up not with two sets of assignable tasks but with two tangles of coloured thread. By and large, the human threads are heuristic and the machine threads are algorithmic. The art of man-computer system design is the art of weaving the two qualities into solid-colour cloth. Despite the artificiality of division, we than divide the discussion of man-computer interaction, for convenience, into three parts:

- What is often called the man-machine interface, the physical medium through which the interactions take place,
- The language aspects of mancomputer interaction, and
- A look at the total process as an adaptive, self-organising process.

THE PHYSICAL 'INTERMEDIUM'

Early in our study of man-computer interaction, we became dissatisfied with the term, 'man-machine interface.' 'Interface,' with its connotation of a mere surface, a plane of separation between the man and the machine, focuses attention on the caps of the typewriter keys, the screen of the cathode-ray tube, and the console lights that wink and flicker, but not on the human operator's repertory of skilled reactions and not on the input-output programmes of the computer. The crucial regions for research and development seem to lie on both sides of the literal interface. In order to remind ourselves continually that our concern permeates the whole medium of interaction, we have avoided 'interface' and have used, instead, 'intermedium.' The man-computer intermedium subsumes the computer's displays and the mechanisms and programmes that control and maintain them, the arrangements through which people communicate information to the computer, and the relevant communication organs and skills of the men. Once we assume that definition of the domain, it is impossible to draw a sharp line between the non-linguistic and the linguistic parts.

The blurred line that we shall in fact draw is intended to put most of the questions of apparatus on one side and to put most of the questions of method, procedure, and format on the other. However, the intermedium extends beyond the console to include the user's entire work space and the physical aspects of his personal documentation system and perhaps even his laboratory system or his application system. We shall not examine those extensions in detail, but that does not mean that we consider them unimportant.

THE TYPEWRITER SCHEMA

The second main area in which improvement of controls and displays is required is the area of alphanumeric keyboards and hard-copy displays. Those devices are obviously important for the future of pro-cognitive systems. The main functions to be fulfilled by devices derived from the typewriter schema are obvious ones. Such devices must provide for 'digital' communication from the user to the computer. They must also provide a visible record of the information that has been fed into the computer, and this record should be easy to modify. The computer should be able to make marks on the record.

The user should have the option of producing either soft copy or hard copy, and even the option of turning the soft copy into hard copy after editing. The device should accept input as fast as a well-trained operator can provide it, and it should translate signals from the computer into typed characters at a rate of at least 100 characters per second. The typewriter like devices that are currently available provide five schemata that are useful as bases for thinking in this area. Let us abstract from these schemata the parts and qualities we should like to have melded to get) 1er for use in pro-cognitive systems./ The first schema is offered by the familiar teletypewriter. Although there are several models of teletypewriter, the general features are sufficiently characteristic that, for some of our purposes, we may think simply of 'the' teletypewriter.

Compared to most other man-computer communication devices, it is rugged, reliable, and inexpensive. However, it has no lower-case letters, it is slow, and it has a strange 'touch' for anyone accustomed to office typewriters. Many people who have had experience with on-line man-computer interaction look forward to the manufacture of a device like current models, but with 128 or more characters, with the capability of typing at very high speed, and with a touch more like that of an ordinary electric typewriter. We realise, however, that, in the present state of the art, these features are to a large extent incompatible with high reliability and low cost.

The schema offered by the familiar electric typewriter, or by the electric typewriter that has been designed or adapted to be used with a computer, is a montage of 44 type keys, six to twelve operation keys, two cases, fairly clear marks on paper in one or two colours, limited control of the carriage from the keyboard, fair reliability, and a high level of noise. The ensemble of 88 characters is almost large enough for serious intellectual purposes. The font contains both capital and lower-case letters.

These things are important. Perhaps even more important are the intimate familiarity with typewriters and the significant skill in typing that are fairly widespread in the population. It is worth pausing to ponder how few well-developed skills there are that are both complex and widespread. Almost everyone can get about in three-dimensional space. Almost everyone can speak and understand one of the natural languages - perhaps not grammatically, but fluently. But relatively few people can do anything else that is even remotely comparable in informational complexity and degree of perfection. Of the remaining candidates for inclusion in the list of widespread complex skills, we may with some misgivings accept writing, and perhaps the playing of musical instruments. After this comes typing. And typing ends the list. It is possible that, in future decades, typing will move up past music and that it will become almost as widespread as writing and more highly developed. The third typewriter schema is offered by typewriter like devices that are used in association with computers and that type 60 or more characters per second.

These are usually called 'printers.' The aspect of the printer schema that is of interest is simply the rapid rate of typing. It is worth while to have in mind that characters *can* be marked on paper at high speed by a device the size of a typewriter. The fourth schema is offered by devices commercially available but not in widespread use, separated keyboards and typing units. When a typewriter is associated with a computer, there ceases to be any reason for the conventional, direct connection between the key that is pressed and the type bar that strikes the paper. Obviously the pressing of the key should direct a code to the computer, and the computer should acknowledge the code by activating the type bar and thus printing the character on the paper.

As soon as the tacit assumption of a direct linkage between key and type bar is recognised and discarded, there is no longer any need to maintain a one-to- one relation between key pres sings and character markings. It should be possible, in a 'debreviation' mode, to type 'clr' on the keyboard and have 'The Council on Library Resources, Inc.' appear on the display. The final schema in the typewriter field is the 'Stenotype.' The component that seems to be of most value, for these purposes, is simultaneous multiple key pressing. If it turns out, as seems likely, that very large ensembles of characters are desirable in man-computer interaction with the body of knowledge, then it will become much more important than it is now to be able to specify the desired character by pressing a pattern of keys on a small keyboard. That is a much better solution than pressing a single key on a keyboard with several thousand keys.

DISPLAYS FOR GROUP-COMPUTER INTERACTION

Because our thinking is anchored in familiar experiences, we are inclined to think of interaction between men and pro-cognitive systems as a collection of dyadic man-computer interactions. More and more, however, the problems of science, technology, industry, and government are being solved by groups of men rather than by individuals. Although the 'team approach' is a topic of controversy in some fields, its value has been proven in others. Consideration should be given to the development of tools and techniques to facilitate group interaction with the body of knowledge.

In the current technology there are two general approaches to group-computer interaction. The first and most widely used provides a separate console for each member of the group and relies upon the computer, together with auxiliary communication circuits, to mediate the interaction among the members of the group as well as the interaction of the members with the computer and its store. The second approach, taken in some military systems, uses large 'wall' displays, located in view of several or all of the members of the group and intended to provide a common frame of reference for their decisions and actions. In pro-cognitive systems based on individual consoles, the main items of equipment that would be needed for group communication, not already discussed under the heading of man-computer communication, would be derivatives of the telephone and television.

Communication by telephone and perhaps by television would be closely correlated with communication through the computer system. This procedure does not pose any novel requirements for the display and control equipment of the system. In a pro-cognitive system with group displays one would expect to see large-scale displays similar in principle to the individual display screen already discussed, even with derivatives of the light pen to provide communication between the human members of the team and the computer. The most significant characteristic of the group display seems to us to be resolution.

The total number of resolvable points is no greater in the large-scale kinematic displays available at present than it is in the smaller individual displays. In some large scale static displays, such as wall maps, however, there is high resolution, and in them the advantage of size is apparent. On a good wall map, one can see the general features of a continent from the middle of the room. In order to examine the boundaries of countries or states, it is necessary only to step a little closer.

From a normal reading distance, the names of cities and towns can be made out and the courses of rivers can be followed. It is interesting to extrapolate to very high resolution and dynamic presentation. If display capabilities should increase as rapidly as memory capabilities, one may someday watch a display on a very large wall, examine the weather situation in the Midwest, and then with a magnifying glass follow the movement of an individual automobile from Bethesda to the Pentagon, reading the names of the streets and highways along which it moves. It seems to us that there is some merit in trying to develop such large-scale, high-resolution dynamic displays for group computer interaction, though at the same time we appreciate the difficulty of the technical problems involved.

CONSOLES AND WORK SPACES

The design of consoles and the arrangement of work spaces is not likely to be regarded as an exciting part of library planning, but it is an essential step in overcoming what C. W. Churchman calls the 'brain-desk barrier.' During the course of our experience with facilities for man-computer interaction, the point was driven home to us that convenient arrangement of the elements of the physical inter medium is an extremely important factor in the determination of the effectiveness of the interaction and not something readily purchased or easily achieved. The individual ingredients of the current difficulty of man-computer interaction are trivial in themselves, but they add up to a significant total.

The first inconvenience is likely to be the position of the keyboard of the computer typewriter. Most computer typewriters are located on 'console' desks that are higher than typewriter tables. The keyboards of most computer typewriters stand higher above their resting surfaces than the keyboards of ordinary typewriters do. That makes the keyboard much too high. Raising the chair seat makes the typist's knees hit the table. The computer typewriter to a conventional typewriter table puts the typewriter too far away from the oscilloscope screen, the light pen, and the switches that control the computer. In the computer-posted displays that we have seen, the oscilloscope screen stands only 10 or 20 degrees off the vertical. This is true for displays that have light pens associated with them as well as for screens that function only as displays. Evidently, the designers had in mind the blackboard and not the writing desk.

In fact, one's blackboard habits carryover to the vertical oscilloscope screen, and one writes and draws in a large scale inappropriate to the small size and high resolution of the display. Moreover, it is tiring to hold a hand at eye height for a long time without support. The other elements of difficulty are of the same general nature: Light pens are too thick and heavy for facile writing; they could be and should be the size and weight of ordinary pens. Conventional 'line printers' have no lower-case letters; it is difficult to read long passages in capital letters. One has to turn the lights out to read the oscilloscope and then turn them back on to read print or typescript. And so forth. Each individual difficulty can be remedied easily, but it may take a strong, well-organised effort to perfect all the necessary elements and combine them into an effective physical inter medium.

MAN-COMPUTER INTERACTION LANGUAGES

If the problems of the physical intermedium of mancomputer interaction are lacking in intellectual challenge, the problems of language for man-computer interaction abound in it. The entire spectrum of language from binary machine code to the great natural languages will be involved in man's interaction with pro-cognitive systems. We may distinguish four different involvements of language in a neo-library pro-cognitive system.

Language is employed:

- By the programmers who prepare and improve the computer programmes that implement the basic operations of the system;
- By the information specialists who endeavor continually to improve the organisation and operation of the system;
- By the substantive users of the system in their interaction with the body of knowledge; and

- In the representation of the body of knowledge in the memory of the system.

The science of applied linguistics is so new, and formal languages designed to facilitate the programming of computers are burgeoning so fast, that it is difficult to summarize the present situation and almost impossible to make a long-term projection worthy of confidence. This part of the discussion, therefore, is confined to a brief examination of the roles of language in the four areas of man-computer interaction.

PROGRAMMING LANGUAGE

Even after it has been developed and is in operation, the pro-cognitive system of the year 1994 has a continuing need for programming specialists. Their task is, essentially, to maintain and improve the basic programmes of the system. Requirements arise that cannot be stmet effectively without making alterations in the basic system programmes. To change even one short statement in a large system of programmes is a serious matter, to be undertaken only by the most skilled and experienced professional programmers. The programmers of the pro-cognitive system, therefore, plan modifications carefully, test them thoroughly outside the main stream of operation of the system, and then monitor the situation closely when they introduce the modifications into actual operation. Basic programmes for the pro cognitive system are written in a high-level programming language. The programmes are available to anyone who wishes to examine or use them, not only as services that will function at the user's request, but also in the form of annotated statements in the programming language.

When a system programmer modifies a system programme, he operates upon it through another programme designed to facilitate the preparation, testing, modification, documentation, storage, and retrieval of programmes. This 'programming-system' programme provides several separate services, each of which can be brought into operation by simply typing its name. Each service makes available to the programmer a specialised language attuned to its own structure and functions. Together with his physical intermedium, the programming languages guide and implement the programmer's interaction with the system. Let us observe a programmer at work, modifying a basic graphical display programme in order to make it operate with a new display device that provides eight times as much linear resolution as the older 'standard' displays provide. We shall concentrate more on the functions and operations than on the syntax and terminology.

The programmer sits down at his console, turns it on, and calls the programming system. It reports for service, and he requests the programme retrieval and editing programme. It reports, and he asks it for the names of all the screen-display programmes that are regularly used. Of the 20 offered, he selects four as likely to include the one he must change, and he asks to see their abstracts. From the abstracts, he selects one and asks to see its listing in the high-level language in which it was written. From the listing, he can tell almost at once that he has the programme he wants, for the listing is heavily annotated, and it is immediately clear that the number of lines in each scan is the familiar number and that the division of the screen into sectors is the same as the one currently in use throughout the system. Using the 'moving window' * to scan through the programme, the programmer gets an over-all picture of the display routine and then returns to its beginning, where he finds a statement labeled 'Interrogate display' and a comment to the effect that, through interrogation, the programme checks the type designation of the screen on which it will display information. Such a check is made because at one time or another several different types of display have been in the system. What is being introduced is a fifth or sixth type.

The programmer figures out that the result of the interrogation is a code, that the first ten digits of the code are checked against a standard to provide authentication, and that the last four digits of the code are used as the argument of a 'transfer-table' or 'jump-table' operation. He therefore temporarily dismisses the entire programming system, calls a document- retrieval programme, and retrieves the engineering specification of the new display device. He looks at the document long enough to satisfy himself that he has the correct display programme. He then asks the question-answering system the identification code of the display described in the document. Just as the question-answering system is displaying the answer, he finds the passage in the document that gives the code. He makes sure that the two displays of the code are identical. He sees that the last four bits are 1101. He makes a note of that and recalls the programming system, which comes back into action with the retrieval and editing programme operating in the mode in which he last used it. The programmer notes next that the name of the transfer table is 'Display-selector transfer table.' He types:

```
Insert in Display-selector transfer table
+ 13 a jump to Patch.  Prepare Patch:
Deposit in user's scratch-pad register
(Insert here designation of user's
scratch-pad area used in the first deposit
operation following the jump-out from
Display-selector transfer table + 12) the
octal constant [Insert here (the octal
constant inserted in last-cited deposit
operation)/10].
```

Then on the next line he types:

- Jump to the return used by Display selector transfer table + 12.

Then finally he asks to see a screen display of the newly prepared patch programme. In the first register of the patch, the programming system has composed the instruction 'Deposit,' the octal constant '4000,' and the symbolic address 'Scratch-pad area, Display + 6.' In the next register it has deposited the instruction 'Jump' and the symbolic address 'Initialise display.' Seeing this, our programmer thinks a moment about the '4000' and decides that it is a plausible value for the constant. He then types:

- Display 'Initialise display'.

And looks at the part of the programme to which the 'Jump' leads. The programme statements in that segment seem appropriate to him. He therefore decides to test the modified programme. The modification has been so short and simple that he sees no reason to test it under 'trace,' which would have the effect of running it slowly and protecting other programmes against interference in the event that it should misbehave. However, it does occur to him to take one more precaution before testing. He decides to give the patch a retrievable label and to store away a copy of the modified programme so that he can retrieve it and work on it further if the test is unsatisfactory. He therefore types:

- Assign the label, 'Constant for display 13' to the statement locally labeled 'Patch'

The programming system pauses a moment and then replies:

- The label, 'Constant for display 13', has already been used.

It occurs to him immediately what the trouble is, and he types:

- Assign 'Constant for display 13, H. I. Johnson'.

The programming system then replies:

- Done.

In order to test the programme, the programmer takes advantage of a substitution technique provided by the testing part of the programming system. He calls for the testing service and then asks to have a set of test data displayed on his old display screen, which is still connected. As soon as he has confirmed that the data are displayed on his old display screen, he substitutes one of the new display devices for his old one and requests the test programme to substitute the programme he has just modified for the regular programme. The system will effect the substitution as soon as it comes to the part of the regular programme that matches the part he has just modified. This is a fairly complicated operation, but it is easier and surer for the system to find the place where the substitution should be effected than it is for the programmer to specify it precisely. The programmer then calls for a redisplay of the data. This time the data show up on his new display, the format is the same, the resolution is better, and everything seems to be working well. Now the programmer acts on the insight he had achieved a minute or two earlier -the realisation that one or more than one other programmer has been working on the modification, programming it in parallel with him, so that two or more versions of the modification can be compared before the modification is introduced into the operating system. He therefore asks the programming system:

- Is another programmer modifying a screen display programme?

The programming system says that no one is working on such a modification now, but that O. B. Smith worked on one earlier in the day. Our programmer asks to talk with O. B. Smith. The system makes the connection. The two programmers discuss their modifications on the telephone. Each calls for both versions of the modified programme in order to check that they are identical in their essentials. It turns out that O. B. Smith had happened upon the label, 'Constant for display 13,' only an hour or two earlier than H. I. Johnson and had thereby set up the collision of labels that had been detected by the system. The two versions of the programme do match, except in respect of arbitrary labels. The two programmers together delete the retrievable patch label. They enter a note in the system log, indicating that they have made a modification and giving its location, purpose, and nature, and their names and the date.

Then they replace the old programme with the modified programme in the system files and in the operating system. In that final step they use - without stopping to think about it—a sophisticated capability of the system. Before substituting the modified version for the old one, the system checked to see that no one was at the moment in the process of using the old one. In the foregoing account, attention was focused on the programming system and the language and procedure used in modifying a programme - not on the programming language in which the system programmes were originally written. There is little to say about the basic programming language except that it is a powerful and sophisticated descendent of present-day computer-programming languages and the product of long-continued, intensive research. The example was intended to illustrate how closely interwoven are the threads of hardware, system design, programming technique, and programming language. It touched also upon the capability of the programming system to interrelate the efforts of members of the system programming team.

ORGANISING LANGUAGE

The system specialists in their continual effort to improve the organisation of the body of knowledge and the usefulness of the pro-cognitive system must deal with a variety of languages and procedures. Whereas the language of the programming system dealt with programmes written in a consistent, high-level programming language, the 'organising language' dealt with documents written in the various natural languages, with mathematical models and computer-programme models, with computer programmes themselves, and - most intensively—with large, coherent systemisations of knowledge represented in the 'representation language' that constitutes the foundation of the question-answering system. Associated with each of these diverse objects is a set of information structures and procedures with which the organising language must resonate. Therefore, the organising language is divided into parts, anyone of which may be brought into play almost instantly by anyone of the system specialists who can direct it on the task with which he is concerned.

One of the main tasks of the system specialists is to transfer information from the document store associated with a subfield of knowledge to the organised body of knowledge of that subfield. This operation involves, but is not wholly restricted to, translation from natural language to the representation language. We say that it is not wholly restricted to such translation because many of the documents entering the pro-cognitive system consist mainly of meta-information and are intended not to express substantive findings so much as to set such findings into relation with problems, to define their scopes and domains, and to offer qualifications and suggestions about their applications and their correlation with the body of knowledge.

The substantive findings are typically expressed in the form of a high-order formal language, or in the form of operable computer programmes or in the form of data structures such as lists, tables, and matrixes. The fact that the incoming information is already to a large extent formalised and organised simplifies the problem for the system specialist. During the future period to which this discussion refers, many scientists are beginning to use in their own work the formal language in terms of which the body of knowledge is represented in the pro-cognitive system. However, the rapid advance in the understanding of languages and the burgeoning of linguistic techniques and formalisms are still in progress, and the time when one great formal language will dominate pro-cognitive intercourse appears still to be decades away. The organising language contains a section that handles translation from natural language to the representation language. This section provides translators for each of the main natural languages. These translators work in both directions. One of the major items of routine business is to translate a document into the formal representation language, then to translate it back into a long series of short statements in the natural source language, and then to review the new version in a conference with the author of the document. The system specialists who handle that part of the work are educated in the scientific or technical disciplines they deal with, as well as in the information sciences.

The process of translation is carried out mainly by algorithm, but, even after two decades of progress, there are still many problems and difficulties that must be solved or circumvented by human specialists. The problem of capturing and representing precisely the intention of an author is still so difficult that the conference between the specialist and the author of a 10-page paper may take as much as an hour. By the time the conference is finished, however, the natural-language text has been perfected to the point at which it can be translated into the representation language without the loss of any information the author considers essential.

When the translation algorithms operate upon the final natural-language text, they ordinarily require no human intervention. Whenever a problem of translation persists, however, it is made the subject of a conference between the system specialist and experts who specialise in translation algorithms. Over the years, these conferences have contributed much to the perfection of the translation algorithms. In this part of the work the language employed by the system specialist is essentially a language for controlling the operation of language algorithms, editing text, testing the logical consistency of statements in the representation language, and checking the legality of information structures and formats. The part of the language concerned with editing is to a large extent graphical. Both the system specialist and the author point to words and sentences in the text, move them about with the aid of their styli, insert or substitute new segments of text, and so forth. The language used in controlling algorithms is essentially standard throughout the pro-cognitive system. When an incoming document contains many references to associated information structures, the task of the system specialist expands. He has to introduce the links that will connect the textual document with the associated structures and the associated structures one with another. Inasmuch as the work we are discussing is done in a second-echelon center, this does not involve the actual introduction of the new information into the over-all body of knowledge, but - operation for operation - it amounts to almost the same thing. The main difference is that there is even more caution, more insistence upon verification in the top-echelon centers. In linking the various structures, the system specialist makes statements of the following kind:

```
Table 3 is a two-dimensional matrix with
alphanumeric row and column headings and
with row and column marginal totals.  The
entries are floating-point decimal num-
bers.  Check the format.  If it is all
right, file it, and construct a bidirec-
tional link to "Table 3" and the title.
```

The system will know, of course, to file it in the data base. Encountering a series of equations in a documtent, and seeing that they are sufficiently complete to constitute an operable computer routine, the system specialist makes a series of commands such as the following:

```
Assign an arbitrary PROCOL independent
routine label to these [He points] equa-
tions.  Construct a bidirectional link
between the text and the routine.  Assume

ranges for the variables.  Assume assign-
ments of variables to axes.  Display rela
tions on screen while running program.
Run the routine.
```

The system of equations as a 'PROCOL routine.' While observing the display, he may, for example, make some modifications in the ranges of variables, and substitute z for x as the independent variable. In such operations, he uses the graph-control sublanguage that is standard for the entire pro-cognitive system. One of the main features of the language mechanism used by the system specialist is a built-in 'understanding' of the several kinds of information structure that system specialists usually handle. When the information structure is a matrix, certain operations, certain storage locations, certain kinds of link, certain kinds of test, and certain kinds of display are appropriate. When the information structure is an operable programme, a different set of things is appropriate. When the information structure is a textual string, still different things are appropriate.

The linguistic development that has made all this possible has been the development of an interpretive mechanism that examines the class memberships of the entities mentioned in the declarations, commands, and questions, determines from those memberships what operations and interrelations are appropriate and uses that information to guide its implementation of the instructions. The format of the illustrative commands given in the foregoing paragraphs is intended, of course, only to suggest. No such language is currently implemented on a computer. The suggestion is that such a language will in due course be implement able. The use of pronouns cause no serious difficulty. Most of the power of the language stems from the interplay of the facts already mentioned,

- That the language mechanism 'understands' the information structures that will be encountered in its work, and
- That the operations to be performed upon the information structures have been carefully programmed and associated with the verbs of the language.

The design of a specialised language is in large part a matter of identifying the information structures and the fundamental operations of the special domain of application. It includes also the formulation of a sufficiently sophisticated syntactic analysis to permit flexibility of expression and sensitiveness of response to tense, voice, mood, and so forth. The language must, of course, be intimately correlated with the physical inter medium and with the repertory of processing techniques that are available. 'Techniques,' as used here, is not the same as 'operations.' There may be several different ways to carry out a given operation.

To the substantive user, the difference may appear only in speed or in cost. To the system specialist or the programmer, on the other hand, the selection of a particular technique may have profound implications. Selecting the wrong technique for the performance of a fundamental operation might seriously handicap future development of the system. One of the main responsibilities of system specialists, therefore, is to exercise good judgement about the selection of techniques. The selection of operations, on the other hand, is determined largely by the requirements of the task at hand. We have discussed one particular kind of task in which system specialists are involved. Let us now turn to another kind of task.

It is part of what we have called 'mulling over' the body of knowledge - looking for undetected relations within it and for possibilities of improving its organisation. Let us concern ourselves here with one small facet of that endeavor. Consider the work of a system specialist who is exploring the possibility that there may exist, within a part of the body of knowledge as currently represented, a number of basic abstract correlations that have not yet been detected. Let us suppose that he has available the language and processing mechanisms capable of transforming patterns of information from the standard representation language into various other representations, based upon other information structures. By 'information structures,' we refer, of course, to trees, lists, matrixes, relational nets, semantic nets, multidimensional space analogues, and so forth. The foregoing are currently available examples, but during the next decades there should be great development - both in proliferation and in sophistication - of information structures. The language employed by the system specialist handles the standard representation language approximately the way a present-day query language handles a simple hierarchical file. The system specialist might say, for example:

```
Designate as A, B, and C, respectively,
the parts of the representation that con-
tain models involving DNA and RNA, models
of transformational grammars, and
information-compression codes.  Transform
each of the parts, A, B, and C, into
"trie" representation, list-structure
representation, and semantic-net represen-
tation.  Within each of the latter,
truncate each representation tentatively,
retaining the highest-level 1,000,000
```

```
bits.  Now, consider subdivisions of the
representation that are locally complete
and approximately 10,000 bits in size.
Correlate all the subrepresentations of A
with each subrepresentation of B, and do
the same for B and C and for C and A.
Display all pairs of patterns that have
correlations greater than 0.8.
```

In the foregoing series of commands, there were many points at which substantive knowledge of information structures and technical operations had to be 'understood' by the language mechanism. Since many of the structures and most of the operations are of particular significance to system specialists, the organising language contains specific terms for them. System specialists have many other tasks besides the two that have been discussed. They preside over the introduction, into the top-echelon representation of the body of knowledge, of those contributions that are locally organised and tested in the second-echelon centers. They call to the attention of experts in the various substantive fields the correlations and systematisations they find plausible in their continual examination of the body of knowledge, and they work with the substantive experts in reorganising the representations of substantive areas. They seek continually to improve the representation language. Approximately once each decade they have to adapt the representation to a new and improved hardware base. In so doing, they work closely with the system programmers. Indeed, there are some system specialists who are programmers, and some programmers who are system specialists. There is no sharp line between the two, any more than there is a sharp line between system specialists and specialists in substantive areas of science and technology.

USER-ORIENTED LANGUAGES

The existence of so very many subfields of science and technology, each with its local jargon, its own set of frequently occurring operations, and its own preferences for data structures and formats, makes it necessary to have many different user-oriented languages. However, there is a homogeneity that underlies the diversity. We have seen the basis for this underlying homogeneity in our discussion of programming language and organising language. The homogeneity is inherent in the fact that there are only a few syntactic classes, only a few dozen information structures, and only about a hundred *kinds* of operation - though there are very many different operations - in the entire spectrum of activities of the pro-cognitive system.

The various field-oriented and problem oriented languages employed by the substantive users of the system are therefore all related, one to another, and they are similar in their basic essentials to the languages used by the programmer and the system specialist. One of the tasks of the specialist that is relevant in the present connection is to keep the user-oriented languages compatible with one another. User-oriented languages naturally tend to develop in their own particular directions, and every effort is made not to impede such development when the needs are truly special. It usually turns out, however, that consultation between a substantive user and a system specialist reconciles achievement of the goal of a new specialisation with preservation of order within the over-all system. This is true because the substantive user only rarely invents a new linguistic technique that is superior, for his purposes, to every other technique already established within the system and because any new and useful one that he does invent soon finds application in other parts of the system. The interaction between a substantive user and the pro cognitive system may be intellectually as deep as the user's penetration of his field of study, but it should be simple.

It tends to be simple because there are only a few kinds of action for the user to take at his console. Almost everything posted on a display, for example, is put there by the computer. If the user wants to make a mark or turn on a light, he tells the computer what, when, and where, and the computer proceeds to carry out the act. In order to match the small set of control actions a man can take with the vast assortment of things there are to be done in the world of the pro-cognitive system, it is necessary to take advantage of the concept of determination by local context that is so highly developed in the natural languages.

In the system of user languages, the first step in that direction is the selection of a sublanguage - a field-oriented or problem-oriented language designed to handle the kind of task with which the user is concerned. The second step, taken within the sublanguage, is to enter a 'mode.' We have already touched briefly on modes of display associated with the display screen and the light pen. When the pen is used merely as a pointer, the meaning of its message is conveyed partly by the location of the spot to which it points. However, the meaning is determined also by the nature of the display that is currently being presented and the particular details of that display.

The part of the determination that is associated with the nature of the display is 'mode' determination. The simplest on-line man-computer interaction systems we know of have only two modes: a 'control mode' and a 'communication mode.' In the control mode, the signals the operator directs to the computer select one or another of a set of subprograms. In the communication mode, the signals merely enter a buffer space in the computer's memory, and what the computer then does to the signals depends upon which subprogram is brought into action. For example, in an on-line 'debugging' system called 'DDT,' the programmer, trying to find out what is wrong with his programme, might type:

- Sto/

The solidus is a control-mode signal that means 'I have just transmitted to you three characters or their equivalent that constitute the label of a register in memory. When you have received them, look them up in your address table, examine the register with the corresponding address, and type out in octal notation the number you find in it.' In response, DDT would type the number:

- sto/ 123456

If the programmer wanted to change that number to 123321, he would simply type 123321 and press the carriage- return key. The carriage return is another control character. It says, 'Substitute the number now in the buffer for the old one, and do nothing else about this register unless it is mentioned to you again.' The programmer might then check to see that the new number had in fact replaced the old. To make the check, he would press the period key and the solidus key. The computer would then respond with the number in the second line:

- sto/ 123456 123321
- ./123321

It is evident from the foregoing that DDT uses a shorthand notation that is much less explicit than the notations used in the examples given in connection with programming language and organising language. This is partly because the language of DDT is not very far removed from machine code, whereas the hypothetical languages are high-level languages. Nevertheless, there is an advantage to the terseness of the DDT control language that should not be lost to increasing sophistication. The point here is that one part of what the user types is essentially an instruction to the system, telling it what to do to an object, and another part is the object on which the system is to act. This fundamental distinction will probably never disappear. However, it will not long remain as simple as it is in DDT. One of the first necessary complications of the distinction between the control mode and the communication mode has already appeared in several on-line languages and is also found in DDT. It is the 'execute' command. The execute command instructs the system to consider the object communicated no longer as an object to be processed but as a command to be implemented. The computer therefore executes the communicated message as an instruction. This corresponds approximately to removing the quotation marks from a string of characters of ordinary text. Several groups have recently built into ALGOL the capability of removing the quotation marks from a string of characters and executing the string as an ALGOL procedure.

We may expect a continual development of on-line interaction languages until the residual distinction between control and communication mode is carried partly by the syntactic structure of statements and partly by context. In the work with programmes discussed earlier, for example, the system programmer first examined the programmes, treating them as objects, and then tested them, causing the system actually to carry out the procedures. The convenience of having local context or mode implicitly define terms and particularise procedures for him may to some extent be countered by the responsibility, thrust upon the user, of continually keeping track of the prevailing mode. However, one of the basic facts of man-machine interaction is that, although the responsibility for keeping track of mode or situation causes great difficulty in monitoring, it causes almost no difficulty in truly symbiotic interaction.

In truly symbiotic interaction, the human partner is always active, always involved in directing, always 'ahead of the game.' In monitoring, on the other hand, he tends just to sit there, waiting for an alarm to alert him to action. When the alarm goes off, he does not know what the situation is, and it is difficult or impossible to find out in time to do anything effective. It does not help the monitor much to display to him the developing situation, either in summary or in detail, for it is almost impossible for him to think ahead constantly if his thinking has no effect on what happens. In our conception of man-computer interaction in pro-cognitive systems, however, the man is no mere monitor.

He is a partner - indeed he is usually the dominant, leading partner. On-line interaction introduces into the language picture the possibility of 'conversation.' This possibility, together with the need to bring on-line languages abreast of conventional programming languages, opens an inviting field to research and development. It seems to us desirable to move rapidly beyond the simple dichotomy between the control and communication modes and to develop a syntax in which it will be possible to express commands, state facts, and ask questions in any convenient sequence. The most economical approach to that objective appears to be to direct all the operator's signals, except one special 'terminator' signal, into a buffer. The operator can put as long a string as he likes into the buffer.

When he wants the signals to control action or to be acted upon, he presses the terminator key. The computer at once recognises the terminator and calls a translator, a programme that sorts the contents of the buffer into commands and data and puts them into a format determined in part by the syntax of the language and in part by the needs of the programmes to be controlled or employed. The translator initiates the requested actions by executing the first command. From then on, processing follows the course determined by the commands in interaction with the programme.

What is needed, we believe, is a synthesis of the good features of the several approaches that have been mentioned in the foregoing discussion. In order to control - complex processes, an on-line interaction language must have a sophisticated syntax and a large vocabulary. At the same time, to cater to the user's convenience, it should minimize the requirement for complex or manifold control actions, and it should encourage the kind of convergence upon understanding achieved in conversation. To facilitate learning, and to promote efficient utilisation of programmes, on-line interaction languages should be compatible with one another and should fit together into a coherent system.

REPRESENTATION LANGUAGE

The representation of information for storage and retrieval has already been discussed at length. Here we merely reiterate our conviction that both formalisation and sophistication of language seem important for effective representation and efficient processing of a large corpus. We suspect that 'the' representation language, if a single representation language ever becomes dominant over all its competitors, will be essentially a language system. It will have several sublanguages, specialised for different applications. Some of them may have as many syntactic categories as the natural languages and will distinguish among several thousand sharply defined semantic relations. Some of them may 'understand' the complex interrelations among the semantic relations and the syntactic categories and deal competently with several dozen clearly defined information structures. Others will be simpler but less powerful.

We must distinguish between a language or sublanguage and its implementation through computer programming. One language or sublanguage may have several implementations, differing in compactness of packaging and speed of processing, but yielding the same answer to a given question and the same solution to a given problem. There will probably be a demand for two or more implementations of certain sublanguages in the pro-cognitive system.

The over-all language will be a system because all the sublanguages will fall within the scope of one meta-language. Knowing one sublanguage will make it easier to learn another. Some sublanguages will be subsets of others. There will be translators, as suggested earlier, to convert sets of data or domains of knowledge from one representation to another. One sublanguage will resonate with one discipline or problem, another with another. But the whole apparatus of representation will be internally consistent. It will be a coherent system - if the day ever arrives.

Meanwhile, every effort should be made to find a way out of the present chaos of fragmentary and incompatible schemes for representation. Standardisation of terms and formats will doubtless help. The main hope, however, appears to lie in the development of community computing systems. The economic impracticality of having a different system for every user will force convergence. There will be an active market place and a strong incentive to form coalitions. Perhaps one coalition will become a monopoly. Monopoly should not be allowed to stifle research on languages and representations, but it should be encouraged to foster coherence within the operating system.

COMPUTER TECHNIQUES AND PROCEDURES IN LIBRARY

The following studies are concerned with early steps along the course from present digital-computer system to future pro-cognitive systems. Let us consider the studies in the order of their locations along that course. The first ones were intended merely to make it convenient to carry out some of the functions that are required in research on library and pro-cognitive problems or in the efficient use of large collections of documents. The last ones in the sequence were intended to explore functions that we think will actually be involved in future pro-cognitive systems.

AN 'EXECUTIVE' PROGRAMME TO FACILITATE THE USE OF THE PDP-1 COMPUTER

One of the first needs of the study was a computer programme to facilitate the programming and use of the laboratory's digital computer. The computer is a small but excellent machine, Digital Equipment Corporation PDP-I, specialised to facilitate interaction with users who work 'on line.' The PDP-1 has an oscilloscope display with light pen, several electric typewriters, a set of programmable relays, an analogue-to-digital converter, and an assortment of switches and buttons. Its primary memory is small but it is capable of transferring information rapidly between the primary memory and a secondary drum memory that holds about 90,000 eighteen-bit words.

Associated with the computer are two magnetic-tape units. With the computer, it is possible to implement, in a preliminary and schematic way, several of the functions that were described in Part I as functions desirable in a pro-cognitive system. One encounters two main difficulties in trying to do, with the PDP-1 computer, research oriented towards a future period in which information-processing machines will have more advanced capabilities.

First, although the machine is reasonably fast, and although its secondary and tertiary memories make it possible to work with significantly large bodies of information, the machine is not capable of performing deep and complicated operations on really large bodies of text with the speed that would be desired in an operational system. The result is that it may take 30 seconds or a minute to get something that one would like to have almost instantly, that the display flickers on the oscilloscope screen, and so forth.

Second, there is not available, at present, on any machine, either a programming language or a man-machine interaction language that makes it easy to do, or possible to do rapidly, many of the things envisioned in the discussion of pro-cognitive systems in Part I of this report. Our approach, during the study, was simply to put up with, and make allowances for, the shortcomings of the hardware system. It was easy to do that in informal experiments conducted by members of the research group; it was not realistic, however, to hope that all the observers of demonstrations would make the necessary allowances, and the shortcomings of the equipment effectively precluded formal experimentation.

Nevertheless, the equipment situation was at least tolerable, in terms of absolute assessment, and it seemed superb when we compared our man-computer interaction situation with any but two or three of all the others with which we were acquainted. The unavailability of highly developed languages and, of course, the interpreter and compiler programmes that would be required to make them useful - was, however, a seriously inhibiting factor. During the period of our study, two good programming-language systems came into being: DECAL, which is a quite elegant and powerful language and compiler of the ALGOL type, suitable for a small computer, and MACRO, which is an ingenious language and assembler system that incorporates several of the features that DECAL lacks and lacks several of the features that DECAL incorporates.

However, neither DECAL nor MACRO was designed for on-line programming, and neither was designed particularly to handle the problems that seem likely to present themselves to users of pro-cognitive systems. Those considerations led to the effort, which was never quite completed, to develop a composite programme oriented and user-oriented system to facilitate our research in man-machine interaction.

The system is called 'Exec,' which stands, of course, for 'executive program'– and thus expresses something about the mode of operation: statements of the input language, coming into the computer, are examined by the executive programme, and, depending upon whether or not they fall into the class requiring interpretation, are either interpreted and executed with the aid of a set of subroutines associated with the executive programme or simply executed as machine instructions. Exec was written originally in the symbolic language called 'FRAP' and had, as its main function, simplification of the preparation of programmes and subroutines to be translated and assembled by FRAP.

When DECAL became available, Exec was rewritten in DECAL, and slight modifications were made to facilitate the use of Exec in the preparation of programmes and subroutines to be translated and compiled by DECAL. The original intention - to develop Exec to the point at which it could operate as an on-line language as well as an adjunct to a programming language—was not accomplished.

One of the main themes in the work on Exec was to simplify and regularise the 'calling' and 'returning' of subroutines. In most computer-programming systems, and especially in the computer-programming systems that will be required in the implementation of plans of the kind, a computer programme is a complex arrangement of parts. The highest echelon of the structure does little more than represent the chapter headings of the general plan.

The actual work—the detailed processing of data - is handled by subprograms or 'subroutines' that break the task down into successively simpler sub packages at successively lower levels of detail until, finally, there is nothing left for the lowest-echelon subprograms to do but to perform simple, explicitly defined operations upon the few codes or numbers that are supplied to them.

In this process of successive delegation of responsibility, the transactions that appear repeatedly are the 'calling' of a lower-echelon subroutine by a higher-echelon subroutine and the 'returning' of control from the lower-echelon subroutine to the higher-echelon subroutine. Calling usually includes transmission of instructions, and also the designation of the arguments upon which the lower-echelon subroutine must operate, from the calling subroutine to the called subroutine. The transmission of information down the line we shall call 'briefing'.

Transmission of results up the line we shall call 'debriefing.' In the conventional way of handling calling and returning, a subroutine eventually returns control to the subroutine that called it, but it may first call one or more lower-echelon subroutines. Fortunately or unfortunately, depending upon one's point of view, there are many different ways in which subroutines can be called and briefed and in which they can return control and do their debriefing. As indicated, one of the main purposes of Exec is to simplify and regularise this whole process.

In order to simplify the process of calling and returning, Exec is interposed between the calling subroutine and the called subroutine at the time of calling and between the called subroutine and the calling subroutine at the time of returning. With each subroutine is associated a compact code, that provides Exec with a description of the needs.of the subroutine.

Exec can therefore handle in a systematic, centralised manner several of the functions that would otherwise have to be handled by each subroutine. In taking a burden off the routines, Exec takes a burden off the programmers who prepare them. The arrangements in Exec for calling and returning are set up in such a way that the chain of subroutine calls can be recursive. That is to say, it is possible for subroutine *A* to call subroutine *A*, or for subroutine *A* to call a subroutine *B* which, directly or through one of its minions, called subroutine *A*.

To permit recursive operation, one must handle 'temporary storage' - storage of the scratch-pad jottings made by each subroutine during its operation - in such a way that results written by *B*, for example, do not destroy results that *A* calculated before calling *B* and will need to use after *B* returns control. The functions just described have been implemented in a few programming systems - notably in the systems called IPL and LISP.

In IPL and LISP, however, one either works wholly within the system or does not use the system at all. Exec extends the basic programming language and provides the new capabilities and conveniences within the structure of DECAL. In implementing the handling of subroutines, we made use of the technique of the 'pushdown list'. A pushdown list is an arrangement for storing information that resembles the spring-supported tray on which plates are stored in restaurants. If one puts a plate onto the top of the stack, it pushes all the others down, and if one then takes the plate off the top, the others pop up again. Exec, itself, employs one pushdown list.

Another pushdown list is available to the programmer or user through simple commands. He has only to give the name of the entity to be stored into the pushdown list or returned from it and to say whether he wants to push it down or pop it up. In the process of handling a call to a subroutine or a return from a subroutine, Exec examines the subroutine's heading code – determines whether or not, and how, to fulfill each of a number of functions, and then carries out those required. These functions include protecting contents of certain special registers of the processor against destruction during the running of the subroutine, finding the arguments needed by the subroutine and displaying them for its use, accepting the results obtained by the subroutine and communicating them to the calling routine, and protecting the contents of various temporary storage registers and 'flag' registers against modification by the called subroutine.

Exec protects information by putting it into the pushdown list. A second general purpose of Exec is to provide the advantages of generality and the advantages of specificity both at the same time and within the same system. If a computer programme is written in such a way as to make it useful in a particular situation. On the other hand, if the programme is written so that for example, it alphabetises or orders any kind of strings of alphanumeric text in any file or table, then he has to communicate to it, or have the routine that calls it communicate to it, that it should operate on words and that it should alphabetise according to a specified alphabet. In Exec, an effort is made to accommodate very general subroutines and to make it maximally convenient to communicate to them the information required to prepare them for specific applications. This is done by setting up and maintaining a description of the prevailing context of operation. In the terms of the example, his description may contain a specification that the currently prevailing string class is the class of 'words.'

It contains the specification that the *x,* in any subroutine prepared to operate upon 'Table *x,*' should be interpreted as 3. The subroutine, therefore, automatically performs on the operation intended by the programmer, despite the fact that the programmer was thinking in terms of abstractions and not in terms of the particular present task. With arrangements of the kind just suggested, Exec makes it possible to use a subroutine that contains the expression, 'next string,' for example, to operate on the next character, or the next word, or the next sentence, or the next paragraph, or the next section, or the next chapter, and so forth. Exec keeps track of three 'string classes' simultaneously, class *u,* class *v,* and class *w.* At any time, the programmer can set anyone of the string classes to anyone of seven levels. He can write, for example, '*SSCU* word,' meaning to *set* the string class *u* to have the value, *word.* From that time on, until the instruction is superseded, all the subroutines that deal with the string class hierarchy *u* will consider the *u* strings to be words.

The procedure for designating tables is similar to that for designating strings. If the programmer would like to have programmes written in terms of Tables *x, y,* and *z* operate on the contents of Table zones 2, 5, and 7, he writes '*ntox* 2, *ntoy* 5, *ntoz* 7.' * When Exec sees those instructions, it does more than merely substitute 2 for *x,* 5 for *y,* and 7 for *z.* It finds the descriptions, in its file of table descriptions, that characterise the three numbered tables, and it substitutes these descriptions for the pre-previously prevailing descriptions of Tables *x, y,* and *z,* respectively.

When a subroutine operates on the contents of the table, it examines the table's description and controls its processing accordingly. This makes it possible to accommodate diverse formats and conventions. Inasmuch as the adjustments are made 'interpretively' during the running of the programme, the user can change his mind and reprocess something in a slightly different way without having to go through extensive revision and recompilation of his programmes. This is an advantage that the present technique has over the technique, based on the 'communication pool,' that has been developed in connection with the programming of very large computer systems—systems programmed by teams so large as to discourage the effort to enforce the use of a single, standard set of conventions and formats.

The part of Exec that we have been describing is approximately an interpretive communication pool. The third set of functions with which Exec is concerned has to do with the display of alphanumeric information on typewriters and on the oscilloscope screen. Although these are very simple functions, they involve enough detailed programming to be a nuisance unless they are handled in a systematic way. Exec makes it convenient to separate specification of the information to be displayed from specification of the equipment through which it is to be displayed. It uses standard programmes to handle strings that are long enough to be considered messages or texts, but it provides special arrangements to facilitate preparation of labels, headings, and the like.

For example, the programmer can call for the typing of any particular character *x* on whatever typewriter is currently specified to be typewriter *b* simply by writing *'type x.'* If the programmer wants the character to appear upon the screen of oscilloscope *a*, he writes *'scpa x.'* With the aid of Exec, the programmer can define in equally short instructions the size of the print, the vertical position at which the text should begin, and other parameters of the visual display.

Exec's arrangements for displaying capital and lower-case letters on the oscilloscope are primitive, but it is a step in the right direction to have both capital and lower-case letters. At present, a 'lower-case' letter is simply a small capital letter. We settled for that stopgap solution only in the interest of economy. The fourth and final set of functions handled by Exec has to do with display, by the computer, of what the computer is doing. One technique developed for this purpose, a technique called 'Introspection,' because it was developed as a separate project. The arrangements described here are integral to Exec. One of the main causes of difficulty in man-computer interaction is that the computer does not give the man any good clues about what it is doing until it completes a segment of processing and spews forth the results.

When the computer is running, its lights flash so fast that they are scarcely interpretable. It seems important to provide a way of having the computer give a running account of its processing. A part of Exec called the 'Reporting Subsection 'an optional part - is brought into play each time a subroutine is called and each time a subroutine returns control to its caller. When the reporting subsection is brought into action, it examines the list of things that it should do. This list can be changed while Exec and other programmes are running. Ordinarily, the first thing on the list is to give the address, and, if it is available in the directory, also the name, of the subroutine that is being called or that is returning control to its caller. Since the subroutines operate very rapidly, the names and addresses would appear to be presented simultaneously, one on top of another, if they were shown in a fixed location on the screen.

Therefore they are displayed in a format corresponding to that of a conventional outline. If a chain of subroutines is called, each one operating at a level just lower than its caller, the names and addresses appear on successive lines of the display with increasing indentation. Then, as the subroutines return control, each to its caller, the names and addresses are displayed again in such a way as to redisplay the outline pattern from bottom to top. To the display just described can be added, at the option of the operator, a display of the contents of the active registers of the computer. In addition, the operator may see the contents of whatever parts of the computer's memory he wants to examine. He designates the various parts of memory to Exec by typing on the typewriter while the programme is running. He can change his prescription at will.

The current version of Exec allows him to specify nine different sectors of memory, either symbolically or in terms of absolute addresses. When he indicates that he wants to see 'the subroutine,' Exec interprets 'the subroutine' to mean the particular subroutine that is being called, or that is returning control to its caller. That will, of course, be one subroutine at one moment and another at another moment. When the operator wishes to examine a table or a programme in detail, he touches the space bar of the typewriter.

That causes the system to pause in its progression through the sequence of things to be displayed, and to hold the current display until the operator releases it by touching the tab key. The Reporting Subsection provides a few additional conveniences - minor ones introduced from time to time on an *ad hoc* basis - but the foregoing will suffice to give an idea of the existing arrangement. Let us mention a few of the steps not yet accomplished, however. It seems worth while to connect to the Reporting Subsection the 'Introspection' programmes that will be described later.

It is necessary to complete the arrangements that associate the tables that reside in the primary memory to corresponding structures in secondary and tertiary memory and, in the manner of the Atlas computer system, to arrange it so that information structures are automatically shifted up through the memory hierarchy whenever they are addressed. It is necessary, also, to expand the mechanism that associates symbols with machine addresses. That mechanism is only a simple table-searching system, but it is inherently capable of effecting the translation required to make conveniently readable the reports of 'what is currently going on in the computer.'

We found it useful to distinguish, in Exec, between 'intrinsic' and 'extrinsic' subroutines. Exec is highly 'subroutinised' and has the partly hierarchical, partly recursive, structure that we have described as essential for pro-cognitive systems. Each sub-function of Exec that appears to have any likelihood of proving useful in future applications is separated out and set into the form of a subroutine.

In the process of writing subroutines to handle substantive problems - subroutines that made use of Exec but were not at first intended to be part of the Exec system - we encountered repeatedly several sets or clusters of functions. By associating with Exec the subroutines prepared to handle those functions, we were able to build up a system of considerable convenience and power. The part of the system not intrinsic to Exec was too extensive to be held in primary memory at all times. However, it was clearly desirable to bring parts of it into primary memory - coherent clusters of it corresponding to major functions - whenever required in the execution of a programme. The easiest way to accomplish dynamic storage and transfer of subroutines, and to handle the associated bookkeeping, was to take care of it automatically through Exec's ability to examine calling sequences and subroutine headings. We did not make much progress towards that end during the course of the study.

However, we did work with the problem enough to see the great convenience and power that reside in a coherent structure of computer subroutines and a largely automatic arrangement for calling them and transferring information among them. Evidently, the more sophisticated the arrangements, the larger the fraction of the subroutines that will be intrinsic to the arrangements. We visualise a system in a continual process of development, with a set of intrinsic subroutines, a set of extrinsic subroutines, and a continual flow from the extrinsic set to the intrinsic set as more and more functions are brought within the scope and capability of the system.

WEB BASED LIBRARY SERVICE

A digital Library service manages and develops electronic services, the library Web sites and library staff. According to White, it can be defined broadly as 'an information access service in which users ask questions via electronic means, *e.g.,* e-mail or web forms'.

Library service on the internet requires many of the same qualities as traditional references: accuracy, promptness, courtesy, an understanding of the information need. It provides users with the convenience of accessing information in their own time, saving them traveling cost and time and new options for answering reference questions. The provision of these services is not constrained by the traditional opening hours but can be offered on a 24-hour, seven-days-a-week basis known as 24/7. And while there may be a disadvantage in not having a face-to face encounter, there are many advantages to this new medium and the greatest advantage is that many more users can be helped by using electronic library services. Advantages and disadvantages of electronic access over printed form access are showed in table. Web based services are established due to the following reasons.

- Ensuring the needs of users and the accessible information sources are suitable matched at all times.
- Delivering those information sources to the user in a timely and appropriate fashion.
- Ensuring the information provided is high quality, accurate and appropriate.

- Assisting the user in interpreting the materials, if necessary.
- Promoting user awareness of new services and information sources as they develop.
- Providing users with individualised guidance and support as they build their information search and application skills.

Table. Advantages and Disadvantages of Printed Form over Electronic Access

Sl.No.	Advantages of Print Form	Electronic Form
1.	Format is tested and standardised	Format is in the early stages of development
2.	Easy for users to use	Requires some training for users to use
3.	No special equipment needed	Special equipment required (hardware, software, printers, etc.,)
4.	Easy to locate (if shelved properly)	Access is currently unreliable (URL problems, internet connection problems, etc.,)
5.	Use is limited only to copyright	Use is limited by laws copyright laws and licensing agreements
6.	Archiving is effective and	Archiving is 'up in permanent the air'
Sl.No.	**Disadvantages of Print form**	**Electronic Form**
1.	Operating costs are considerable cataloging, claiming,	Operating costs are (ordering, minimal (no and binding) cataloging, binding, or clalmlng)
2.	Requires shelving	No shelving required
3.	Often mutilated, stolen, or	Cannot be mutilated, misshelved stolen, or misshelved
4.	Requires extensive storage space	Saves considerable storage space
5.	Allows only one user at a time	Allows for multiple users with simultaneous access
6.	Slow delivery via 'snail mail'	Immediate receipt of issue
7.	Issues are easily lost in the	No more missing mail or missing issues
8.	Slow publication	Fast publication

DIFFERENT RESOURCES FOR WEB BASED LIBRARY SERVICES

Today, users may have access a variety of textual information resources. There are different kinds of webbased reference resources and services for accessing information from libraries such as OPAC, Gateways, Portals, Subject Portals, Electronic Journals, Online Databases, Subject Directories and Search Engines. These resources overlap considerably in the type of information they cover, and sometimes it is difficult to distinguish between some of them. A library should have a good collection of these resources like selected Web links, subscription resources, and library materials in well-organised pages for serving better services to their users.

Many libraries and organisations are providing digital reference service through collaborative services. Existing library consortia are adding digital reference to current shared services, and networks of libraries. Some regional library consortia are offering member libraries the opportunity to share reference questions with each other using the Internet and other technologies.

OPAC

OPAS's - On Line Public Access Catalogues, form an important part of many digital library's collections. It allows users to search for the bibliographic records contained within a library's collections. Now days, some OPAC also provide access to electronic resources and databases, in addition to the traditional bibliographic records.

GATEWAYS

A gateway is defined as a facility that allows easier access to network based resources in a given subject area. Gateways provide a simple search facility and a much-enhanced service through a resource database and indexes, which can be searched through a web based interface. Information provided by gateways is catalogued by hand. Gateways cover a wide range of subjects, through some areas, such as music and religious studies, currently lack subject gateways. Some well-known gateways are as follows:

- Internet Public Library (IPL),
- Bulletin Board for Libraries (BUBL),
- National Information Services and Systems (NISS),

PORTALS

In the library community, portals may be defined as an amalgamation of services to the users where the amalgamation is achieved through seamless integration of existing services by using binding agents such as customisation and authentication services, search protocols such as Z39.50, loan protocols such as ISO10161, and e-commerce.

The result is a personalised service which allows the individual to access the rich content of both print-based and electronic systems. Portals are either commercial or free web facilities that offer information services to a specific audience. The facilities include web search to communication to e-mail to news,etc.There are three kinds of portals; Consumer (or horizontal), Vertical and Enterprise.

- Consumer portals are aimed at consumer audiences and offer free e-mail, games, chat,etc., Examples are Yahoo!, MSN and AOL.
- Vertical portals, target a specified audience, such as a particular

industry, and offer many of the consumer portal features. Example includes VerticalNet.

- Enterprise portals on the other hand are similar to consumer portals, but they are offered only to corporations or similar organisations. Examples include Epicentric and Corporate Yahoo! These portals can be best understood as electronic pathfinders for users, pulling together in one place in a web site selected links to subjects or interest-oriented resources located on the WWW.

SUBJECT PORTALS

Web Search Engines had been developed initially by computer scientists, by borrowing techniques from information retrieval search such as best match searching and relevance ranking. Information professional are increasing bringing their skills to help organise the growing wealth of Internet resources.

A good example of their influence is the development of subject-specific web search engines known as subject portals, where evaluation of material covered is a major concern. Two prime UK subject portals are SOSIG Social Science Information Gateway, covering social science resources and OMNI Organising medical networked information covering medical resources. Subject portal sites can be very helpful, but they should be used with care. Users should bear the following points in their mind:

- The aim of the subject portal is to list and review the most important sites on the web relevant to that subject. The sites are usually constantly peer-reviewed to ensure that the site is relevant and up to date.
- New sites are appearing all the time. Relying on a subject portal site to find everything users require may mean that they miss an important site that has recently appeared and has not yet been reviewed by the producers of the particular subject portal.
- A subject portal is a one stop shop for information on the topic it covers. Users don't have to carry out extensive Internet searches in order to find the information require. They can simply go to the required subject portal site.
- Subject portals save users having to have long lists of bookmarks (saved addresses of web pages), which are often, cumbersome and time consuming to arrange and keep up to date. However, if users do prefer to use bookmarks they can arrange them in an order to suit the way they work and not have an order forced on them by the subject portal.
- A subject portal site is only as good as the reviewers who peer-review the site listed. The reviewers need to have a policy of keeping the portal sites up to date and of constantly reviewing the sites they list,

to make sure that they are still relevant and still contain good, timely information.

- A subject portal may be available to everyone who needs to use it to only certain groups of users. A good portal should be publicly available to anyone who needs it.

ELECTRONIC JOURNALS

Electronic journals form a large part of the collection of a library for providing web based services. Today many journals are available electronically - some are full text and some contain only bibliographic information with abstract. Major advantage of electronic journals is that they are constantly updated and easy to access but disadvantage is that breaching of copyright law is very easy.

They are available as bitmaps, PostScript, PDF, ASCII, SGML and HTML. Library services may be delivering to users on CDRom, through e-mail or through web. Some international societies and associations have developed their own digital libraries through which users can get access to all their publications. Services are available to the members of society or associations through subscription.

ONLINE DATABASES

These are large collections of machine-readable data that are maintained by commercial agencies and are accessed through communication lines. Many libraries subscribe to them for easy access and use of current information. The disadvantage is that only bibliographic data is presented and not full text. The information cannot be accessed when the system is down for any reason. Examples Ei Compendex, SciFinder Scholar, Web of Science, Current Contents,etc.

SEARCH ENGINES

Search Engines are huge databases of web page files that have been assembled automatically by machines where as the subject directories are human-compiled and maintained. Search engine indexes every page of a Web site and subject directories linked only homepages.

Search Engine is the popular term for an information retrieval (IR) system. A search engine is computer software that searches a collection of electronic materials to retrieve citations, documents, or information that matches or answers a user's query. The retrieved materials may be text documents, facts that have been extracted from text, images, or sounds. A query is a question phrased so that it can be interpreted properly by search engine. Depending on the type of software, it may be a collection of commands, a statement in either full or partial sentences, one or more keywords, or in the case of Non-text searching, an image or sequence of sounds to be matched.

SUBJECT DIRECTORIES

Subject directories differ from search engines in that search engines are populated by robots that finds and index sites whereas humans making editorial decisions that populate subject directories. Subject directories are basically index home pages of sites and can be classified as general, academic, commercial or portal.

Among the well known subject directories are the Argus Clearinghouse and Yahoo. Strengths include relevance, effectiveness and relative high quality of content. Weaknesses are that they lack depth in their coverage of the subjects.

NEW WEB BASED LIBRARY SERVICES

VIRTUAL LIBRARY TOURS

Web sites of libraries provides virtual library guide to the physical facilities including collections, services and infrastructure available in the library. The combination of library maps and floor plans, library departments and photographic views are used for the tour. Virtual library tours are also using new technologies such as QuickTime movies etc and are beginning to replace image maps on main campus Web sites.

ASK-A-LIBRARIAN

Ask-A-Librarian services are Internet-based question and answer service that connects users with individuals who possess specialised subject knowledge and skill in conducting precision searches. Most 'Ask-a-Librarians' services have a web-based question submission form or an e-mail address or both. Users are invited to submit their queries by using web forms or through e-mail. Once a query is read by a service, it is assigned to an individual expert for answering. An expert responds to the query with factual information and or a list of information resources.

The response is either sent to the user's e-mail account or is posted on the web so that the user can access it after a certain period of time. Many services have informative web sites that include archives of questions and answers and a set of FAQs. Users are usually encouraged to browse archives and FAQs before submitting a question in case sufficient information already exists.

REAL TIME SERVICES

A new and exciting method of digital reference service that libraries are attempting to provide more and more now is live reference. These are real-time, interactive reference services in which the users can talk to a real, live reference librarian at any time, from anywhere in the world.

User and librarian can interact using chat technologies, and unlike with e-mail reference the librarian can perform a reference interview of sorts by asking the users to elaborate or clarify if needed before proceeding to answer the question. The librarian can perform Internet searches and push Web sites onto the user's browser, and can receive immediate feedback from the users as to whether their question have been answered to satisfaction.

BULLETIN BOARDS

A bulletin board is an electronic communications forum that hosts posted messages and articles connected to a common subject or theme or interest. It allows users to call in and either leaves or retrieves messages. The messages may be directed to all users of the bulletin board or only to particular users. But all messages can be read by all users. Several libraries are using bulletin boards for their web-based library services. The bulletin board system is also used as an interactive interface to invite suggestions on activities and services of a library. It can also be used as an interface to distribute library services.

WEB-BASED USER EDUCATION

Web guides and teaching tools are found everywhere on the Web because they are easily updated, accessed, and printed on demand. The web-based user education provides a high degree of interactivity and flexibility to the users.

The library web sites can use web-based user education for imparting training to users in teaching the basic library skills along with glossary of library terms, using Library OPAC, locating books, magazines, biographical data and other library materials, understanding how to navigate the libraries Web site and how to select the most relevant database, instructions for searching CD ROM and guidance in locating web-based databases and other electronic resources and instructions on subject searching training, using Boolean operators and searching internet resources through search engines.

WEB FORMS

Library web sites have some web forms for suggestions and comments on the Library Services. Different types of Web Forms are available on web that may be an Indent form for acquiring some publications, interlibrary loan request form for document delivery, Ask-a-Librarian forms, on line reservation form or user survey form, etc.

INDIAN SCENARIO

The Indian libraries also have realised to give web based services to users and they have recognised that working together can accomplish for more than they can do individually. Many Indian libraries in India are not geared up for accessing e-journals due to various reasons including user ignorance, infrastructure and initial funds. The library and information networks in India were initiated in early eighties. The growth during this period can be linked to some of the policies that Government of India pursued. Some institutions like CSIR, ISRO, DRDO, DAE, ICAR, SIRNET, NICNET, NISSAT, INFLIBNET, MHRD and IIM libraries are actively working continuously to improve the present situation. They spend annually a huge amount of money towards library acquisition, especially towards journals, e-journals and e-databases.

Some initiative include, Indian Institute of Management for accessing bibliographic databases, CSIR laboratories for Science Direct, FORSA for accessing Astronomy and Astrophysics journals, Hyderabad Knowledge park members of J-gate, INFLIBNET (UGC–INFONET) initiative for full text and databases like BIOSIS and CAS and INDEST for a host of full text sources and few bibliographic databases for the benefit of IITs, IISc, NITs and Engineering colleges. In India, library consortia are emerging as one of the important service to users. The Indian consortiums will help the library to provide better services to the users by investing Meagre amount. To expand the access for more number of e-journals, e-books and other eresources, we have to develop the digital library infrastructure as a platform for e-learning.

FUTURE OF WEB BASED SERVICES

Library Web services will continue to spread out, offering more full-text electronic journals and indexes that do not now include full text will begin to do so, or link to external resources. Bibliographic access to full-text periodicals either through cataloging, databases, or vendors will be in improved form. There will be more Web forms for user feedback, and perhaps a virtual librarian who interacts in real time chat or video conferencing. More Document delivery services to distance education or users and Savings on Interlibrary Loan and user convenience are incentives. Information resources through creative consortia purchasing will be popular. A well-developed user education modules or tutorials, especially to support independent exploration of library and Web resources. Somebody will have to figure out how to keep Word users from saving print documents as XML, without thinking in terms of Web, not print, space. XML will be embraced as a way to control page appearance and Behaviour, but it will take a while for people to figure out how to use it well and there will be trends we haven't thought of yet.

CONCLUSION

The standards for organising web-based resources are still in the early stages of development, and librarians are forced to utilise standards for print resources that were not designed for electronic resources. Additionally web-based information resources are volatile in the sense that may be moved from one site to another or may be removed altogether from web. Web-based library services will become more widespread and sophisticated as the web becomes common place throughout the world, and to be successful players in the E-world. Libraries must continue to address the web design and implementation issues. As we actively transfer library services, our central purpose remain the same, to serve and teach users to find, evaluate, and use information effectively. The librarians should be expert to hold the hands of the users who are moving towards new communication paradigm a shift from face to face human contact to human machine interaction, from paper to electronic delivery, from text centered mode to multimedia and from physical presence to virtual presence. Despite these changes in communication technology, the reference interview will remain at the heart of the reference transaction. To meet these challenges the librarians may play a leadership role in providing better Web Based library Services facilities to their current techno savvy users.

9

ICT Advancements and the Future of Libraries

The rapid developments of ICT since, the birth of computers and the Internet has contributed so much in changing the way we live our daily life. They affect the way we do things, which includes the way we do our jobs. They even affect the way we relate to one another in terms of personal relationships, as well as professional ones. Almost everything we do in daily basis has something to do with ICT. It ranges from simple stand-alone applications to collaborative and networked systems. Nowadays it's almost unimaginable to write an article without the help of a word processor application, online dictionary or thesaurus, reference management application, and online journal databases.

All these advancements have offered invaluable help for people from any professions in terms of working more effectively and productively. Some ICT advancements however can cause fundamental changes in the traditional roles and functions of certain professions. They fundamentally alter the ways in which people or institutions provide products and services. Libraries—especially academic libraries—and their librarians have been living through these inevitable, yet often subtle, transformations. Nowadays most librarians are familiar with—or at least aware of—approval plans, selector services, new acquisitions of library materials with embedded electronic bibliographic records, copy cataloging, self-check-in/out, Internet search engines, virtual reference services, etc.

All these roles and/or functions (acquisition, cataloging, reference, etc.) were traditionally the domains of (local) librarians. Local librarians used to have the authority over or in charge of performing these roles and/or functions. However the new environment affected or created by ICT advancements has created new 'arrangements', where these basic roles and/or functions are gradually being taken over by ICT, or at least transferred to other institutions outside the libraries. In short, traditional roles and/or functions of librarians are being challenged by the rapid technological changes, which usually also leads to social changes. Librarians need to 'redefine' their roles and/or functions in the new landscape of the future information society. Davenport stated something that I believe is a good response to the challenge.

She suggested that librarians should have "expanded, more collaborative roles in the creation and dissemination of knowledge," which will empower (academic) libraries to assume new role and/or function as learning space instead of information storehouse. It is now up to librarians on how to assume this 'new' role and/or function in the new landscape. Digital libraries (DLs) and/or institutional repositories (IRs) offer opportunities for librarians and libraries to re-assert their influence in the creation and dissemination of knowledge. DLs/IRs is a strategic move for libraries to maintain their relevance in the new landscape of ICT-savvy society. However before going into any further discussions, we need to be on the same page on what we call digital libraries (DLs) and/or institutional repositories (IRs).

EDUCATIONAL DIGITAL LIBRARIES

The democratisation of content creation via ubiquitous Internet tools and infrastructure has fueled an explosion of user-generated digital content in the commercial and educational markets. Federal agencies in the United States, such as the National Science Foundation, are actively seeking ways to integrate teachers and learners into the education cyber-infrastructure. The overall purpose of this education cyberinfrastructure is to connect people with information and with web-based tools to improve productivity, teaching, and learning. By connecting teachers and learners with tools, they become co-creators of educational content. Educational digital libraries, part of this cyberinfrastructure, have been created as places to deposit and disseminate educational content, which often takes the form of online learning resources of varying levels of granularity.

Digital library content can be created easily and deposited rapidly, placing it outside the peer review processes typically employed by publishers and professional societies, but it is unclear whether teachers are using high quality online learning resources in the classroom. To date, educational digital library developers, catalogers, teachers and school administrators have depended on one or a combination of the following proxies to establish an imprimatur of content quality: the reputation and oversight of a funding organisation, the credentials of the content creator, or the collection development policies of specific digital libraries.

However, the definition of 'quality'for organisations like those often reflects internal policies and goals, resulting in reviews or judgements that are not comparable across institutions. Further blurring the boundaries between creator-reviewer, teacher-learner and publisherconsumer, many sites employing user ratings and comment tools, such as YouTube, Flickr, iTunesU, and ccMixter provide an alternative to the evolving education cyber-infrastructure, creating a rich and diverse environment for disseminating user-generated educational content. Most educational digital libraries do not rely on even a quasi-review for assessing the quality of the content created for, or by, their users as the above sites do.

However, in the omnipresent climate of accountability within the U.S., K-12 education system at the federal, state and local levels, education digital libraries are being challenged to prove their value. For these reasons, it is useful, if not necessary, to develop a method to review the quality of online education resources. And, since, social networking tools make sharing a by-product of content creation, it is necessary to develop a standardised set of measures that can be employed across a range of education digital library environments while leveraging existing and emerging social and technical networks to enrich, facilitate, and automate the review process.

This stage describes the development of a guide to assess the quality of educational learning resources within the context of the Instructional Architect, a web-based content-authoring tool for K-12 teachers in the United States. We describe the motivation for developing this Quality Guide, the process for creating it by synthesising the rubrics of other education digital libraries, and the results of testing and using the Guide with K-12 teachers in the context of professional development workshops.

Analyses of its usability and reliability indicate that the Quality Guide influences how teachers design instructional activities using online learning resources. But, defining 'quality' remains a difficult task since, the perception of quality is dependent on a reviewer's, or user's, purpose for the learning resources and context of their use. Over the past 10-15 years, as part of the many global initiatives created to provide access to online educational resources, educational digital libraries in the United States have been developed for K-12 and higher education audiences with support from state and federal agencies: from private foundations, and from universities.

These institutions funded projects create, or provide access to, curricula that integrates online educational resources and training programmes to empower teachers to incorporate learning technologies into their daily preparation and practice and, ultimately, to design their own learning resources. Educational digital library developers have gathered online learning resources of varying levels of granularity (*e.g.*, from images to entire lessons) and of varying sources of authorship (*e.g.*, grant-funded subject matter experts; K-12 teachers; graduate students) into central online portals to enable discovery and re-use by other educators. While traditional libraries use collection development plans to guide acquisitions that are based on knowledge of their users, educational digital libraries acquire resources created as a result of projects with museums, practicing teachers, researchers and from Internet users.

The challenge is to balance collecting and providing access to many online learning resources while maintaining a level of resource quality, cataloging, and curation that distinguishes educational digital libraries from generic Internet search engines and non-educational social software. However, it is often as difficult for teachers and learners to define quality as it is for the courts to define pornography. As U.S., Supreme Court Justice Potter Steward once noted, 'I know it when I see it." The problem (or the solution?) lies in the perspective of users who are confronted with a variety of resources of indeterminate origin.

For school administrators, teachers, and learners, a high quality resource could consist of an entire lesson that meets several state standards; a web-based animation that accurately depicts a science concept. Grappling with the idea of 'quality', several education digital libraries have already created rubrics to assess their content. As we tried to apply these criteria to the content in the Instructional Architect, we observed that portions of each rubric were applicable in different settings, and other portions were specific to each digital library with little room for re-use outside of the original context. As such, our goals were:

- To synthesise the various dimensions of existing rubrics in order to identify a standardised set of criteria that could potentially be used by any digital library with online educational resources; and
- To create a guide that could be used to assess the quality of materials in the Instructional Architect projects.

This stage briefly describes our process for developing the standardised set of assessment criteria; evaluating its utility and usability with middle school science and math teachers; developing a Quality Guide for use with Instructional Architect projects; testing its reliability; and, exploring how the Guide could foster teachers' skills in designing learning resources.

PREVIOUS RESEARCH

Many education digital library builders have developed rubrics to help assess the quality of online educational resources generated by teachers, faculty and learners. However, the motivations and methods for implementing the rubrics vary as do the implied assumptions about the value of the results for each education digital library. Established publishing houses and professional societies institute peer review processes to maintain a reputation for producing quality publications thereby increasing subscriptions and membership.

For newly-funded education digital libraries, under pressure to prove their value, rubrics and a process to measure quality, were created to first establish a reputation with users. Similarly, other education digital libraries used rubrics to support access to high quality resources in a digital library or repository because use of a collection development policy for inclusion of quality resources adds value and buy-in from peer reviewers and users. Still other sites developed a rubric to guide authors in creating high quality online resources by gathering feedback from target users. The methods by which education digital libraries collected data using rubrics and how they used that information also varied. Muramatsu and Agogino used a rubric to gather feedback from targeted users to inform collection development, while Recker, Walker, and Lawless gathered data through automated mechanisms to provide teachers with suggestions based on resources they had previously viewed and used. Establishing peer review panels and processes was not a *de facto* choice for every education digital library. Enlisting users-as-builders, or reviewers-as-builders, is a characteristic of the grass-roots environment in which many education digital libraries evolved over the last decade in the U.S.

However, many digital library developers found that gathering reviews from users was difficult, though providing incentives, in the form of awards or other methods was one way to increase acceptance and adoption of the rubric and review process and of the education digital library in general. The process of creating and testing an assessment rubric can be time consuming. Many rubric creators believe it is important to map out stakeholders and end-users, review previous work by other digital libraries and learn how to gather data. Testing a rubric with users, for formative evaluation, further refines the rubric, yielding usability information as well as real time feedback from target users which ultimately assists with the process of implementing the rubric with a larger group of users.

FACILITATING INSTITUTIONAL VISIBILITY

Academic libraries have always contributed to the institutional visibility of their host institutions. They have unconsciously played 'silent' marketing role, promoting their host institutions in the process. Their unique nature as public spaces has allowed them to be visited by various members of the community, inside and outside of campus boundaries. Libraries are the very few institutions in the world where ordinary people would feel comfortable to visit even though they don't have any membership or institutional affiliation. Academic libraries should capitalise on this aspect to facilitate institutional visibility.

Before the advent of the Internet and DLs/IRs, this would mean providing their traditional collections and services, and physical spaces to the campus communities and the society. The Internet, open access movement, and DLs/IRs have provided new opportunities for academic libraries to raise their contributions to the facilitating of institutional visibility of their host institutions. Digital contents in IRs should be provided freely to enable a wider dissemination to the global audience, which in turn will translate into a significant increase in institutional visibility. There is no longer any physical barrier that limits the scope of the dissemination of the IRs' contents as in physical library collections. This is also the experience of DI. Table shows the web access profile for 'petra.ac.id' domain.

Where Visitors Go on Petra.ac.id.

Table.Domain Profile for 'petra.ac.id' from Alexa

Subdomain	Per Cent of Site Traffic
Digilib.petra.ac.id	59.6
Dewey.petra.ac.id	20.5
Petra.ac.id	5.1
Genesis.petra.ac.id	4.3
Careercenter.petra.ac.id	1.8
Puslit2.petra.ac.id	1.1
Fportfolio.petra.ac.id	1.1
It.petra.ac.id	0.7
Puslit.petra.ac.id	0.7
Communication.petra.ac.id	0.4
John.petra.ac.id	0.4

This is a very significant contribution that PCU Library–through DI–has made to the overall 'Internet marketing' of the university. The access statistics from Alexa is confirmed by the weblog of the DI server as shown in table. More opportunities to facilitate institutional visibility can be gained when we share metadata of our digital contents with other IRs. This can be achieved by utilising the OAIPMH or even a 'low-tech' approach by exporting the metadata and exchange them using spreadsheet application such as Microsoft Excel.

Table. Web Access Statistics of Desa Informasi

Month	Unique Visitors	Number of Visits	Pages	Hits	Bandwidth
Sep-09	160,097	355,177	3,125,802	6,686,167	191.36 GB
Oct 2009	224,082	607,877	5,305,997	11,296,525	315.91 GB
Nov 2009	215,583	563,184	5,005,537	10,664,877	325.83 GB
Dec 2009	201,370	510,646	4,581,746	9,751,878	283.93 GB
Jan-10	212,415	538,796	4,538,643	9,769,348	295.05 GB
Feb-10	197,727	450,327	4,293,240	8,789,435	360.64 GB
Mar-10	247,483	615,001	5,058,876	10,573,688	431.89 GB
Apr-10	237,076	577,638	4,845,910	10,138,585	454.83 GB
May 2010	207,424	484,272	4,225,088	8,831,741	436.39 GB
Jun-10	199,156	454,782	3,975,456	8,281,444	496.72 GB
Jul-10	174,474	360,614	3,175,481	6,503,735	398.71 GB
Aug 2010	157,810	317,685	2,804,185	5,897,145	338.25 GB
	2,434,697	5,835,999	50,935,961	107,184,568	4,329,51GB

This approach is being utilised by DI while an upgrade to an OAI-PMH compliant system is still in progress. The Indonesian Ministry of National Education under its Directorate General of Higher Education has launched a collaborative programme to create a 'union catalog' of metadata for local contents from higher education institutions across Indonesia called Garuda. Networking opportunities like this provide increased visibility of our IRs and host institution. Rankings by independent organisations that measure web sites and online resources provide additional incentives for developing IRs.

One of them is the Ranking Web of World Universities that measures world universities' commitment to open access by looking at digital contents on their web sites. Using certain methodology it has managed to rank world universities based on several parameters. DI opens up its digital contents to be indexed by Google, which has enabled Webometrics to measure the 'Size' and 'Rich Files' stored in DI. Webometrics rankings are important for us in Indonesia since, they are being used by Directorate General of Higher Education as one of several metrics to measure performances of Indonesian higher education institutions. PCU has been ranked #5 along with big state universities in Indonesia. A good rank will surely contribute to the increased visibility of the host institutions. This fact strengthens the assertion that IRs serve as one of "meaningful indicators of an institution's academic quality ... thus increasing the institution's visibility, status, and public value".

FACILITATING SCHOLARLY COMMUNICATIONS

Although reforming scholarly communication system has been one of the 'two strategic issues' that IRs try to address, McDowell concluded that "IR has been relatively unsuccessful in fulfilling 'original' role.' This assertion was supported by his survey, which found that "the percentage of peer-reviewed works—pre-and post-prints, e-journal articles, and e-books—is considerably around 13 per cent". It is obvious IRs has been facing serious challenges in the scholarly communication arena.

There are several reasons why IRs is not the preferred choice for disseminating researches. Aschenbrenner *et al.,* observed that "journal publication patterns are already well in place and they are often (rightly or wrongly) considered the most reliable route to scientific credit". Foster added to that observation by identifying the current established system that "rewards faculty members with tenure and promotion based on their success at getting published in respected scholarly journals" as the main reason why 'professors do not have much incentive to put their material in an experimental online archive'.

There are also some faculties "who believe that self-archiving may threaten their rights over their work, their relationship with their favourite publishers, or their status in their disciplinary communities." This trend has led Salo to assert that "libraries whose support for repositories rests purely on hopes of collecting peerreviewed literature would be well-advised not to bother with them".

Another challenge in the scholarly communication arena comes from the fact that most IRs are functioning only as digital resources management system, without 'the more complex services on which users depend'. IRs might be useful and/or powerful for organising and managing digital resources, but "want something that will support the authoring process, not just the finished product". IRs also needs to strive to 'become a natural part of the user's daily work environment'. This might explain why IRs can achieve relative successes in acquiring contents from students, but not from faculties or peer-reviewed publication authors. Salo noticed that slight exceptions might apply for "younger scholars may be attracted to self-archiving as a way to game a prestige system otherwise stacked against them".

Besides all the shortcomings of IRs in the scholarly communication arena, I believe IRs has managed to reduce the total monopoly of conventional journal publishers. Many journal publishers have revised their publishing and copyright policies to allow authors to selfarchive in institutional or subject repositories. The new policies wouldn't have had materialised had it not been because of open access movement (or spirit) embodied in IRs. There are currently open access (book and journal) publishers offering alternatives to conventional publishers. More and more universities and research institutions are jumping into the open access (and IRs) bandwagon by instituting Open Access Mandates in their institutions.

Although in its current state IRs might not achieve big success in (radically) reforming scholarly communication, I believe that IRs has contributed—to certain extent—the efforts in "advancing the positive transformation of scholarly communication over the long term". The same challenge is faced by DI in acquiring journal articles from faculties. DI—as an IRs system—has not yet accommodated any authoring or collaborative process. In its current state, DI acquires contents for eDIMENSI (scientific journal articles) collections through a formal cooperation with the Research Center at PCU. The Research Center is the formal agency at PCU that manages the review, editorial, and publication processes of DIMENSI journals using the Open Journal System (OJS).

The cooperation allows the Library to batch download the newly published articles and feed them into DI. It might be the future direction to merge the two systems into a single platform, which will streamline much of the processes involved in both entities (Research Center and Library) and open up opportunities to create new collaborative features in the future.

FACILITATING COLLABORATIONS

An important aspect of IRs that is often overlooked is its potential as a collaborative platform for the campus communities. If we agree that IRs is, as Lynch stated, "a set of services that a university offers to the members of its community for the management and dissemination of digital materials created by the institution and its community members" then academic libraries have an invaluable asset in their hands.

This asset has a functions and/or roles that span traditional boundaries of campus communities, units, and academic disciplines. Due to this nature, academic libraries that implement and manage IRs will soon discover themselves introduced to a rich variety of local contents produced by different campus communities covering a wide range of academic disciplines. Cross-pollination or cross-fertilisation of knowledge is a natural consequence of exposures to such rich and diverse local contents. Contents produced by a campus community can be re-used as learning resources by other campus communities. Marketing or promotional efforts can be conducted by academic libraries to introduce these local contents to all academic departments and provide insights on possibilities of their uses for each department.

Libraries can also expand features in their IRs to be able to link to e-learning systems used on campus. The linking will enable students and faculties to access our local contents directly from the e-learning systems that they are using for teaching and learning, thus increasing exposures of the contents to various campus communities. These efforts will expose local contents from a specific campus community to a wider audience.

Thematic exhibitions will also provide rich exposures for students, who otherwise would have been 'confined' to their particular field of studies. The experience will enrich students' learning experience. Thematic exhibitions of local contents can sometimes create unique opportunities for inter-disciplinary conversations. Liauw told of an interesting story as an example of how thematic exhibitions can create such conversations.

A thematic onsite exhibition featuring photography documentary of Sedulur Sikep—an ethnic minority in Central Java, Indonesia—was held in 2006, displaying works of a student from Visual Communication Design Department. The exhibition sparked interests from other academic disciplines to conduct other researches on the ethnic minority. An English Department faculty was interested to conduct further study on the linguistic aspects of the ethnic minority. Another faculty from Interior Design Department expressed interests in doing further studies on the ornamental design on the ethnic's settlements.

This example shows that academic libraries should treat their local contents and exhibition spaces as assets to be used to facilitate collaborations and conversations across academic disciplines. Wider collaborations among different campus units and academic departments can be facilitated when academic libraries capitalise on their local contents in IRs to reach out to the society. Academic libraries can create and carry out various programmes and activities jointly with other campus communities. Surabaya Memory (SM) provided a good example on this aspect. Digital resources in SM have been used as part of the teaching and learning process by Architecture Department, Tourism and Leisure Management Department, and Hotel Management Department.

However SM has also become a collaborative platform for PCU Library and other campus units to reach out to the society in Surabaya city. Every May (anniversary of Surabaya) SM conducts thematic exhibitions in a mall in Surabaya. During the exhibition, which usually lasts four to ten days, various competitions, cultural performances, and heritage walks are held to celebrate the city's anniversary.

All these programmes and activities have been made possible by the collaborations between the Library and various academic departments. The Event Management course at Hotel Management Department has been using SM as real world projects for its students. The students are assigned to help the Library in preparing and supervising the exhibition, looking for sponsors, creating events and performances during the exhibition, etc.

The Cultural Tourism course at Tourism and Leisure Management Department has also been using SM as real world projects for its students by conducting heritage walks throughout the year for campus communities as well as the general public. IRs can also serve as collaborative platform to build networks with various parties outside the university boundaries. SM has been functioning as a networking tool for PCU. Various co-operations and collaborations have been initiated between PCU communities and outside parties through SM.

Furthermore SM has served as a common platform for campus communities at PCU to reach out to the society. It is obvious from that IRs can facilitate collaborations if academic libraries are willing to go beyond merely populating their IRs with digital contents. Collaborations with various campus communities will strengthen the libraries' roles on campus and help libraries tremendously in advocating their services to the campus communities. Libraries can even increase the institutional visibility of the whole institution with their IRs projects.

DEVELOPMENT OF IT SKILLS FOR INFORMATION PROFESSIONALS

As a result of Information explosion the libraries and information centers (LICs) have become a necessity. A continuous flow of information in all the sectors of human activity through research and innovation has brought drastic changes in the present society. At present age Knowledge and information are strategic inputs in all walks of life, along with the traditional ones of man, money and materials. Knowledge and information will continue to play a significant role in the socio-economic development. Hence there is expansion of the employment market for library and information professionals. But despite increase in the number of jobs, the total market demand for LISc professionals at present is far less than the total output. Moreover, the quality of output is not fully compatible with the requirements of the expanding job market. Librarianship today has arrived at the information age where the role of information is increasingly emphasised as an economic resource, a marketable commodity and as a social wealth. In this context the role of librarian is very much important. He/ she will have to act as a facilitator, advisor, consultant, instructor, navigator, searcher, researcher, evaluator, organiser, preserver, promoter, communicator, technical expert, as well as a manager, leader, entrepreneur and visionary.

And for the success of library and information centers as effective communication system, the development of manpower to do such work is vital. One of the important aspects of manpower development in this connection is improved education system for library and information science. Mangla 'Library and Information Science programmes should be so designed as to equip the student:

- With knowledge and techniques to handle the immediate job requirements in an efficient manner; and
- "To develop programmes, procedures and services on modern lines in future where the use of various modern techniques, computers etc., could provide better, quicker and efficient service".

Skill in Information Technology (IT) can be gained only when one gets hands-on training and experience in laboratories under simulated conditions or in real life situations. The graduates and post graduates turned out by library schools of West Bengal do not possess adequate skill and expertise to interact confidently with IT specialists, evaluate what is recommended by them and full fill their requirements.

NECESSITY FOR PRACTICAL IT TRAINING

New Information Technology

Technological innovations have given rise to new ideas relating to collection, processing and dissemination of information. These innovations and ideas including Artificial Intelligence, Robotics, Speech Synthesis, Electronic mail, CD-ROM, CD Networking, Barcode systems, Electronic publishing, Hypermedia, Multimedia, Tele facsimile, Radio data paging, Networks etc. share a common technology revolving around electronics, computers, Telecommunication, Printing and Reprography, popularly known as Information Technology.

Futurist Alvin Toffler has rightly predicted that computers will enhance our 'mind power' just as the industrial revolution has enhanced our 'muscle power'. At least complete practical knowledge of computer applications in LICs is essential for a LISc professional. LIS being an information collection, organisation, and dissemination agency, technological innovations especially in the field of IT, have implications both for LIS, and the workforce required to service information users and their needs. Development in educational technology and the changing pattern of education and learning also indicate challenges for the library and information community to upgrade their IT skills.

Revolution Concept of Library

The LIS education aims at providing trained manpower to manage different types of libraries, information and documentation centers which, over a period of time have undergone changes in terms of needs, functions, types and range of services offered, as well as tools and techniques being used when offering the services. Application of information and communication technologies has revolutionised the whole concept of libraries, the system of information storage and retrieval and ways to access the information. Therefore, the objectives of LIS education also need to be redefined. The students need to be more practical oriented and should be equipped with intensive and extensive knowledge on the use of IT in libraries. Application of technology has opened up new vistas and thus, all LIS schools should think seriously in terms of the changing context. Students need to be given adequate knowledge of computers (including hardware), computer and communication technologies, networking, operating systems, Internet concepts, and database management systems, with adequate practical exposure to handle these technological devices.

Table. Traditional Library Concepts and Modern Concepts of Information Science

Traditional Concepts	Modern concepts
History and Development of Libraries	Library Automation, Library Application Software
Preservation and conservation of Library Materials	Multi-media information sources
Cataloguing of Books	Online Public Access Catalogue
Library Systems and services	Design and development of Databases; Database Management Systems
Library Orientation	Computerized Information Retrieval; Online Search and Retrieval of Information; e-journals & e-books
User needs and user surveys	Internet basics etc.
Inter Library Loan	Networking & Resource Sharing; Consortia

Areas of Practical IT Skills Developments in LISc Curriculum

LISc courses offered by Indian library schools in different universities have become partially irrelevant since long. The debate about changing the LISc curricula has been going on for the last few years, but nothing concrete has yet been done at the national level, except for some cosmetic changes.

Dominance of Practice

The issue of the relationship between theory and practice is not properly addressed in the Indian context. An expert once stated that we are drowning in theory at library schools and not giving enough exposure to practice. The dilemma lies in the choice between teaching students the knowledge and skills needed in their first posts to which meet the immediate needs of employers and instilling principles from which they can expand their skills and knowledge base as their career develops. It is also seen that during the challenge of managing the complex and diverse new environment, some of the schools have been merged with different disciplines like information management and technology, information studies and mass communications. Given the pace of change in the nature of library and information services, there is a still need to not only in preparing library professionals but also in establishing practitioners, a commitment to lifelong learning because the circumstances are demanding greater professional and technical awareness.

As professional obsolescence becomes a real and ever present danger, only a systematic continuing education provides a method of combating such obsolescence. In the western countries many schools have made a thorough revision and development of course programmes and also introduced new courses to meet the needs of employers in industries, and the public and private sectors. The introduction of new programmes should therefore be seen too some extent as reflecting the 'Pull-Push Effect' of recognising the increasing need for the professional workforce to match the growth and significance of information industry and the expanding higher education system to provide the appropriate workforce. To design a model curriculum for a dynamic inter-disciplinary subject like Library and Information Science on the national level is quite difficult, and such attempts will raise awkward questions regarding inclusion or exclusion of particular topics and the emphasis to be given to individual topics. Hence, relevant topics, which are already implemented in LIS education emphasis on both theoretical and practical aspects but the information professionals are not getting hands-on training and experience in laboratory under simulated conditions or in real life situations (*i.e* trouble shooting).

Networking

- *Node failure:* In an automated library all the work station should be connected through LAN to the server, if the application is not being accessed from any of the work station then this situation is called node failure.
- *How to detect this problem:* Using of 'ping' command from run, if 'request time error' is coming then there must be an issue with the connectivity.
- *Syntax:* ping 'IP address of the work station' -t
- How to resolve issue:
  - Make sure the computer is turn on
  - Check the local area connection must be enable
  - Check the Ethernet cable must be plug in
  - Check other end of that Ethernet cable should be plug in into a network switch.
  - Check the IP address should be in the same class compare to the server IP if DHCP server is not there.

Database

- *Information retrieving/updating/deleting error:* In a server based library, application library software will be running in which all the information will be stored into the database. Sometimes we face a problem at the time of retrieving, updating and deleting records.

- How to resolve the issue:
  - Make sure the database are running
  - Make sure the database path is correct
  - Make sure that there is no issue with the front end application
  - If needed you can restore the database from database back up taken in every alternative minutes through 'database attachment'

Printing

- *Error:* Printer is not working.
- First needs to check the type (network/desktop shared) of printer, if it is a network printer then the following steps are:
  - Check printer is properly connected to the LAN switch through an Ethernet cable. RJ45 connector is working or not.
  - Check Power is turned on
  - Check the IP address, Subnet and default gateway of that printer by using network command in the printer's display. Also check the port details.
  - Check Printer's IP is pinging or not.
  - Check that is there any issue like paper jam, no paper in the tray etc.
  - Make sure that work station's 'printer spooler' service is running by using a command 'services.msc' from run.

Therefore, it is right time to inject some practical IT training with proper resources *i.e* Library Open Source Soft ware, Database, Servers and Network equipments etc. and fine tune the LIS courses accordingly. It will make the LIS courses consistent with the Job market.

Bibliography

Anil Parnami: *Library Information : System and E-Journal Archiving*, Cyber Tech, 2011.

B.S. Aggarwal: *Issues in Library Information Science* , Oxford Book Company, 2007.

Bhupendra Narayan Singh: *Library and Information Science in the Digital Age*, Anmol Pub, 2011.

Bikika Laloo Tariang: *Library and Information Science Education*, Ess Ess Publications, 2012.

C Praveen Singh: *Modern Strategies in Library and Information Science*, Alfa, 2008.

G. Devarajan: *Applied Research in Library and Information Science*, Ess Ess Pub, 2005.

G. Devarajan: *Research in Library and Information Science*, Ess Ess Pub, 2002.

K.L.M. Swaminathan: *Library and Information Science*, Sarup and Sons, 2001.

K.T. Dilli: *Library and Information Science in a Digital Era*, Atlantic, 2009.

Kanchan Kamila: *Library and Information Science*, Ess Ess Publications, 2012.

Khalid K. Faruqi and Mehtab Alam: *Library Information Systems and E-Journal Archiving*, Authorspress, 2005.

Krishan Kumar And Jaideep Sharma: *Library and Information Science Education in India*, Har-anand Publications, 2009.

Kusum Verma: Library Information and Society, Vista International, 2005.

Kusum Verma: Library Information Services and Systems, Vista International Pub, 2008.

L.B. Rakesh: *Library and Information Science in Digital Age*, Alfa Pub, 2006.

P K Singh: *Current Trends and Techniques in Library and Information Science*, Shree Pub, 2007.

P. Balasubramanian: *Advanced Computer Application in Library and Information Science*, Deep and Deep, 2011.

P.S.G. Kumar: *Foundations of Library and Information Science*, B.R. Publishing Corporation, 2012.

Punit Ralhan: *Advancement in Library and Information Science*, Oxford Book Company, 2009 .

Purushotham Tiwari and R.S. Kochar: *International Encyclopaedia of Library and Information Science*, APH, 2010.

Purushotham Tiwari: *Dictionary of Library and Information Science*, A.P.H. Pub, 2011.

R P Bajpai: *Current Trends in Library and Information Science*, Shree Pub, 2007.

R.G. Prasher: *Library and Information Science: Parameters and Perspectives*, Concept Pub., 1998.

Ram Shobhit Singh: *Library Information Systems and E-Journal Archiving*, Anmol Pub., 2008.

S.R. Das: *Managing Library Information Systems*, Arise Pub, 2008.

Sambhu Nath Halder and Sibsankar Jana: *Library and Information Science in Changing Paradigm*, Ess Ess Publications, 2013.

Suryakant and O.S. Shekhar Singh: *Library and Information Science*, Ess Ess Pub, 2011.

T. Saravanan: *Library and Information Science*, APH Pub., 2008.

Tariq Ashraf and Sanjay Kumar Jha: *Library and Information Science*, Bookwell, 2008.

V.G. Choukhande: *Library and Information Science Research*, Shivneri Pub, 2008.

Vaishali Khaparde: *Library and Information Science*, Ess Ess Publications, 2012.

Index

A

Acceleration 136
Accommodate 182
Accomplish 100, 104, 177, 259
Accomplished 24, 251
Acquiring 95, 175, 179
Appropriate 75, 110, 115
Archiving 268, 269
Asynchronous 157, 159
Augmentation 39

B

Bewildering 129
Bibliometrics 150
Bureaucratic 114, 167

C

Calculus 205, 206, 213
Cognition 133
Competencies 225
Computerrelated 94
Conferencing 117, 118
Connotations 131, 149
Consortium 166
Constellation 169
Continually 229, 233, 241

D

Dictate 66, 69
Dimensions 26, 28, 81, 82, 209
Disadvantages 208
Discouragingly 205
Disparate 182
Dissemination 70, 108
Distractions 124
Dreadful 135

E

Earmarked 187
Echelons 207, 208, 210, 211
Efficiency 84, 87, 271
Efthimidiadis 135
Exemplified 123, 134
Explosion 129, 131, 133, 136, 198, 204

F

Facilitated 270
Fortunately 39
Futurist 92

G

Granularity 263, 264

H

Hierarchy 176, 207, 208, 210, 211, 250

I

Immediately 60, 235, 236
Imperialistic 63
Impetus 129
Implement 223
Implementation 66, 111, 114
Inadequate 107, 109
Individualism 212

L

Legislation 198, 199, 200, 201, 203, 204
Leitmotifs 129
Leveraging 100, 264
Lexical 127, 131
Linguistics 206, 234

M

Mandate 73
Manifestation 129, 150
Matrixes 238, 241
Meanwhile 216
Mechanisms 79
Mentioning 210, 211

N

Navigability 64
NEXIS 70
Nonexclusive 207

O

OPACs 140, 148, 150
Ordinarily 208, 238, 251
OrganiSation 80, 171, 174, 177, 179, 180
Oscilloscope 233, 246, 247, 251

P

Paradigm 133, 141
Parallel 20, 21, 22, 23, 24, 33, 236
Plausible 215, 236, 241
Pragmatic 131, 132, 133, 141
Preliminary 88, 246

Q

Quantifiable 176

R

Raphael 213
Realization 32, 236
Recognizes 22, 245
Repositories 263, 268, 269
Rubrics 264, 265, 266

S

Schema 26, 81, 82, 206, 229, 230, 231
Semantic 83, 84, 209, 214, 241, 245
Semantics 122
Separated 207, 231, 252
Stakeholders 96, 97

T

Tactile 185
Taxonomies 83, 175, 212
Telegambling 93
Thematic 270
Turbulent 109, 166, 167, 168, 169

U

Ubiquitous 94, 181
Unambiguous 215
Unarbitrary 213

V

Valiantly 134

W

Webster 127, 137, 149

Y

Yazykov 90